The Turf

A Social and Economic History
of Horse Racing

Wray Vamplew

Emeritus Professor of Sports History, University of Stirling.

Visiting Professor, Manchester Metropolitan University.

Special Projects Editor, International Journal of the History of Sport.

Second edition, with new preface and epilogue.

EER

Edward Everett Root, Publishers, Brighton, 2016.

Edward Everett Root, Publishers, Co. Ltd.,
30 New Road, Brighton, Sussex, BN1 1BN, England.
www.eerpublishing.com

edwardeverettroot@yahoo.co.uk

The Turf. A Social and Economic History of Horse Racing

Classics in social and economic history series, 1.

ISBN Hardback 978-1-911204-04-6.
ISBN Paperback 978-0-9542075-7-1.

First published in England in 1976. This edition, 2016.

The cover picture has been reproduced from Hawley Smart,
From Post to Finish. A Novel (London and New York, Ward,
Lock, & Co., n.d.), an edition produced for sale on railway
bookstalls. Illustration by O.R. Bould, 1885. Courtesy of the
John Spiers Collection of Victorian & Edwardian Fiction.

Cover designed by Pageset Limited, High Wycombe, Buckinghamshire.
Printed and bound in England by Lightning Source UK, Milton Keynes.

To Lester Piggott
'Genius Genuine'

It has to be said of the 'sport of kings' that, so long as it is surrounded by that army of gamblers, which now so fatly flourishes on all our racecourses, it will continue to be what it has long since become, a monstrous game of speculation.

L. H. Curzon, *A Mirror of the Turf* (1892)

Contents ⌐

New Preface 2016]

Horseracing is unique among British sports. It was the first truly national sport with a history stretching back to at least the days of Henry VIII. It has two distinct codes, the traditional flat racing, which is the subject of this book, and National Hunt racing which emerged in the nineteenth century. Although amateur jockeys have topped the National Hunt Riders table in the past and 'Mr' George Thursby gained four places in Classic races at the beginning of the twentieth century, those days are long gone and there is now little room for amateur participation at any level of the sport. Finally perhaps more than any other sport horseracing has been associated with, even dependent upon, gambling.

Some of these issues are the subject matter of *The Turf* which essentially looks at how racing proved to be a dynamic sports product that changed its character over time. The pre-modern version of the sport was predominantly rural, highly localised, and was free to watch but, by the end of the nineteenth century, racing had national rules and many courses were enclosed and were charging gatemoney. What had happened was a combination of commercial widening (more fixtures), commercial deepening (new revenue sources such as spectator fees), product improvement (as with the enclosed courses offering Saturday racing which added more events to the calendar but did not change the essence of the sport), and product development (changing the nature of racing by replacing the traditional long-distance heats for older, staying horses by sprints for two-year-olds).

At the time of the publication of *The Turf* there had been little academic work on horseracing. Previous writing had been non-academic and generally anecdotal rather than archival. It is reasonable to suggest that *The Turf* paved the way for a new way of looking at the sport. Some of the literature published since then is outlined in the Research Epilogue.

In fact when *The Turf* was published there had been relatively little academic interest in sports history, but the past forty years have seen it become a significant area of academic study, though the Americans continue to refer to it as sport history in the singular; but then they do math in their schools! Sport history societies have been established in Britain, Australia and Europe, all with their own academic journals to emulate the pioneering North American Society of Sport History.

In addition to the acknowledgements in the original publication, I would like to pay special tribute to two fellow (if this is not a sexist term) sports historians with a special interest in horseracing, Mike Huggins and Joyce Kay. Both have commented on my work (and hence improved it) and have generally created a stimulating environment for bouncing ideas around. I also thank John Spiers for his generous invitation to make *The Turf* available to a new generation of readers.

Wray Vamplew
Edinburgh
January 2016

Introduction ⌉

In 1896 the University of Pennsylvania Press published a volume by a Professor Church entitled *Games of the Far East*. A shocked reviewer, worried at what the academic world was coming to, sarcastically wondered if he should now look 'to the Clarendon Press for an exhaustive book on cricket, to Cambridge for a treatise on football, to St Andrews for a history of golf'.[1] Edinburgh, without a race-course of its own (despite the *Racing Calendar*'s geographical liberties with Musselburgh) may not be the place from which to expect a work on horse racing; but at least these days a study of sport is considered academically respectable. Indeed sport is now acknowledged as a major social institution, an acceptance symbolized in Britain by the appointment of a government minister with special responsibility for sport and the establishment of a Sports Council to pursue a campaign of 'Sport For All'. Several social scientists have assisted our understanding of the importance of sport to society: in Britain, Eric Dunning (*The Sociology of Sport*) and Peter McIntosh (*Sport in Society*); in the United States, Harry Edwards (*Sociology of Sport*) and John Loy and Gerald Kenyon (*Sport, Culture and Society*); and, of course, the many contributors to the *International Review of Sports Sociology*, published in Poland under the auspices of the United Nations.

Inevitably some of the growing interest in the role of sport and other leisure activities in contemporary society has focused on how man has spent his non-working hours in the past. However, in my experience, these historical inquiries were hidebound initially by institutionalism. I well remember a history of leisure seminar which I attended some years ago where a picture was emerging of the working man's leisure time being taken up in attending a trade union branch meeting, or studying at the local Mechanics' Institute, or perhaps practising a choral arrangement at church or chapel. At this point one heretic suggested that perhaps our hero merely went home and dug his garden. Nowadays, I am glad to say, there is a greater realization that institutional records do not reveal everything about man's leisure activities. Saturday afternoon at a soccer match, an evening's hard drinking, and, if capable, a demanding of his conjugal rights may be as atypical of the working man at play as the institutional archetype cited above, but it must be considered. Unfortunately, data deficiencies mean that we may never know the true pattern of leisure in the past. Particularly this may be the case where sport is concerned. Some work has been done, notably by Robert Malcolmson (*Popular Recreation in English Society 1700–1850*), but analytical studies are still rare. Eventually I hope to reduce the deficiency by producing a social and economic analysis of sport in nineteenth-century society. This monograph on horse racing is a spin-off from the longer-term project, done in the belief that a study of one sport will enable others to be put into perspective.

There were several reasons for the choice of racing as a case study. One was a sneaking suspicion that there might still be some truth in a nineteenth-century comment that 'in all probability the three principal jockeys of England will earn, or at any event receive, more money in a year than the whole professional staff of a modern university'.[2] Another was my life-long interest in matters of the turf: indeed I cut my statistical teeth at the age of ten, or thereabouts, calculating the returns on the tips of leading racing correspondents, and, with the benefit of hindsight, devising betting systems which would have drastically increased my pocket money. There were academic as well as personal grounds for my choice. Racing was one of the first sports to have a mass audience. It was also one of the early employers of professional sportsmen. Moreover racing was (and still is) a sport which appealed to all ranks of society, to the upper-class owner, the middle-class trainer, and to the working-class *habitué* of the betting shop. In addition racing raises some interesting economic issues. Was the ownership of racehorses investment or consumption? Was the infrequent use of racecourses an inefficient utilization of resources? And what of gambling which many people would regard as highly irrational economic behaviour?

In this book I attempt a social and economic analysis of the major changes in British flat-racing between the 1830s and the 1930s. I have pursued four main themes. Part one is concerned with the changing character of the sport. In the eighteenth century racing was a free, social event, the highlight of the sporting calendar for the local community, but by the late nineteenth century most race meetings were highly commercial enterprises, demanding payment from all spectators, many of whom came from afar, thanks to the railways. Part two deals with the morality of racing, with the rule-makers and the rule-breakers. Certainly racing was a corrupt sport *par excellence*: it is no coincidence that one meaning of 'jockey' is to cheat or deceive. Part three concentrates on four categories of participants in racing: jockeys, trainers, owners, and breeders. Issues discussed include their recruitment, motivation, and whether they could make money out of racing. The final part relates to gambling and its symbiotic relationship with racing: the opportunity to make money by gambling keeps many participants in racing and in turn racing provides a ready betting market for others besides those actually involved in the industry.

Few authors can work in isolation. I have obtained ideas and criticism from many people, not least the members of the university seminars at which I gave papers. (Incidently I wonder if it is a reflection on university finances that I received far more invitations to talk on horse racing and gambling than I ever did when I was a serious student of econometric history.) At one seminar I was introduced to David Swannell, Jockey Club handicapper and deputy clerk of the course at York. I am deeply indebted to him for reading most of the draft manuscript. Here, in order to safeguard his position, I should make the usual statement that as the author I have sole responsibility for all errors and insults. In these days of threatened academic redundancies perhaps my colleagues at Edinburgh would also be grateful for such a release. In particular I would like to thank Frank Bechofer, Roger Davidson, Colin Jones, Berrick Saul, Chris Smout and John Ward. My research was made both easier and more pleasant by assistance from several quarters. David Swannell gave me full access to both York Racing Museum and the records of York Race Committee; William McHarg generously put the records of Ayr racecourse at my disposal; and Dr W. A. L. Seamen of the Durham County Record Office very kindly allowed me to consult the racing correspondence of

John Bowes prior to its being catalogued. I am also grateful for help and assistance from the Jockey Club, the Racehorse Owners Association, the Jockeys Association, the Bookmakers Protection Association, the National Sporting League, Racecourse Technical Services Ltd, Geoffrey Best, Simon Brown, Colin Finlayson, Jo Hignett, John Hutchinson, Ann Kettle, Sandy Ochojna, Margaret Williamson and numerous librarians, and particularly from the members of the inter-library loan service at the University of Edinburgh.

As horse racing can be an expensive form of research I am also grateful to those who rendered financial assistance. First and foremost the Carnegie Trust for the Universities of Scotland, who were most generous. Secondly, the Travel and Research Committee of the University of Edinburgh, who paid some of my travelling expenses, though I believe one or two eyebrows were raised at a grant for visiting Ascot, Newmarket, and Sandown Park. Finally, in his own way, the incomparable Lester Piggott helped finance the project.

WRAY VAMPLEW
University of Edinburgh
October 1974

Promotion:
The Development of Racing⏋

The construction and wide extension of railways, the
facility, rapidity, and safety with which horses
are conveyed in boxes to the scene of the action and
back to their training stables, and lastly, the
electric wire, have revolutionized the whole system
of racing and of training, early maturity and quick
returns being at present the order of the day.

J. Kent, *The Racing Life*
of Lord George Cavendish Bentinck (1892)

The influence which the institution of the Park
Meetings has had on the sport . . . can
hardly be exaggerated. These meetings have, in fact,
revolutionized racing. By the elimination to a
very great extent of the undesirable following with
which the old-fashioned open meetings were
afflicted, it has been made possible for ladies to
participate in the sport, and there can be no
doubt that in every way the Turf has benefited by
the inauguration of enclosed meetings.

E. Moorhouse, *Badminton Magazine* (1913)

1]   *Racing before 1840]*

No doubt Henry VIII had his own views as to what constituted the 'sport of kings'; nevertheless it is horse racing that commonly carries this appellation. Yet to suggest that racing was the prerogative of an élite is wrong: it was the sport of all, a common interest of peer and peasant, of lord and labourer. Indeed, although William IV himself had no great passion for the turf – he was 'bored to death at Ascot'[1] – he acknowledged its worth as a social institution:

> I consider this to be a national sport – the manly and noble sport of a free people, and I deeply feel the pride of being able to encourage these pastimes, so intimately connected with the habits and feelings of this free country . . . we are here to enjoy these liberties and sports which I will, with my utmost power, ever protect and foster, and, in so doing, never lose sight of the welfare and enjoyment of every class of my people, from the highest to the lowest.[2]

Horse racing emerged naturally out of an environment in which horses played an important role: as well as providing a means of transport, they were also status symbols, their quality an overt display of the owner's wealth. Ownership inevitably engendered rivalry which in turn led to the organization of races, initially merely matches between two horses but later formalized races with several entrants.* Some races would also serve an economic function in letting owners show off their horses prior to offering them for sale. Many race meetings in the eighteenth and early nineteenth centuries were not just for thoroughbred racehorses. At all but the major fixtures there might be events for half-bred horses, hunters, and, occasionally, even ponies. One reason for this variety of competitors was the transport situation: as long as horses had to be walked to meetings they tended to race only locally, thus restricting the

---

* It can be conjectured that the widespread ownership of dogs, particularly among the lower classes, also led to competitive sports such as ratting, baiting, coursing, and fighting.

number of entrants at any particular gathering. The use of heats was another device to obtain a full day's racing from a limited supply of horses. The winner of an event was the first entrant to win two heats; this could often require four or even more races. Another reason for the variety of horses participating was that most race meetings at this time were primarily social events, and not just for the privileged leisure classes. They were a high point of the social calendar for the bulk of the local populace who, starved of organized public entertainment, came determined to enjoy *their* meeting.* If it was possible to participate at more than spectator level, then they wished to do so; hence farmers raced, and frequently rode, their half-breeds and others their thoroughbred hunters and racing stock. What greater ambition could there be than to ride one's own horse to victory at one's local meeting?

Races before 1840 were not gate-money events. Spectators paid no entry fee: everyone was free to watch and to watch was free. Unless onlookers wished to view from the grandstand (not that there always was one), they paid nothing to see the races. This has led one sports historian to argue that racing was organized solely for gambling purposes, for if entrance money was not charged then clearly racing had no need of spectators.[3] It is true that racing could take place without an audience, but if the crowd had not been part and parcel of the local meetings, then surely they would have been more than the annual or semi-annual events that they were. At Newmarket, where racing was exclusive to the upper classes and the masses were actively discouraged from attending, meetings were far more frequent. Here, and at a few other select meetings, gambling may have been the fulcrum of the sport, but elsewhere racing was intimately associated with local holidays: travelling shows, gaming booths, beer tents, cock fights, boxing and wrestling matches, open-air dancing, and, for a privileged few, balls and dinner parties, all contributed to a full day out.[4]

Money was made out of the race crowd: the proprietors of the

---

* R. W. Malcolmson (*Popular Recreation in English Society, 1700–1850*, 1973), has shown the wide range of recreational activities pursued by the common people, but to a great extent this was self-made entertainment. What organized entertainment there was tended to be irregular and frequently on a one-off basis.

grandstand were paid by those who wished to segregate themselves from the masses; and most spectators wanted more than a
view of the horses when they went racing, a fact well appreciated
by the lessees of the gambling booths, beer tents, and food stalls.
Nevertheless, there seems to have been no attempt to charge
entrance money. Perhaps the race committee, usually local
notables or their nominees, was deterred from such a practice by
feelings of paternalistic responsibility towards the community.
Racing was an integral part of a local holiday; if spectators
wished to purchase food and drink or to have a gamble that was
up to them, but the basic ingredient of the day should be free.
There were also practical problems to the introduction of gate
money. Entry fees to the grandstand could be collected as access
was relatively easily restricted; two or three burly gatemen
could take care of that. For the racecourse as a whole, however,
restricted entry was not so easily attained. Enclosure would
have been necessary and this was not possible where racing took
place on common ground. Elsewhere it was legal but expensive
and the returns might not be commensurate with the outlay. If
they were not to be grossly uneconomic, enclosed meetings
would have to be held more regularly than were the existing
social gatherings so as to cover the increased overhead costs.

But there was no guarantee that sufficient spectators could be
attracted. Clearly there was plenty of time available for recreation. Conditioned by the climate and the ecclesiastical calendar,
agricultural work – the dominant economic activity well into the
nineteenth century – was unevenly spread over the year. In
addition, the discretionary authority over working hours
enjoyed by independent farmers and task-work labourers
imposed an intermittent daily or weekly working rhythm. Craft
and domestic industry workers, both rural and urban, also had
some choice in their working routine, and whenever men had
such control the 'work pattern was one of alternate bouts of
intense labour and of idleness'.[5] With the Industrial Revolution
there came an acceptance by industrial capitalism that time was
not now passed but spent. However, it was only in large-scale,
machine-powered industries that working hours were almost
totally inflexible and, even in the 1830s, relatively few members
of the occupied population were factory employees. So the

position regarding time for leisure activities 'up to and including most of the Industrial Revolution [was] holidays at home, and plenty of them, for the great majority'.[6]

Whether they had the money as well as the time is not so certain. Professor Flinn has charted the way through the diverse price and wage series covering the century before 1850 and argues that 'from such figures as we have . . . it would be a brave historian who would assert that real wages were generally advancing' before 1788–92. Indeed he goes further and suggests that 'there are relatively few indications of significant changes in levels of real wages either way before 1810–14'. He sees some substantial gains – perhaps in the order of 2 to 3 per cent per annum – in the deflationary period 1813–25, but considers that they were made at the expense of employment. Finally from 1825 to 1850 he argues that 'the gains in real wages were slight'.[7] The very fact that there has been controversy over the course of real wages in the period studied lends support to Professor Flinn's claims of only modest gains: one can argue about the existence of fairies at the bottom of the garden, but the presence of giants can hardly be a subject for debate.

Even if both time and money were available, there was still the transport problem. The poor state of inland communication limited the spectator catchment area of any particular course. When all is said and done, it was far easier for the race committee to continue along traditional lines than to attempt to create an enclosed meeting. This was a task for entrepreneurs which the committees decidedly were not; their function was to organize a meeting for the benefit of the local community and this could be done adequately without great capital expenditure.

Nevertheless, money was essential to the organization of a meeting. At the very least trophies or prize-money had to be provided and by an Act of 1740 no event could be worth less than £50 to the winner. Running heats could get several races for the price of one, but £50 was still needed. How was this money raised?

Most of the prize-money came from the owners themselves in the form of stakes and forfeits. In addition the race committee would tour the neighbourhood requesting subscriptions to the prize fund from hoteliers, publicans, victuallers, brewers, and others who stood to benefit financially from the meeting.[8] Patronage could also be expected from the local gentry and, of course, from the borough or county member; indeed so common was this political contribution that its absence at Brighton in the 1830s was publically commented upon.[9] Further funds came from the stands, both directly from entry fees and also in the form of ground rentals from the owners of private stands, paying either for their own exclusiveness or for the privilege of charging others for theirs. Much depended on who owned the course: at Goodwood, which was the property of the Duke of Richmond, the meeting's sponsor, an annual average of £746 was raised from this source between 1829 and 1843;[10] whereas at Epsom, where the race committee held no territorial titles, no funds were forthcoming till 1845 when Henry Dorling first combined the role of course clerk with that of chairing the Grandstand Association.* Occasionally, additional money could be raised from the stands by leasing them to the organizers of cricket matches, prizefights, and the like.[11]

Practically every race committee relied on the ancillary activities of the meeting to provide contributions to the racing fund; in fact letting space for gambling booths and refreshment tents was considered vital by most race organizers.[12] Whether let by auction or by fixed fee, the number of booths was generally limited so as to encourage the proprietors in their expectations of profit. The gambling booths always fetched more than the beer tents but together they could raise substantial sums, dependent, of course, on what the proprietors felt the crowd would spend: at Ascot in the early 1840s, ground rents produced £1,200 but at Egham they raised less than £100 because, in the words of William Hibbert, the clerk at both

---

* As Epsom was a manorial property, it was the Lord of the Manor who obtained any rentals. The Grandstand Association developed from a speculative venture of Charles Bluck, a Yorkshireman who in 1828 saw the financial potential of replacing the various ramshackle sheds by a modern grandstand. Once he had obtained a lease to do this (for twenty years at £30 per annum), other, more respectable, individuals stepped in, organized an association, bought Bluck out for £1,000 (a profitable speculation indeed!), and spent £14,000 erecting the largest grandstand in Europe with accommodation for 5,000 persons, including seats for 2,500 on the roof. The Association concerned itself solely with the grandstand and, until Dorling became chairman, had no voice in the organization of the meeting. (Rosebery Papers, Box 108 (Papers Regarding Epsom Commons), National Library of Scotland Acc. 4070; E. E. Dorling, *Epsom and the Dorlings*, 1939, pp. 54–8.)

meetings, 'the company is so different'.[13] Sometimes the race committee sub-contracted the whole business of booth rentals to speculators in return for a fixed payment; at Epsom, Timothy Barnard paid £700 for the privilege.[14] These men were profit maximizers and even charged the itinerant thimblemen and three-card tricksters five shillings or half a sovereign; as Barnard said, 'when you rent a racecourse you must make the most you can of it'.[15] The general public, however, benefited from the speculators as they could expect additional entertainment to be provided for them, since, as one speculator rightly remarked, 'if there was nothing but the bare horse racing, the races would all be over in an hour or two' and this would not have encouraged the booth proprietors to pay high rents.[16]

Professor Harold Perkin has argued that between 1780 and 1850 Britain underwent a 'moral revolution' and 'ceased to be one of the most aggressive, brutal, rowdy, outspoken, riotous, cruel and bloodthirsty nations in the world and became one of the most inhibited, polite, orderly, tender-minded, prudish and hypocritical'.[17] The sporting writer, Charles Apperley (alias 'Nimrod') noted in the 1830s that this gradual refinement of manners had contracted the circle of rural sports: hawking had disappeared, shooting had lost its wild character, hare-hunting had fallen into disrepute, and cockfighting was soon to be made illegal.[18] This was part of an attack on traditional ways of life, an attempt to discredit what were regarded as barbaric hindrances to social and economic progress. Perkin sees the campaign to soften manners as part of the capitalist middle-class drive to impose its own values on a society in which 'the aristocracy and working class were united in their drunkenness, profaneness, sexual indulgence, gambling and love of cruel sports'.[19] This was partly the traditional puritanism of the English middle ranks, mutated but not mute, in the service of industrial capitalism: the sharp attack upon popular customs, sports, and holidays which began in the last years of the eighteenth century was clearly associated with the capitalists' desire for a labour force willing to offer regular work and unlikely to abuse its free time in drinking or violent sports, neither of which were conducive to efficiency or productivity.[20]

In the early nineteenth century humanitarian Christians also made efforts to remodel traditional leisure patterns: the R.S.P.C.A. (1824), the Temperance Movement (1829) and the Lord's Day Observance Society (1831) all originated in the Evangelical hope that they would help civilize manners and make the masses more receptive to religious instruction.[21]

Racing was a traditional rural sport* and it too changed, though it is debatable whether this had anything to do with the assaults of the progressives. Admittedly the barbarous system of long distance heats was generally abandoned and races for heavyweight jockeys were increasingly difficult to find, but both these developments are explicable by factors which produced other changes such as the racing of younger horses† (shown in Table 1) and the substitution of sweepstake races for matches and races for plates and other trophies (shown in Table 2).

TABLE 1. AGE OF HORSES RACING: 1797 AND 1832

	2-year-olds	3-year-olds	4-year-olds	5-year-olds
1797	48	161	122	262
1832	200	395	237	407

Source: *Racing Calendar*

TABLE 2. TYPE OF RACES: 1807 AND 1843

	Matches	Plates	Stakes
1807	189	269	263
1843	86	191	897

Source: Estimates of H. Rous, *On the Laws and Practice of Horse Racing*, 1850, p. x.

* Of course, racing was an urban as well as a rural sport. It seems to have developed as a town dweller's recreation concurrently with being a countryside pursuit, though no doubt its urban growth was reinforced by the migrants to towns bringing their traditional sports with them.

† At the beginning of the eighteenth century few horses raced before the age of five. Races for two-year-olds and three-year-olds developed from the mid century, but though the latter soon became generally acceptable, as symbolized in the foundation of the Derby, Oaks, and St Leger in the 1770s and 1780s, the former received no such stamp of approval till 1827 when the Criterion Stakes was begun at Newmarket. Yearling races were tried at Newmarket in 1791 but they were received unfavourably.

What influenced racing to innovate was either some predominantly non-economic, evolutionary mechanism or a growing commercial attitude on the part of owners. Both cases can be argued. Long distance heats may have died out simply because they became farcical with the first two miles of a four mile heat being taken at little more than walking pace;[22] and perhaps there was a growing awareness that younger horses could produce races just as exciting as any by fully mature animals; and it is possible that the rise of the sweepstake race was a reflection of a desire to prove that one's horse was a true champion, capable of taking on all-comers and not merely a few selected challengers. But all of these changes can also be explained in terms of commercial motivation. Sweepstake races meant that owners risked less for the chance of winning more. Racing younger horses meant that investment in expensive bloodstock could yield a return much earlier than before. And once younger horses ran, shorter races and lighter jockeys almost inevitably followed: owners did not have to be in racing for the money to realize the foolishness of risking the breakdown of valuable horseflesh. Lighter weights were also associated with the growing popularity of the handicap race, which was both a method of getting more races out of the limited local supply of horses and a way of pleasing owners by giving all horses a chance to win. However, in order to increase their particular chances some owners, seeking prize-money or hunting trophies, began to employ professional jockeys; the enthusiastic, amateur owner-rider began to do likewise, either because he could not make the lighter weights or because he recognized the futility of competing against specialists.

Although the non-economic explanation cannot be rejected out of hand, it does require several independent developments to take place whereas the alteration in owners' attitudes is sufficient in itself to account for all the changes. Some support for the growing importance of commercial attitudes in racing can be found in the difficulty encountered by the élite Newmarket and Ascot meetings in attracting sufficient runners in the early 1830s because of the inadequate prize-money offered.[23] And in 1842 a public subscription was established at York for the purpose of making additions to the prize-money as such added money had 'materially contributed to the prosperity of racing at other places'.[24] We are left with the problem of explaining why this new attitude developed. It is not an easy question to answer: one can tentatively suggest that the changing norms and values of a rural society in transition came to be reflected in all the activities of that society. Britain had undergone an agricultural revolution, in the process of which economic behaviour had increasingly become conditioned by the profit motive. It is not beyond the bounds of credulity to suggest that some owners took this attitude into their leisure pursuits; others then adopted their practices, if not their motivations, simply to compete effectively in racing.

The degree of change should not be exaggerated: even in the 1830s many race meetings were still one-day, annual-holiday affairs, social functions rather than economic events. In 1823, 87 out of 95 racecourses had only one meeting a year. In 1840 the figure was 120 out of 137. (There may be an illusion of an increasing volume of racing because of the incomplete coverage of the *Racing Calendar* in these years). In 1848, by which time the *Calendar*'s coverage was more comprehensive, 61 meetings were one-day events, 56 lasted at least a day longer, but only 13 courses hosted more than one meeting. At most of the one-day gatherings, the spectators came from the local communities to enjoy the fun of the fair. Owners too tended to be local, racing more for prestige than for prize-money, usually with horses of only modest pretensions, and often in heats so as to ensure a full day's racing. Nevertheless, even at these minor meetings some owners came from afar, either to win prize-money or to enhance the reputation of their horses. This led to several race committees, anxious to retain the local character of their meetings, fighting off the invaders by excluding grooms and professional jockeys from riding and accepting as entries only horses from within a certain radius or which had hunted with a particular pack of hounds.

Some meetings emerged as social events for more than local inhabitants. Ascot was universally acknowledged as first among the provincial (i.e. non-Newmarket) meetings. It was the society meeting of the year at which the nobility and gentry from far beyond the surrounding county made 'a practice of attending . . . with all the style which wealth regulated by good taste can command'.[25] Epsom too attracted the élite spectators, especially on Derby Day when half the male peerage of the realm could be seen in the saddling enclosure. Goodwood, under the aegis of the Duke of Richmond, was also a great aristocratic meeting and Doncaster served the same social function for northern notables and nobility, though by the 1830s it was losing its reputation because of unchecked roguery on and off the course.[26] Other meetings, of lesser rank but of more than local importance, included Warwick, Manchester, Liverpool, Chester, Cheltenham, Bath, Worcester, York, and Newcastle.[27]

Although all these meetings attracted a high class of spectator, they were also local meetings for the lower classes. Only at Newmarket was racing almost exclusively for the upper-class owner and spectator. At Epsom on Derby Day a crowd of over 100,000 could be expected, but at Newmarket the attendance rarely exceeded 500 'and they [were] mostly of the higher classes, the majority on horseback, with perhaps a few close carriages and barouches for invalids and ladies'. Here racing existed 'in perfection' with no crowd or booths to obscure the view and 'none of those discordant sounds which make a perfect Babel of other racecourses'.[28] Newmarket was the racing man's Mecca, a place where racing was the only thing of importance. Over 400 horses (of a racing population of some 1,200) were in training here, all there to participate in Newmarket's seven annual meetings, each of which lasted several days.[29] Royal patronage, Jockey Club authority,* and ideal but testing conditions for training and racing had all contributed to raise Newmarket to its pre-eminent position.

Racing in the 1830s was not the same as that of the 1730s: there were more horses running, and especially more young horses; stake races were replacing matches; shorter distances were being raced; and specialist, professional jockeys were taking over from the amateur owner-rider. Nevertheless, two important factors restricted further development: these were the limited amount of prize-money and the transport situation.

Prize-money had risen from £115,950 in 1807 to £143,204 in 1839 and was a jump to £198,990 by 1843,[30] but till the

* See below, Chapter 6.

spectator was made to pay at the gate a potential major source of funds was not being tapped; and if the commercial motivations of some owners were the driving force inducing changes within racing, then inevitably developments would be delayed. There had been an attempt in 1837 to introduce the enclosed course to London but it had ended in disaster. John Whyte erected a barrier around his Hippodrome circuit in Bayswater, near Kensington Gardens, and proposed charging for admission. The auguries seemed good: not only was there a dense population within easy travelling distance, but he had also established a training centre nearby at Notting Hill. However, the soil at the training quarters proved to be deep clay and unusable at times, thus depriving the Hippodrome of a ready supply of runners. Worse still were the objections of local rate-payers, who determined to destroy the meeting by exploiting a right of way across the course and encouraging the local riff-raff to smash down the barriers and invade the ground. However, even when Whyte redesigned his course it failed; not enough spectators were willing to pay the minimum shilling entrance fee.[31] If others had considered following the entrepreneurial example of Whyte – though no evidence suggests that they were – his failure must have put them off. Almost forty years elapsed before another attempt was made to establish an enclosed, gate-money course.

The second major problem was transport. All owners wishing to race any distance from their training quarters, whether for economic or other reasons, had to set their horses walking well before the race: from Goodwood to Epsom or Ascot took four days, to Newmarket a week, and to Doncaster almost a fortnight.[32] Long journeys reduced the time that a horse was available for either training or racing and throughout the trek there was always the risk of a horse being injured and going lame, as happened to *Plenipotentary*, favourite for the 1834 St Leger.[33] One can only imagine the constant worry of John Scott's lad who accompanied *Cyprian* on the long walk from Malton to Epsom for her Oaks triumph and then back north for the Northumberland Plate at Newcastle. Nevertheless, despite the difficulties, by the late 1830s the desire of owners to race further afield had led to the emergence of half-a-dozen racing circuits, within which the better horses travelled to take on each other and also local challengers. However, except for large stakes and prestige events, racehorses rarely left their chosen circuits; racing was still a national sport pursued at local or regional level.

2] The Railway Revolution: Racing 1840–70]

Sir John Easthope, chairman of the London and Southampton Railway Company, was a keen follower of the turf and it was little surprise to find his company advertising, only days after the opening of their Kingston line, that they would run eight special trains to accommodate those wishing to see the 1838 Derby. Any surprise was the company's. Despite the long walk to the course from Kingston, there was a huge response; so large as to catch the company unawares and with only one train left to go there were still about 5,000 potential spectators milling around Nine Elms station. When it became apparent that their hopes of a day at the races had been dashed the crowd stormed the station; gates were lifted off their hinges, windows were broken, and eventually mounted police had to be called to disperse the mob and restore order. Undeterred, or perhaps encouraged by the obvious demand, the railway company ran a special excursion to Ascot races only a few weeks later; again it proved a tremendous attraction.[1] The age of the racing special had begun.

There was still a long way to go. In 1839 Britain had less than a thousand miles of track in operation, scarcely enough to serve the nation's hundred or so racecourses adequately. The incompleteness of the system especially hit the long distance traveller: many racing men journeying north for the St Leger preferred to come the whole way from London by coach rather than reach Derby by rail and then search for vehicular transport to Doncaster.[2] Neglect and inconvenience diminished in the next decade as Britain experienced a railway mania: between 1846 and 1850 over 3,600 miles were opened which took the operating total to about 6,000 miles, an extent of railway sufficiently well integrated to justify being called a network. By 1870 further construction had raised the total mileage to 13,500.

Sidney Smith concisely summed-up the advantages offered by

the railway: 'everything is near, everything is immediate – time, distance and delay are abolished'.[3] Among the appreciative passengers were racegoers. Doubtless, some of them were ardent and hardy enough enthusiasts to travel to meetings even without the benefit of the railway: before the South Yorkshire line was opened many spectators from Sheffield walked through the night to Doncaster and then walked the eighteen miles back home again.[4] Nevertheless the race trains encouraged others to attend, and not merely at their local meeting: trains of impressive length brought spectators to major meetings from well beyond walking distance. All courses within proximity of a station found their spectator catchment area both widened and deepened by the speed and convenience of railway travel.

Racing did not need these extra spectators: a crowd created atmosphere but this heightened its own enjoyment rather than positively benefiting racing. Nevertheless, although the new attenders, like the old, did not pay entrance money, they contributed indirectly to the prize fund since their spending persuaded the booth proprietors to pay increased rentals. Most race committees therefore welcomed them. The one great exception was at Newmarket: here racing was for the privileged few, and more especially it was for those on horseback. Facilities for spectators were meagre: three forlorn edifices, two of which were wholly or in part appropriated for use as jockeys' dressing and weighing rooms and the third was a small private stand for Jockey Club members.[5] The Heath was regarded as the preserve of the well-to-do followers of racing: indeed their pleasure was increased by the absence of the mob. Here the turf was an intense business with no fairs, nigger minstrels, or fortune-telling gipsies to distract the audience.[6] The pleasure-seeking, holiday racegoer was not wanted: in fact when the Great Eastern Railway began to run cheap excursions to Newmarket, the Jockey Club stewards countered the invasion by taking full advantage of Newmarket's many courses and staging the finish of consecutive races literally miles apart so that only the mounted gentry could effectively view the racing.[7]

Clearly, when in 1847 the Jockey Club gave its warm support to a railway line designed to put Newmarket on the national network, it was not with a view to attracting spectators: the

Club was concerned with saving the legs of horses not humans. [8] Race horses were first taken by rail in 1840 and it soon became appreciated that the days of sheeted racers marching to meetings with tiny grooms at their heads were numbered. [9] Newmarket-trained horses could always race locally and frequently without long treks, but their prestige as champions was dependent on meeting the best horses and there was no guarantee that these would be at Newmarket. The Heath's stranglehold on the Derby had been broken and its reputation as the premier training centre was being challenged: between 1788 and 1832 all but three Derby winners were trained at Newmarket; in the next thirty years only three winners came from the Heath. [10] If Newmarket became isolated from the racing world it might forfeit its crown by default.

The railway was a major breakthrough in the transportation of horses. However, there had been earlier demonstrations that horses need not always be walked to meetings. The star role is usually given to Lord George Bentinck, * who, when he could not get the odds he wanted on *Elis* for the 1836 St Leger, made no apparent efforts to send the animal to Doncaster. *Elis* was still in his Goodwood training quarters only days before the race and the betting fraternity naturally assumed that he would not run. The odds on *Elis* widened till they reached a level which satisfied Lord George; whereupon he placed his bets and then despatched *Elis* northwards in a van† drawn by four horses, far fewer than the victorious *Elis* left to his rear at Doncaster. [11]

Despite the publicity, Lord George was not the first to van a race horse. Twenty years previously Mr Territt's *Sovereign* had arrived at Newmarket having come from Worcester in a padded bullock van; Territt was a grazier and often sent his quality fat bullocks to auction on horse-drawn floats. [12] The time-lag between Territt and Lord George is not easy to explain. It probably had something to do with expense: a pair of post-horses could cost upwards of two shillings a mile and *Elis*'s trip

---

* For more on Lord George see below, pp. 88–93.

† The Earl of Suffolk, *Racing and Steeplechasing*, 1886, pp. 44–5, says that Lord George borrowed a van which Lord Chesterfield used for show cattle, but modern writers (R. Mortimer, *The Jockey Club*, 1958, p. 66; R. Longrigg, *The History of Horse Racing*, 1972, p. 120) suggest that he had it constructed specially.

reputedly set Lord George back about £100.[13] Such outlays could not be warranted by the level of prize-money, especially when horses could be walked anyway: the lessened risk of going lame was most likely offset by the chances of injury due to inefficient suspension systems. All that vanning saved was time and this was money really only to gamblers; it must be conjectured that Lord George was the first among them to appreciate the possibilities. Owners had little to gain. Perhaps vanning would have allowed horses to race more frequently, but the racing circuits that had evolved enabled horses to undertake walking tours, competing at meetings arranged to fit in with their travels. Vanning allowed them to race outside their chosen circuits but it was expensive, especially relative to the prize-money that could be won. Nevertheless the publicity given to Lord George's venture did stimulate a move into vanning. In 1838 it was reported in the *Sporting Magazine* that 'the system of transporting horses by van is being felt everywhere, and Scotland particularly reaps the advantage in common with every far-off district'.[14]

The era of vanning was short-lived. Within four years of *Elis* travelling to Doncaster by van, the clerk of the course at Newcastle was anticipating the arrival of southern horses sent north by rail.[15] The railways could offer all that vanning could, and more. They were much cheaper and would have been worth utilizing even if the level of prize-money had remained unaltered, but in fact the railway companies helped raise the level of prize-money from £198,990 in 1843 to £315,272 in 1874. They did this indirectly by bringing more spectators and directly by sponsoring races. This increased prize-money attracted larger fields which in turn further raised the volume of prize-money via entry fees and stake money. Railways were also much faster than vans: horses need not leave their training quarters till the day before the race or even the morning of the race day itself, thus cutting down the risk of a horse being 'got at', something always easier without stable security. Once the railway network passed the incipient stage there was no real alternative for most owners and trainers.* Horses could easily race outside

---

* The Druid, *Post and Paddock*, 1895, p. 5, dates this point of no return at the mid 1850s.

the traditional circuits without undue cost or waste of time; in fact the railways produced a shift in the circuits so that eventually, instead of half-a-dozen regional ones there emerged a nationwide circuit of major meetings and a fluctuating set of lesser events, extremely local in character and seldom having a permanent date in the *Racing Calendar*.[16]

It is no exaggeration to say that the railways revolutionized racing. Many meetings became nationally rather than locally orientated, attracting both horses and spectators from all over the country. More horses were raced: Table 3 shows that there were more than double the number of racehorses running in 1869 than in 1837. The easing of the transport problem played

TABLE 3. AGE OF HORSES RACING: 1837 AND 1869

	2-year-olds	3-year-olds	4-year-olds	5-year-olds	Total
1837	215	326	210	462	1,213
1869	842	673	402	617	2,534

Source: *Racing Calendar*

an important role in this, as did the rise in prize-money, itself influenced by the coming of the railway. The expansion of two-year-old racing – the numbers almost quadrupled in thirty-two years – was certainly attributable to the railway: these immature horses could not stand the strain of long distance walking.[17] The ease of travel encouraged specialization within racing: the leading jockeys could enhance their positions by riding at more meetings; the best officials similarly could act nationwide; and owners could select their training quarters without regard to the proximity of a racecourse. This latter point badly affected northern trainers who found that their old patrons continued to race in the north but preferred to keep their horses at Newmarket, partly because of the facilities there but also because it was near London where they would be in residence for a good part of the racing and social seasons. By the end of the century neither Malton, Middleham, Hambleton, or Richmond could boast of horses anywhere near the calibre of *Daniel O'Rourke*,

Alice Hawthorn, Voltigeur, West Australian, Caller Ou or
Beeswing, their classic celebrities of the 1840s and 1850s.[18]

Although prize-money increased, many racing men thought
that the level of added money could have been higher. The
revenue of many courses was substantially greater than the
prize-money they contributed. Doncaster Corporation, who ran
the Town Moor course, voted only £1,200 to the prize fund in
1850 but received £7,000 from the grandstand receipts.[19]
Private enterprise meetings were no more generous despite
their incomes rising with the growing popularity of racing,
aided, of course, by the railway special. Indeed Admiral Rous,*
virtual perpetual president of the Jockey Club for over two
decades, claimed that many meetings were held 'not for the love
of sport, but for the certainty of making a good investment and
a lucrative speculation'.[20]

By now more people could afford to go racing. It is generally
acknowledged that real wages rose after the 1840s.[21] Even
E. J. Hobsbawm, no optimist in his interpretation of the effects
of the Industrial Revolution, admits 'there may or may not have
been deterioration between the middle 1790s and the middle
1840s. Thereafter, there was undoubted improvement.'[22] There
was certainly improvement in the 1860s; perhaps an increase of
10 per cent in average real wages compared with the previous
decade.[23] But did the mass of the population have the time to go
to the races? One leading social historian has argued that by the
1830s or 1840s the industrial worker had internalized the time
thrift ethic and accepted long and unremitting hours of labour.[24]
Nevertheless, in other sectors there was still ample opportunity
for daytime, midweek leisure activity. Agriculture, with its
irregular work patterns, was still the largest single employer in
1850; outwork survived in several manufacturing industries; the
ports and docks had an army of casual labour; and large numbers
of self-employed craftsmen maintained control over their working hours. Even in the factories some workers simply took time
off to attend their neighbourhood race meeting;[25] here, presumably much depended on the state of the labour market and
local trade union strength.

* For more on the Admiral see below, pp 93–4.

Rising incomes, sufficient leisure time, and improved transport facilities encouraged the emergence of new meetings: in the 1850s there were sixty-two new events, in the 1860s ninety-nine, and in the first half of the 1870s fifty-four. A few were revivals of languished social gatherings, but most were commercial speculations, designed to extract money from the racegoer via the stands, booths, or facilities offered by the town. As yet, however, there were no enclosed, gate-money events: the high rate of failure among new meetings shown in Table 4 suggests that there was still no certainty of a market large enough to warrant the necessary expenditure.

TABLE 4. SURVIVAL AND FAILURE OF NEW MEETINGS, 1845–69

		Length of life		
Meetings founded	1 year	Less than 5 years	Less than 10 years	10 years or more
1845–9	25	16	18	22	3
1850–54	43	18	21	33	10
1855–9	19	12	12	13	6
1860–64	38	11	16	27	11
1865–9	61	16	33	48	13

Source: calculated from data in *Racing Calendar*

What annoyed Rous even more than the low level of added money was the growing practice of trying to attract entrants by advertising large prizes but then 'defrauding' the winner by deducting up to 25 per cent on pretexts such as police expenses and fees for officials.[26] Writing in typically explosive style to the clerk at York, he declared:

I shall be obliged to blow up all the clerks of the course, not forgetting you, about that abominable system of offering to give good prizes with the right hand and stealing a portion back with the left. Even at York you cannot give a fifty-sovereign plate without stealing back a fiver.[27]

One meeting stood alone in its generosity and freedom from

the Admiral's criticism. 'Ascot,' he declared, '[is] the only course in England where liberality is shown.'[28] Here the executive was both willing and able to offer good prizes without deductions. In 1839 a new grandstand had been financed by a subscription of one hundred £100 shares. Each year five shares were paid off, so that, at the end of two decades, all the fees paid by the 3,000 or so spectators using the stand were available for the race fund. In 1859 £16,200 was given as added money and, after the remaining shareholders were reimbursed, even more substantial sums were raised.[29]

In striking contrast to Ascot was a group of metropolitan meetings organized by local publicans and bookmakers. These men had no intention of offering added money; their races were for what Rous scathingly dismissed as 'wretched £30 plates and small prizes'.[30] Such rewards did not attract many horses, so the promoters frequently provided their own, and indeed often fixed the race, deciding beforehand which horse would win.[31] It was the size of the crowd not of the field which concerned the organizers: racing to them was a means for selling more beer or taking more bets. On the fringe of London but beyond the pale of respectability, these meetings attracted the worst elements of the metropolis. In 'facilitating the movement of bands of indolent roughs', the railways brought ruffianism to many courses, but especially, critics claimed, to Harrow, Kingsbury, West Drayton, Croydon, Lillie Bridge, and, roughest of all, Enfield, Bromley, and Streatham.[32] Rioting and hooliganism were accepted features at all these meetings, though it was worse at some than others: at Bromley a pitched battle was fought between welshing bookmakers and angry punters; at Streatham, a rioting mob tore up railings and flung them at a jockey accused of not trying; and at Enfield a similarly suspected rider was saved from lynching only by armed racecourse officials.[33] Organized by publicans for sinners, these 'suburban saturnalia' were little more than schemes of fraud, robbery, and mob rule.[34] Eventually Parliamentary legislation was used to put them down.*

Other meetings went more quietly: in the period 1840–70 an average of six meetings a year disappeared from the *Racing*

* See below, p. 99.

Calendar. Some were fly-by-night speculations which vanished as quickly as they arose. Some were traditional meetings, isolated from the mainstream of racing, and, for various reasons, unable to attract either local or distant support. Others, too near a railway, attracted unwelcome spectators with the result that the local patrons no longer felt any responsibility to the meeting: instead of sponsoring races or watching their horses run, 'the Master of Hounds is busy among the cubs, the Lord Lieutenant is shooting partridges four or five fields off, and the Duke has shut himself up at home'.[35] Not all the traditional social gatherings failed to survive, but, as is shown in Table 5, there was a distinct trend towards longer meetings and to holding more than one meeting a year: commercially orientated racing was taking over. However, although the sport had changed significantly in only thirty years, even more momentous changes were yet to come.

TABLE 5. RACE MEETINGS IN BRITAIN 1848–70

	One-day meetings	Longer meetings	Courses having more than one meeting
1848	61	56	13
1856	37	74	13
1863	35	71	19
1870	58	82	32

Source: calculated from data in the *Racing Calendar*

Railways did much to increase racing's popularity as a spectator sport. Indeed 'on the slightest provocation railway companies placarded half London with lists of cheap trains to any country places where races are held, and in every sporting paper at least half a column is dedicated to excursionists who want to go racewards'.[1] Nevertheless, despite the crowds that flocked to race meetings, no race committee of any significance moved to charge a general entrance fee. Some of the roughest courses witnessed a few brute force attempts to collect gate money, but the general practice at all other meetings was to charge only those spectators who utilized the stands or who viewed from the comfort of private carriages.

In 1875, however, Sandown Park opened its turnstiles as an enclosed course, entry to which required a fee from *all* race-goers. It was an instant success: beginning with two annual meetings, it ran four by 1877 and five by 1880. Within two to three decades racing was taking place at enclosed courses all over Britain. In the south, Kempton Park made its successful début only three years after Sandown's inaugural meeting. Then in the early 1890s new enclosed events began at Hurst Park, Lingfield, and Gatwick. Although all three had difficulty in obtaining suitable dates for fixtures because the Jockey Club gave preference in the *Calendar* to established meetings, they were still successful,* probably due to the ease of access for the metropolitan populace, who traditionally preferred days out to holidays away from home.[2]† Newbury, founded in 1906 by the famous, but by then retired, trainer, John Porter, also drew on London for the bulk of its spectators.[3] In the Midlands, racing companies‡

---

* Initially, however, Gatwick was unprofitable because of undercapitalization and excessive expenditure. G. H. Verrall, 'The Financial Aspect of Racing From Another Point of View', *Badminton Magazine*, vol. 23, November 1906, p. 507.

† Perhaps this explains why in Surrey one could find four of the top five enclosed meetings and also the incomparable Epsom gathering.

‡ Sandown Park began as a partnership but became a limited company in 1885. All other enclosed meetings cited here had company status.

created enclosed courses at Derby (1880), Leicester (1884) and Colwick Park, Nottingham (1892). Further north, Gosforth Park was widely acknowledged as one of the finest enclosed courses of the nineteenth century.[4] The old Newcastle Town Moor fixtures were transferred there in the early 1880s, and essentially Gosforth relied on northern racegoers unlike Manchester whose three strong programmes at Castle Irwell, less than two miles from the city centre, attracted many spectators from the south of England. Here the river Irwell acted as a natural barrier against intruders; unfortunately on occasions it invaded the course itself. One of the directors of the Manchester enterprise, John Davies, was also responsible for founding the Haydock Park Meeting in 1898.[5] North of the border there was only one attempt at an enclosed course before 1900. This was in 1887 when a group of Glasgow sportsmen-cum-speculators leased part of Hamilton Park and fenced it off as a racecourse. However, although there was a population of over a million within ten miles of the course, no more than 12,000 could be attracted to the early meetings.[6] Attendances improved, but in 1907 the Duchess of Hamilton, concerned about working-class gambling, refused to renew the lease. All debts were paid but the shareholders lost their money. Hamilton's fixtures were then taken over by a newly-established course at Ayr.[7]

The success of the enclosed course was dependent on its ability to attract spectators; here two groups attained new significance, ladies and the working class. Prior to the advent of the enclosed meeting relatively few ladies went racing. Of course they attended Ascot where there was the Royal Enclosure and the lawn to accommodate them; Goodwood and Epsom too were part of the social season; but elsewhere, even at Newmarket, ladies were rarely seen except for a few in carriages or in private or stewards' stands: respectability inhibited them from using the free areas or even the grandstands such as they were.[8] This social parameter was accepted by the enclosed courses when they attempted to attract lady spectators. From its inception Sandown encouraged their attendance by the formation of a racing club, carefully vetting the membership to ensure an aura of respectability. Although club membership was a male prerogative,* members who subscribed at the higher rate obtained two ladies' badges and other subscribers could take in two ladies on the payment of a small fee. Similar clubs were formed at all enclosed courses and by the turn of the century several thousand ladies could be expected to attend most important meetings.[9] Racing clubs were not new, but the previous ones at Epsom, Stockbridge, and Lewes were much smaller and did not admit ladies.[10] The establishment of clubs within the enclosed course provided pleasurable racing for the wealthier supporters of the turf and their womenfolk: the races, luncheon, the musical accompaniment, even just strolling around the lawns and flower beds could all be enjoyed in comfort.

The other major new source of revenue was the working class, more of whom became both willing and able to pay to see racing. There are obvious difficulties in generalizing about *the* working class, for it was far from being a homogeneous group; at any time the skilled artisan could probably afford a wider range of recreational activity than the labourer or the factory hand. Nevertheless, most economic historians would accept that, for the bulk of the working class, real incomes rose between the 1850s and the end of the century.† Before the 1880s, however, most of the rise was attributable to money wages moving ahead of prices and was thus probably restricted to those groups with the strongest bargaining power, but, from the 1880s, falling prices brought greater prosperity to the working class on a broad front.[11] Overall, between 1850 and

---

* As elsewhere in society, ladies found their role in racing severely restricted. They were not allowed to act as officials or trainers, and the thought of lady jockeys would have caused apoplexy in Jockey Club circles. For most of the nineteenth century too, female owners generally took male pseudonyms (The Duchess of Montrose raced as Mr Manton, Lily Langtry as Mr Jersey, and Lady Meux as Mr Theobalds), though by 1900 eighty-one ladies had their colours registered. For a general view of the situation see C. Ramsden, *Ladies in Racing*, 1973.

† Calculations based on B. R. Mitchell and P. Deane, *Abstract of British Historical Statistics*, 1962, pp. 343–4 suggest that an index of average real wages rose from 99·8 in the period 1850–59 to 110·1 in 1860–69, 129·6 in 1870–79, 145·8 in 1880–89 and 171·0 in 1890–99. E. H. Phelps-Brown and M. H. Browne, *A Century of Pay*, 1968, p. 170 argue that between 1871 and 1895 real wages rose 1·94 per cent per annum. A discussion of the issue can be found in S. B. Saul, *The Myth of the Great Depression*, 1969, pp. 30–34.

1900 average real wages rose some 70 per cent. Initially spending was probably expanded along conventional consumption lines, but by the 1880s new spending patterns had emerged.[12] Entrepreneurs had responded to the new market stimulus by developing goods and services suited to a 'mass consumer' society, among them commercialized leisure.* Indeed the 1870s and 1880s are important decades in the history of commercialized popular recreation: they witnessed an expansion of the specialist music halls which had first appeared in the 1860s, the rapid development of seaside holidays for the working class, the take-off of gate-money soccer, and, of course, the enclosed race meeting.[13]

It may be that the Sandown Park executive was not attempting to tap the working-class market in any depth since its minimum admission charge before 1914 was never below half a crown,[14] which contrasts remarkably unfavourably with the sixpence charged to see a top quality football match.† Most other enclosed courses, however, took a shilling as the basic entrance fee – the same as the Hippodrome some fifty years previously – this was still expensive relative to soccer but within the pocket of sufficient working men to satisfy the course management. It must be stressed that it is *not* being argued that every working man could afford to go racing: clearly the contemporary social surveys repudiate such a notion. However, it should be pointed out that a basic deficiency of many budgetary studies showing how much was left for recreational and other purposes after meeting necessary expenditure is the reluctance to admit that *all* spending is optional. Human beings are perverse creatures, often finding greater satisfaction in activities other than meeting basic physiological needs. We do not know how

---

* This response lends support to the current re-evaluation of the performance of British entrepreneurs in the late Victorian economy which suggests that they have been overly condemned as failures. See, e.g. D. N. McCloskey and L. Sandberg, 'From Damnation to Redemption: Judgements on the Late Victorian Entrepreneur', *Explorations in Economic History*, vol. 9, Fall 1971, pp. 89–108; P. L. Payne, *British Entrepreneurship in the Nineteenth Century*, 1974. The expansion of commercial leisure also underlines the 'myth' of the so-called 'Great Depression'; dare it be suggested that Britain had not gone to the dogs but to the races?

† When the Football League was founded in 1888 sixpence was set as the minimum admission charge. Most clubs allowed entry at this price except at key cup matches.

many attenders at race meetings nutritionally could not 'afford' to be there.

The executives of the gate-money meetings laid great emphasis on attracting spectators: they were in racing to make money. They had encouraged the attendance of ladies by providing the racing club; they did the same for the working man by offering Saturday afternoon racing. This was partly forced upon them because many existing meetings would not have a Saturday, traditionally a day for taking horses home from a meeting, but no doubt as the Saturday half day had become more common* there was also a positive reason for choosing to race on a Saturday. Nevertheless that the working man had more money in his pockets did not mean that necessarily he would spend it at the races: racing had to compete against other leisure activities, some of them organized by equally profit-motivated entrepreneurs. And even among racegoers the enclosed course did not have a captive market: the railway had seen to that. Although the Jockey Club organized the racing calendar so as to prevent serious fixture clashes between meetings, courses were still in competition with each other for spectators as the average racegoer had limited funds and leisure time at his disposal. If he was to be persuaded to pay for his pleasure rather than frequent a meeting which did not charge gate money, then he must be offered something different for his money: the product of the gate-money meeting had to be differentiated from that of the unenclosed course.

To some extent this was done by offering better facilities: the club for the wealthier supporter of the turf and plenty of space for the humbler admirers of the sport so that they could view the racing without being crowded or hustled, even when, as at Gosforth Park on Northumberland Plate day, over 50,000 spectators presented themselves.[15] Travelling facilities were also considered: almost all the new courses had a railway

---

* A free Sunday presumably followed from a combination of working-class self-interest and religious pressure, but why Saturday afternoon attained such significance for the working man is not clear. Once Sunday had been obtained then any further gain would probably be on Saturday afternoon or Monday morning; possibly employers might offer less resistance where the labour force first attended work rather than when they had to be relied upon to turn up after having had a morning off.

station within easy walking distance, often with a covered walk-way from the platforms to the stands. Primarily, however, the race promoters attracted their audience by offering the type of racing which the crowd wished to see: not for them the long distance races in which the best horse might come in well ahead of the field; instead they preferred two-year-old races, sprints, and handicaps, all of which had a sufficient degree of uncertainty about the result to make for exciting racing. Much of the racing was also of a high standard, featuring top-quality horses and jockeys; and racegoers could always be attracted by a great performer, human or equine. The tracks of the enclosed courses were kept in first-rate condition so no owner need fear injury to his valuable bloodstock, but more positive an attraction to quality horses was the increased level of prize-money offered at the gate-money meeting. Increases in prize-money attracted more, as well as better, horses. Large fields were attractive to spectators and their gate-money underwrote the level of prize-money. The secret of the enclosed meeting's success was succinctly put by a contemporary racing writer: 'good management and good money mean good sport' and, it may be added, good sport meant that the good money was forthcoming via the turnstiles.[16]

However, the so-called 'mammoth' prize should not be exaggerated. This began in 1886 when the Sandown executive inaugurated a £10,000 race, the Eclipse Stakes. It was a great success: the publicity and the quality of the field attracted a host of paying customers. Three other course committees attempted to follow suit: Manchester with the Lancashire Plate (1888), Kempton with the Royal Stakes (1889), and Leicester with the Prince of Wales' Stakes (1889), but none of them lasted any time. Each, for its own reasons, failed to attract sufficient entries or extra spectators to justify the executives' contributions. Greater success was met by the Jockey Club in 1894 when it introduced two £10,000 races, the Prince of Wales' Stakes and the Jockey Club Stakes, both of which had conditions almost identical with those of the Eclipse. In 1900 Sandown Park tried to introduce a second mammoth prize with the Century Stakes but it was not a financial success and was discontinued.[17]

Not all enclosed meetings were successful. Indeed Portsmouth Park, Hedon Park (Hull), and Four Oaks Park (Birmingham), where £100,000 was lost, were conspicuous failures, partially because of an inability to obtain suitable dates.[18] Nevertheless the majority of the new, enclosed meetings were successes; so much so that many older, established fixtures were forced to follow suit and adopt the style of the modern racing company by rebuilding stands for the general public, creating club enclosures for more select racegoers, and charging a shilling for admittance to the outside portion of the course. Even where they did not enclose to the extent of Sandown and its ilk, they offered less free space than before. Unless the attitudes of their executives had changed radically, the old meetings did not follow the new ones simply to make money: in any case, the Jockey Club, worried about the influence of the gate-money fixture, had imposed a dividend limitation of 10 per cent on any race company.* No, the prime reason for the move was a desire to maintain the quality of their racing. To do this they had to increase the level of prize-money offered, otherwise they would not attract the better horses; but larger prizes could only be offered if the funds were available. Although owners were mainly racing for their own money – even in 1905 entry fees from owners provided two-thirds of all prize money[19] – prizes had to be underwritten for there was always a chance that insufficient entries would be forthcoming to guarantee the promised rewards. Contributions could still be solicited from local hotelkeepers, shopkeepers, and railway companies; entrants to the stands could be charged for the privilege; and there was always half the surplus from selling races.† But the best way to make sure of sufficient funds was to charge at the gate, and this necessarily involved some form of enclosure.

* See below, p. 96. The average dividend declared in 1913 was 7½ per cent. *Bloodstock Breeders Review*, vol. 4, no. 4, January 1916, p. 282.

† Selling races were a device to obtain money for the prize fund whilst at the same time giving owners a chance to get rid of relatively poor horses. Entry conditions stated that the winner be sold for a certain sum, usually £100; the money difference between the actual auction price and the nominated selling price was divided equally between the race fund and the second horse. Lord Suffolk, a Jockey Club steward, maintained that 'selling races as at present carried on are the vital principle of most meetings, for they constitute an unfailing source of revenue'. *Badminton Magazine*, vol. 6, May 1898, p. 587.

Without this, it would be difficult to compete against the gate-money meeting.

In the quarter century after the inauguration of Sandown Park eighty-nine meetings disappeared from the *Racing Calendar*; failure to enclose, however, was not the only or even the prime cause of this. Parliamentary legislation in 1879 put down several London meetings, specifically the suburban shams and violent gatherings discussed in the previous chapter.* It is suggested that the promoter of the West Drayton meeting, the self-styled Count Bolo (really a George French), pursued his villainous activities right to the end by burning down the grandstand which he had insured for £600. However, he refused the insurance company's offer of £400 and insisted on the full £600; the company's reply was to build a new stand, which remained a white elephant for many years to come.[20]

More devastating than the Parliamentary action, or so it is generally alleged, were new Jockey Club rules, applicable from 1877, which forced race committees to provide a minimum of 300 sovereigns added money for each day of racing and also to ensure that each race was worth at least £100 to the winner.[21] But it is possible – considering the casualty figures of the 1860s and early 1870s shown in Table 6 – that even without these regulations many minor meetings would still have disappeared. The rules may have stifled the emergence of further mayfly meetings, destined to figure only briefly on the racing scene, but the right of the Club not to recognize meetings and the sanctions applicable to participants at such unrecognized events could equally well have served the same purpose.† Indeed from the early 1880s the Jockey Club became very reluctant to license any new courses, even ones which could have raised far more than 300 sovereigns.[22] Moreover, the deterrent effect of 300 sovereigns has to be questioned: surely, provided that there was local interest in racing, only the most inefficient or unenterprising of executives could not have raised such a sum from solicited contributions, booth rents, stand fees, and selling plates. If there was little local interest or if the executives were ruled by inertia, then, even without the Jockey Club legislation, such meetings would not have survived long in the face of gate-money

* See above, p. 36.　　　　　　　† See below, p. 95.

competition for race entrants. Most of the race committees who were able to raise the necessary money found it difficult enough to compete both in terms of the prize-money and the standard of course offered to the owner.[23] For most meetings the choice was simple: either you erected fences or you went to the wall. Unenclosed meetings generally disappeared or struggled along with racing of an inferior quality.[24]

TABLE 6. RISE AND FALL OF RACE MEETINGS 1860–99

	Meetings founded	Meetings ended	Nett change
1860–64	38	28	+10
1865–69	61	32	+29
1870–74	54	81	−27
1875–79	13	56	−43
1880–84	1	15	−14
1885–89	9	5	+4
1890–94	4	9	−5
1895–99	5	10	−5

Source: calculated from data in the *Racing Calendar*

Few open meetings could hope to do more than survive; except for an elect few, Ascot, Epsom, Goodwood, Doncaster, and York. Here racing continued to flourish. The charisma of traditional prestige events may have been sufficient to tempt owners to race, but if so why was the prize-money for the Derby, the blue riband event of the turf, raised to a level comparable to the better prizes at the enclosed meetings?[25] What protected Ascot and the others was their position in the social calendar: members and would-be-members of high society felt a social obligation to put in an appearance at these meetings. However, certificates of social seaworthiness did not come cheaply: at Ascot, a weekly admission ticket cost at least two pounds with further charges for entry to the grandstands; private boxes and luncheon rooms cost another ten guineas.[26] With such prices, ample funds were forthcoming for the prize fund – in 1900 Ascot gave over £37,000 to its twenty-eight races[27] – and it was prize-money that was the major attraction for owners.

That prestige and a good name for racing was insufficient to preserve an open meeting intact is clear from the experience of Newmarket. Here, despite the testing variety of courses and an acknowledged racing reputation, the Jockey Club found that the level and quality of entrants left it 'no alternative but to march with the times, to build stands, to make enclosures, to substitute the white rails of modern civilization for the old-fashioned ropes and stakes of our forefathers'.[28] Pedestrians and horsemen were still allowed free entry to most of the heath, but heavy tolls were exacted from carriage owners everywhere and from all who utilized the stands and other spectator facilities.[29]

The enclosed, gate-money course brought significant changes to British racing; indeed it forced transformation upon the turf: if race committees did not innovate they frequently disappeared. In general it reinforced and accelerated the long established trend to greater commercialization, but with a major difference: previously most race committees had put the owner before the spectator but now, even if this attitude still prevailed, it became impossible to serve the owner's needs without also considering those of the crowd. By offering the spectator, especially the working man, the kind of racing he preferred – in particular sprints, handicaps, and two-year-old events – the enclosed courses tempted him to pay for his pleasure. His admission money enabled a greater volume of prize-money to be offered: in 1874, the year before Sandown's innovation, £315,272 had been won; by 1905 the total was £495,082. This increase of £179,810 in thirty-one years compares favourably with the rise of £116,282 in a similar time period (1843–74) during the era of the 'railway revolution'. The greater rewards offered encouraged more horse ownership. The number of racehorses in training rose from 2,534 in 1869, the highest number in the pre-enclosed era, to 3,957 by 1902; and one estimate suggests that in the relatively short period 1877–91 the value of investment in racing bloodstock jumped from £1·7 millions to over £3 millions and to between £7 millions and £8 millions by 1913.[30] The pressure placed on the bloodstock industry resulted in stud fees soaring: in the early 1860s a top-class stallion could earn forty to fifty guineas per service; in the early twentieth century fees of 200, 250, or 300 guineas were quite usual and a great horse such as *St Simon* could earn 500 guineas a time.[31] Clearly racing was becoming as much a part of the economic as the social scene, an industry as well as a sport. Working-class support had never been necessary to racing, but once it began to be actively solicited by course executives then both the structure and character of the sport changed.* Even the major open courses which made no attempt to charge the mass of racegoers, but which held their own against the wealth and seductions of gate-money gatherings, found 'it necessary from time to time to alter their programmes and keep step in the quick march of the day, lest they too should be fain to take their place in the rear of the companies'.[32]

---

* One can only speculate as to the demise of the 'social' race meeting, so dominant in the eighteenth century. Many simply lost their traditional local character and patronage as the railways brought participants and spectators from far afield. Possibly, at least for the rural population, the point-to-point replaced the flat meeting as the local social event of the year. Certainly for the urban workers new forms of paternalistic leisure emerged under the aegis of muscular Christianity and productivity-conscious employers, e.g. works' football teams, brass bands, and sponsored outings.

4]   *The American Invasion]*

John Huggins, the walrus-moustached, American trainer of
Volodyovski, the 1901 Derby winner, was once asked if there
were many crooks on the American turf. 'No,' was his considered if sweeping reply, 'they have all come over here to
England.'[1] The anti-racing lobby in the United States seemed
to be winning its crusade to extinguish the sport and conse-
quently owners, trainers, jockeys, gamblers and horses had all
crossed the Atlantic to take part in British racing. This so-called
American invasion of the British turf in the late 1890s and the
early twentieth century added fuel, often bright burning, to the
fire of turf immorality which the Jockey Club was attempting to
dampen down.* Not all the trans-Atlantic visitors came with
criminal intent, but some of them had fraud and turf abuse down
to a fine art, if not a science.

This was not the first time that American racing men had
come to Britain. By the second half of the nineteenth century
there were few barriers, save sea-sickness, to the international
transfer of turf participants. British racing men frequently
crossed the Channel to challenge and 'educate' the continentals,
and it was claimed, admittedly by an English turf devotee, that
many of the top French horses in the 1870s were derived from
British bloodstock, ridden by British jockeys, and prepared by
British trainers.[2] On the other hand, British racing circles had
been shocked by some continental incursions. As early as 1840
the Duke of Orleans won the Goodwood Cup with *Beggarman*.
This may have been viewed as an isolated incident, but not so
Fille de l'Air's Oaks victory for Count de Lagrange in 1864
followed next year by *Gladiateur*'s triple crown for the same
owner. And by the 1870s many major British races were going
to invaders from the Continent.†

---

* See below, Chapter 6.
  † Their victories included the Goodwood Cup (1873 *Flageolet*); the Oaks
(1872 *Reine*, 1876 *Enguerrande*), the Derby (1876 *Kisber*), the Ascot Cup (1871
Mortemer, 1872 *Henry*, 1873 *Boiard*, 1878 *Verneuil*), the 2,000 Guineas (1877
Chamant) the Doncaster Cup (1870 *Sornette*, 1872 *Dutch Skater*) and the St Leger
(1879 *Rayon D'Or*).

The Atlantic was wider than the Channel, but it was still crossed, though here the racing traffic was one-way. Americans brought their horses to England; the English saw little prestige in winning American races.

The pioneer American owner was Richard Ten Broeck, who first arrived in Britain in 1857 along with some of the best horses the American turf could at that time produce. His greatest horse, *Le Compte*, American despite its name, unhappily contracted an illness and was never able to run in Britain. But Ten Broeck's patriotic red and white striped jacket with blue stars and blue cap was carried to victory in the Cesarewitch of 1857 by *Prioress*, and two years later in both the Goodwood Stakes and Cup by *Starke*. Although Ten Broeck, his horses, and occasionally an American jockey to ride them reappeared at intervals, it was not till the early 1880s that American owners created a real stir. Messrs Lorillard, the tobacco millionaire, and J. R. Keene made their debut on the English racing scene, the former's *Iroquois* taking the scalps of leading British contenders in both the Derby and St Leger, and the latter's *Foxhall* completing the Autumn double, beating in the Cambridgeshire one of the best fields ever to go to the post for that race.[3] However, despite these successful incursions, it was in the closing years of the nineteenth century that American owners, particularly J. R. Keene, August Belmont, and father and son Whitney, began to make their great impact on British racing: not just in the races that they won, but also in the introduction of American training methods and racing practices.

Among the American trainers that came over to Britain at this time, two stand out, though for different reasons. In the three years, 1898–1900, John Huggins trained the winners of 162 races valued at over £87,000. In 1900 he had the third highest total of wins of any trainer and the year previously had topped the list; in both years he ranked second for the value of winnings; and, of course, in 1901 he trained the Derby winner. Then, there was Wishard, the man who brought over the two Reiff brothers, Lester who became champion jockey in 1900 and young Johnny, possibly the best lightweight rider ever. But Wishard left his mark for something else, his cleverness with dope. He first came to Britain in the mid 1890s with a few American horses but, enjoying only moderate success, soon left. In 1899 he reappeared and in partnership with W. Duke, another American, he trained fourteen winners. The races were insignificant ones, but Wishard was more interested in betting coups than prize-money, so the type of race was immaterial. In 1900 Duke and Wishard, training independently, each made their influence felt; Duke trained thirty-one winners and Wishard fifty-four, the most of any trainer. In both cases the successes were generally with cheaply bought horses which had lost their form, not that it had ever been startling. Almost miraculously under Duke, and especially Wishard, they more than regained it and went on to win handicap races. American training methods may have had something to do with it: horses were given much more fresh air than was common in British establishments, better shoes were fitted, and 'the general health (of these American-trained horses) improves to an extent which is almost unknown in English stables'.[4] The turf writer, Alfred Watson, editor of the *Badminton Magazine*, believed it was the skill of Wishard rather than any specific training methods.[5] But skill at what? American race meetings lasted for ten days or more and horses ran several times at one meet. Over time this led to the use of dope on tired horses. When the Americans came to Britain they imported the techniques with them. Wishard had made a careful study of drugs and supplemented his training expertise by using dope to give that extra edge to his horses. He was not alone. Although Huggins for one detested the practice, most of the other American trainers had no qualms about using the hypodermic needle.[6] It is noticeable that their success rate dropped sharply after 1904 when the Jockey Club made the doping of horses a turf offence. It must be stressed that till this legislation Wishard and his compatriots had acted within the written laws of racing: doping may have been a dubious moral practice, but there was no official sanction against it. * Some American trainers, however, acted outside the rules of racing: jockeys were bribed, horses scandalously pulled, and handicapping rendered a farce. Finally, the actions of one of them, Eugene Leigh, stimulated the Jockey Club to insist that

* See below, pp. 103–4.

all trainers in Britain had to hold a Club licence, not merely those who wished to follow their calling on Newmarket Heath.[7]

Richard Ten Broeck, the first of the American invaders, once gave an exhibition of amateur jockeyship in a match at Warwick. Puffing away at his cigar and sitting bolt upright in the saddle, he looked set for hacking about the park rather than race riding. When the flag dropped he was left eight lengths; this in a race of only five furlongs. Needless to say he was beaten, though only narrowly, for he came with a tremendous rush at the end. His turf commissioner, George Payne, reckoned that 'if he had not put him £800 on, he should have sworn he had pulled the horse'.[8] Ten Broeck's amateur efforts were unsuccessful: the American professional jockeys who came later did much better. Unhappily some of them differed from Ten Broeck not only in style and success, but also in honesty.

Their level of success was astonishing. The Derby, the race all jockeys want to win, went their way five times in six years: Lester Reiff piloted *Volodyovski* home in 1901; J. H. 'Skeets' Martin followed on *Ard Patrick* in 1902; Danny Maher completed an American hat trick by winning on *Rock Sand* in 1903 and a personal triple when he was first at the post with *Cicero* in 1905 and *Spearmint* in 1906. These classic victories reflected the phenomenal turf success of the diminutive Yankee invaders. In 1900 five of the leading ten jockeys were from America, including Lester Reiff who won the championship and in 1903 when only ten jockeys rode more than fifty winners, again five of them were American. The Americans not only won a large number of races, they won a high proportion of the races they rode in: in 1900 Maher, Johnny Reiff, and Martin topped 20 per cent, Lester Reiff gained 26 per cent and Tod Sloan almost 27 per cent.

Sloan was the first to make his mark in Britain. On his first short visit in Autumn 1897, he made over £2,000 after paying all his expenses, no mean feat considering his taste for the high life.[9] In that year he had fifty-three mounts and won on twenty of them. He returned the following Autumn, again as the punter's friend, winning forty-three out of seventy-eight races and being unplaced only seventeen times. At the first Newmarket October meeting he had twelve winners out of sixteen rides, including five in succession. The shocked British turf experts contented themselves with the view that 'the very great majority of his successes, at any rate, would have been gained with any competent jockey in the saddle' and that if Sloan came over for a full season it would be a different story.[10] In both 1897 and 1898 Sloan had arrived at the tail end of the British season, but in 1899 handsome retainers induced him to come over in time for the opening meeting at Lincoln. Now, said the pundits, he will be shown in his true light. He was. He rode 345 times, won on 108 occasions and was placed in a further 103 races.

Clearly Sloan was an outstanding jockey. Yet it was not just Sloan that was winning. The American invasion had begun in earnest. Other jockeys crossed the Atlantic and were also victorious. Maher, Covington, McGuire, Martin, and the two Reiffs all came and began to be busy and, in varying degrees, successful. The invasion was at its height in 1900 with the American jockeys doing so well 'that English jockeys had become exceedingly doleful with the conviction that they were to be swept practically out of existence'.[11] In racing, at least among jockeys, success can breed success. When a jockey has a good season the demand for his services increases and he has more mounts offered to him; if he can judge horseflesh as well as he can judge a race, his choice of rides can reinforce his initial success. So with the Americans' spectacular success there was good reason for British jockeys to worry about their livelihoods. It could not have eased their minds when the Prince of Wales offered Sloan 6,000 guineas as a retainer.[12] How many other owners would consider it fashionable to emulate royalty? In fact the worst was over. Sloan's gambling led to him not being given a licence to ride in 1901 and Lester Reiff was warned off at the end of that season for not trying to win on a horse at Manchester.* Others withdrew voluntarily and soon only Martin and Maher remained, both of them content to reside permanently in England.

Why were the Americans so successful? One obvious reason was that they were good jockeys; their record in America showed this clearly. Maher was actually champion jockey there

* See below, pp. 57–8.

in 1898. However, being masters of their trade in America would not guarantee them success in Britain, for British race-courses, with their variety of undulations, gradients, and turns, presented a riding challenge not at all like that of the uniformly flat American dirt tracks. Riding doped horses for their com-patriot invaders may have inflated their winning figures, but again it is an insufficient explanation. The key factor was their riding style and racing tactics.

American riders could be distinguished at a glance. English jockeys rode not much different from the style of the hunting field, sitting erect with a comparatively straight knee and a good length of rein; in contrast the Americans pushed the saddle forward, shortened both the stirrups and the reins, and rode with knees bent, crouching along the horse's neck. How this style evolved is lost in the folk-lore of racing. One version is that it originated from the bareback riding of the American Indians. Another, more popular, view was that it was devised by southern negroes whose racing masters threw them up without saddles, forcing them to grip the mane and lie along the neck for balance. Sloan claimed it was all his own idea, discovered when larking about in the training yard.[13] The effects of the American seat were much clearer than its causes.

It was first seen by the English racing public at the New-market Craven meeting in April 1895 when *Eau Gallie*, a three-year-old son of *Iroquois*, went to the post for the Crawfurd Place with Simms, a coloured American jockey, perched up on his neck. Jockeys and spectators alike were vastly amused by Simms's appearance, but the smiles soon vanished once the flag dropped. *Eau Gallie* jumped off, came along at top speed and passed the post without ever being caught, leaving the favourite and the mounts of several leading British jockeys to its rear. Simms won three other races, out of nineteen rides, and then disappeared from the British racing scene.[14] He had no successor the following season and the eccentric American seat was forgotten. Like its coloured exhibitor, it was regarded as a novelty; something to be looked at out of curiosity and then consigned to obscurity.

However, in the autumn of 1897 Tod Sloan arrived. Seated, more or less, in the fashion of the forgotten Simms, Sloan rode winner after winner. Insular British turf experts were reluctant to concede that the Americans could teach them anything about horsemanship; they regarded it as luck that he won races riding in such a preposterous, monkey-on-a-stick style.[15] The punters just accepted that Sloan won. Eventually all but the diehards acknowledged that the American seat cut wind resistance and gave a better distribution of weight on the horse, equal to perhaps a ten to fourteen pound advantage.[16] Nevertheless, while accepting these points, many critics felt that English jockeys could always beat the Americans in a tight finish as they had more control over the horse.[17] The Americans, however, generally tried to avoid such finishes by having their races won long before the winning post. Whereas the English jockeys tended to ride a waiting race* (though not so much in sprint races, of course), virtually hack cantering till the final furlongs, and then staging a gallery finish, regarding a short head victory as supreme artistry,† the American tried to put as much distance as possible between himself and his rivals.[18] The Americans did not ride their horses flat out – no horse has the stamina for this – but they did their waiting at the front rather than in the pack. Most of the Americans were remarkable judges of pace, perhaps because American trainers placed great faith in riding to the clock, unlike British trainers who preferred to try horses against each other rather than against the stopwatch.[19] Of course the similarity of so many American racetracks made comparisons of times much more meaningful than in Britain where 'horses for courses' was a fair working rule.[20] The American jockeys considered every post a winning post and aimed to get to the front as quickly as they could. Their task was sometimes made easier by the starting gate (first used in Britain in 1897‡), an apparatus with which many of the Americans were familiar and thus at an advantage over their

* J. Fairfax-Blakeborough, *The Analysis of the Turf*, 1927, p. 205, claims that William Vane, the starter at Winchester, once beat the field on his hack, so much were the jockeys riding a waiting race.

† An authoritative statement in the mid-nineteenth century declared that 'the duty of a jockey is to win his race if possible, and not to do more than win it . . . a very clever one, if he is opposed to another of less science in a finish will [pretend] he is beat and then . . . he will catch him with a tremendous rush on the post.' *Encyclopaedia Britannica*, 1856, vol. 11, p. 688.

‡ See below, p. 117.

less experienced British colleagues. Sloan's first win in Britain was in such a mechanically started race.[21]

Within a decade of Sloan's revelations the American jockey invasion was over. Two reasons account for this: the compulsory withdrawal of some of the invaders who were warned off by the Jockey Club; and, of more importance since the malefactors could have been replaced, the development of a new style of riding by British jockeys, who took on the Americans and beat them at their own game. When Sloan first astounded British racing men with his eccentric style, one turf authority could not 'believe that, generation after generation, jockeys have been sitting on the wrong part of a horse's back, that the best place for the saddle is not where it has always been, and that at the end of the nineteenth century the theory and practice of horsemanship as applied to racing is to be revolutionized'.[22] He had to eat his words. British jockeys had been made well aware that their style of life was dependent upon their style of riding. If they wanted to beat the Americans then they would have to join them. By degrees, British riders began to shorten their stirrups and to sit further forward and much less erect. Kempton Cannon was one of the first to do this and his increased total of winners soon justified the change.[23] By September 1900 the conservative authority cited above acknowledged that the successful English jockeys 'more or less ride more Americano' and when Kempton Cannon's father, Tom, an outstanding trainer of apprentices, began to teach his boys to ride more in the American style, he conceded that it would be absurd to question the advantage thus obtained.[24] The innovation was widely taken up. Newmarket Heath was filled with jockeys practising the seat on their hacks and trying to forget habits instilled by years of race riding. Those who refused to change had to accept less success and lower incomes. The new style of British riding was an adaptation of the American, not an adoption. Initially, it is true, the pure American style was taken up but, though better than the traditional British upright seat, it was not ideal for the undulating British courses and jockeys found it difficult to rebalance their horses if they changed legs and rolled about. The initial wholesale imitation of the monkey-on-a-stick style, perfected as it was for the billard-table tracks of the United States, led to a host of accidents and objections for foul riding.[25] Soon, however, modified versions of the American seat appeared: the end result was that stirrups in general remained shorter than formerly, but the knees of most jockeys did not overlap the withers of their mounts, nor were reins so tightly grasped or held so close behind the ears as in the original American style, and in general the leathers that had been shortened were lengthened again, though the compromise position lay nearer Sloan's than Fred Archer's.[26] Once the new British style emerged, coupled with the abandonment by British jockeys of their traditional waiting race, the Americans met with considerably less success; Maher was a major exception to this rule, mainly because he himself compromised and altered his early American style.[27] Maher's record remained outstanding: between 1900 and 1914 he rode 1,331 winners with a winning percentage of 25·3. The Americans had invaded, almost conquered, but had eventually been beaten off, though not without leaving a permanent mark on British jockeyship. *

Maher was perhaps unique among the American jockeys. Not only did he remain in Britain to pursue his career, but he was also generally regarded as incorruptible. Lord Durham, archenemy of turf villainy, thought little of Sloan who was frequently suspended, but he had no objections to Maher who seemed 'a most respectable boy'.[28] In fact Maher was so honest that when – unjustly in his opinion – he was called before the local stewards at Leicester he never raced there again, even though he was cleared.[29] Many of the other American jockeys lacked Maher's scruples. They were frequently suspended; indeed several of them were warned off. Some of this was due to the difficulties of keeping horses straight when riding with the American seat, but much was attributable to sheer dishonesty and disregard for the rules of racing, even by the men at the top of their professions. Lester Reiff, champion jockey in 1900, was warned off in October 1901 for not trying to win on *De Lacy* at

---

* The diehards would have called it a disfiguration rather than a mark. S. E. Clayton, an owner for forty-five years, refused to make any concessions: 'no-one can gainsay the fact that the introduction of the American seat has entirely destroyed true horsemanship . . . it wins races, but it is entirely trick riding, and smacks more of the hippodrome and circus than of the racecourse.' 'The State of the Turf', *Badminton Magazine*, vol. 19, December 1904, p. 664.

Manchester.[30] A year earlier, Sloan, the man chiefly responsible for popularizing the new style of riding in Britain, was barred from racing here because of his betting activities. His gambling was an open secret and it was only a matter of time before he was called before the stewards. The actual interview came after the Cambridgeshire of 1900. At the inquiry he claimed that he knew of no jockey that did not bet, and that, in this specific case, his bet of £2,000 was on his own mount, a procedure which was allowed under American rules of racing. He also admitted accepting the offer of a four-figure present from a professional gambler if he won the race.[31] At the time the stewards merely reprimanded him but Sloan had condemned himself. His popularity among the punters was not matched in higher turf circles: his vanity, stupidity, love of gambling, and choice of friends had not endeared him to the Jockey Club and it was intimated that he need not bother to apply for a licence to ride the following season.

It was not just Sloan himself who irritated the racing authorities. The entourage of gamblers that followed Sloan over from America included some of the biggest scoundrels on the turf. It has been estimated that by the use of dope and other dubious methods, the Americans took about two million pounds out of the betting ring.[32] Doping and other incidents convinced 'many excellent people that the American contingent were playing an underhand game' and 'that an exhaustive inquiry was necessary'.[33] The investigation never took place but punitive action against several jockeys, the requirement that all trainers be licensed, and the banning of doping, persuaded the less honest Americans to move on.

The invaders had been repulsed, but the British turf would never be the same again. British racing had been shaken out of its complacency. A few men, small in stature but large in influence, had revolutionized British jockeyship. British trainers had realized that open doors and cool stables were better for horses than the hothouse atmosphere previously prevalent in most English training establishments;* they also learned a good

---

* The change should not be exaggerated. In the early 1870s Admiral Rous was pointing out that stables had more ventilation and less heat than formerly. *Select Committee on Horses*, 1873, XIV, q. 3427.

deal about shoeing racehorses according to the condition of the track. Yet only in retrospect were these features of the American invasion appreciated. Initially the Americans generated more heat than light: they produced antagonism because what they preached and practised upset deeply held theories and cherished beliefs.[34] For some the aversion never faded: the popularity of some American owners, trainers, and jockeys could not compensate for the behaviour of those who flagrantly disregarded the official and unofficial rules of racing.

In 1908, to the horror of the nervous members of the anti-American brigade, a second wave of invaders seemed imminent. Anti-betting legislation, sponsored by Governor Hughes of New York and other sour fanatics, had brought American racing almost to a standstill. Would there be a repetition of earlier deplorable events? Or perhaps it would be worse this time: not only might the rag tag and bob-tail of the American turf come over to practise all kinds of iniquities, but with little racing taking place in the United States, all sorts of horses of dubious pedigree might swamp Britain and do goodness knows what to the bloodstock breeding industry. In the event the fears proved groundless. The Jockey Club refused to hand out licences indiscriminately and only one American trainer had any impact on the British racing scene. This was Andrew Jackson Joyner, already a success in the United States where in six years he had trained 480 winners of races worth over a million dollars. Unlike so many of his predecessors, this utterly straightforward man, again dissimilar from many earlier American trainers, obtained a warm reception from his Newmarket rivals.[35]

American horses were not so warmly welcomed. They raised a major problem for breeders in that their pedigrees could not always be traced back far enough to show that they stemmed from bloodstock exported from Britain.[36] Thus, if English breeders utilized the American horses there was no guarantee that the purity of English stock would be maintained. This had already been an issue in the previous invasion. On that occasion, Messrs Weatherby, the publishers of the *General Stud Book*, the Burke's Peerage of racing, referred the matter to the Jockey Club for advice. The stewards, after consulting most of the principal breeders in the country, decided that if eight to nine crosses of pure blood could be proved, a century or more traced back, and the turf performances of the horse's immediate family be such as to warrant a belief in the purity of the blood, then the horse could be registered in the *General Stud Book* as from volume nineteen, issued in May 1901. The amended rule let in several imported horses and their English offspring which hitherto had been ineligible.

However, the fear that the closure of American racing would result in a flood of horses from that country stimulated a re-think by the British breeders. With little likelihood of a revival of racing in the United States, horses coming to Britain to race would most likely stay here for stud purposes. Accordingly, volume twenty-one of the *General Stud Book*, issued in September 1909, rescinded the previous gateway and, with the endorsement of the Jockey Club stewards, no horse henceforth was to be eligible for the *Stud Book* unless it could be traced to a strain accepted in earlier volumes. The restriction was not enough for the British racing fraternity. The legislation had not been made retrospective so those horses who gained entry from 1901 to 1908 were kept in and their descendants were also given access. The British bloodstock industry was a powerful vested interest group within racing and, at a Jockey Club meeting in Spring 1913, Lord Jersey persuaded his fellow members to pass a rule which prohibited the acceptance into the *Stud Book* of any horse unless it could be traced without flaw, on *both* sire's and dam's side of its pedigree, to horses already accepted.[37] The Jersey Act, as this rule became called, aroused fury across the Atlantic: the stamp of half-breed had been put on many American horses, even though their owners and breeders had laid out large sums of money for them.* American exports of bloodstock throughout the world suffered badly because of this stigma. The British claimed that it was done to preserve the purity of the breed: there was a risk of throwbacks if American horses were promis-

---

* The legislation inevitably seemed ridiculous on occasions, e.g. the French-bred Derby winner of 1914, *Durbar II*, was classed as half-bred on account of his American-bred dam. This horse went on to have an immense influence on bloodstock breeding in France, particularly through his daughter *Durban* who bred that great sire *Tourbillon* whose descendants included the Two Thousand Guineas winner *Djebel* and Ascot Gold Cup victors, *Carcalla II* and *Arbar*. At the time of their victories, all these horses were ineligible for the *Stud Book*.

cuously accepted for the *Stud Book*. Nevertheless, it seems more than coincidental that the restrictive legislation came at a time when American bloodstock sales were hitting at British exports of race horses. No-one will ever convince American breeders that the Jersey Act was not designed to make the international bloodstock trade a British monopoly.*

* The Jersey Act was not repealed till 1949 when entry conditions to the *General Stud Book* reverted back to the 1901 position.

5]   *The First World War and After*[1]]

In May 1915 Britain was at war and *The Times* was on the offensive. Early in the month it thundered out an anti-racing editorial:

> It is the business of the country to see that the movements of its fighting men are not inconvenienced or obstructed by the rush of racecourse crowds . . . Racing still presents its saddening contrasts to the patriotism of those who have devoted themselves to the service of their country.[2]

Racing men were shocked, indeed many were angry, at being labelled unpatriotic. Was not racing *the* method of improving bloodstock and was not quality bloodstock vital to the remounts so much in demand by the military? Were not wounded soldiers honoured guests at race meetings? And had not racing been voluntarily abandoned in the north where it might have attracted workers from the munitions factories?

When war was declared in August 1914 the three-day meeting already under way at Brighton was carried through, but then, as railway traffic became subordinated to military necessity, all meetings were cancelled; a sign of how important the railway had become to racing. No meetings were held for three weeks but on 28 August racing resumed at Haydock Park and Gatwick. Not all scheduled meetings followed suit. An inability to obtain railway facilities, the billeting of troops on racecourses, and, in some cases, local feeling that the pleasures of sport were out of place while there was a war on, led to cancellations at Kempton, Stockton, Hurst Park, York, Derby, Ayr, and Newbury.

Where racing did continue, attendances, especially of the upper ranks of racegoers, were well down on previous years. Eventually the stewards of the Jockey Club felt compelled to reassure turf followers that they were not being unpatriotic.

Racing was being encouraged not 'for the sake of those who go racing for amusement' but because it was an industry providing employment for many deserving people: for the four hundred or so jockeys and apprentices, for the gatemen, groundsmen and caterers employed by the fifty-four racecourse companies, and for the thousands of stablemen and helpers who worked in training establishments, many of whom had enlisted on the promise that their places would be retained. Hence the Jockey Club suggested that racing should continue 'where local conditions will permit and where the feeling of the locality is not averse to the meeting being held'.[3] The stewards' statement did not end the debate. They could show how large the racing industry was but not how efficient; perhaps a cessation or a reduction of racing might have provided a necessary shake-out. Moreover, that workers might be displaced from racing did not necessarily condemn them to permanent unemployment. And, no matter how forcible the arguments for the continuation of racing, could the presence of the crowd really be justified? Almost without exception, major amateur sporting events had been cancelled and most professional sport had also been abandoned, racing and football* being notable exceptions. Many participants had volunteered for the forces, thus rendering championships somewhat artificial, and travel difficulties had made the organization of leagues a nightmare. But basically it was the question of spectators that had turned the balance. They were not to be tempted away from their work or encouraged to utilize hard-pressed rail facilities: in the words of the secretary of the M.C.C. they were now to 'look for their heroes on the great field of battle'.[4] Were racegoers to expect privileged treatment?

Early in 1915 the Duke of Portland struck his horses out of their Epsom and Ascot engagements because he believed it offensive to the allies to hold these meetings, associated as they were in the public mind with the pleasures of society. Holding these meetings, he maintained, also failed to bring home the seriousness of the war to the British people. His action provoked

---

* Eventually the soccer authorities bowed before the informal pressures of the government and, though not abandoning professional football, they reorganized it on a regional basis.

a flood of correspondence to *The Times* and to Newmarket. Once more the Jockey Club met; again it was agreed that racing should be continued in order to protect the interests of those dependent on horse racing or horse breeding for their livelihood. However, problems were beginning to mount up. First the Post-master General announced that it would be impossible to provide the customary telegraphic facilities during the coming season because so many operators had joined the forces. Then the Railway Executive Committee decided that cheap bookings to race meetings would no longer be offered, though they agreed to provide special trains if the rolling stock was available. As was later made clear by Sir Herbert Walker, General Manager of the London and South Western Railway, the Committee felt that it was not up to the railway companies to decide whether or not racing should take place. It was in fact allegations that racing specials were disrupting ordinary rail traffic that led to the furious outburst in *The Times* cited above. Public opinion, already sparked into an anti-racing frame of mind by rumours that wounded soldiers were to be shifted out of their hospital annex in the Epsom grandstand so that the race crowd could use it, and now inflamed by the sinking of the *Lusitania* and German gas warfare, grew increasingly intolerant of a sport, a mere leisure activity, that claimed exemption from the rigours of a wartime economy. Most other organized sport had been voluntarily abandoned; why should racing consider itself different? Morality and morale demanded its cessation.

More and more questions were raised in Parliament. Finally, on 19 May 1915, the President of the Board of Trade requested Captain Greer, senior Jockey Club steward, to suspend racing because of wartime circumstances and the need to avoid rail congestion. The Jockey Club bowed to higher authority and from 20 May all racing was abandoned, except at Newmarket where virtually the whole population of 10,000 or so were dependent in one way or another on racing. A few unlicensed meetings, without Jockey Club control, attempted to continue, but they were stopped by an application of the Defence of the Realm Act in June 1916. After representations had been made to the government, five extra Newmarket meetings were sanctioned and also a couple at Newbury, where there were some thirty racing stables. This concession failed to satisfy many of the racing interests. Protest meetings were held to argue that there would be insufficient racing to preserve the capital invested in the industry; schemes were suggested whereby racing could continue subject to last minute cancellation should rail facilities prove unavailable. All was in vain: the government was not to be swayed.

The reduction in the volume of racing raised severe problems within the sport. Despite attempts to frame conditions which would give all owners a chance, the great number of horses in a small number of races meant that only the best won enough stakes to justify the expenses of training.* Race companies too were badly hit. They had no income but still had to meet overheads and make a contribution to the Newmarket prize-money; at Epsom the clerk of the course was reduced to selling the stocks of wine and spirits in order to pay the rent.⁵ Nevertheless, the Jockey Club believed that the best had been made of a bad job: sufficient racing had taken place to form a just appreciation of the merits of the top two- and three-year-olds; a market, albeit a poor one, had been maintained for breeders; and the complete ruin of the training industry had been avoided.

Early in 1916 the Jockey Club requested the government to permit additional fixtures during the coming season. Perhaps they believed that the recent state purchase of a national stud might have softened the official attitude towards racing.† Whatever the reason, extra meetings were sanctioned, though, to the annoyance of northern trainers, they were at Gatwick, Lingfield, Newbury, and Windsor, courses well away from the munitions-producing areas. Nevertheless, crowds were still not to be encouraged: there were to be no race trains or cheap admissions. ‡ In any case the concession was short-lived. In mid-July public opinion, coupled with an impending petrol shortage, persuaded the government once again to restrict racing to Newmarket.

A similar restriction applied to the 1917 season, for which a

* On 15 June 1915 seven races at Newmarket attracted 214 runners.
† See below, pp. 194–6.
‡ The cost of admission was also raised by the imposition of an entertainments tax in the budget of April 1916.

programme of thirteen meetings was sanctioned. Suddenly a bombshell burst upon the racing fraternity: the Jockey Club stewards announced that all fixtures, after the First Spring Meeting (1–4 May) were to be cancelled. There had been considerable debate about the need to conserve food supplies; the U-boat campaign was at its height and one allied merchantman in four was failing to reach its journey's end. However, the abandonment of racing would not have made a significant contribution to alleviating food shortages, since the total grain consumption of the 2,000 or so horses in training amounted to only two ounces per person per annum, scarcely enough to warrant the risk of destroying the racing industry. More compelling a reason for the cessation was what the government termed 'moral' considerations; in effect that people ought to be at work or in the trenches rather than at the races.

Racing was not banned by formal government edict. After receiving a request to abandon racing from the War Cabinet, the Jockey Club stewards took the initiative and cancelled all fixtures without waiting for legislation on the issue. This angered many racing men, particularly the breeders, who believed that the stewards had given in too soon. Yet there was sense in the action of the stewards. If legislation had been necessary, it would have added ammunition to the arsenal of those sniping at the unpatriotic attitude of turf supporters. Moreover, it would be easier to start racing up again if legislation did not have to be repealed. Notwithstanding that the Jockey Club had always supported the claim that racing was vital to the success of the horse-breeding industry, the bloodstock breeders were unhappy at the apparent willingness of the Club's stewards to comply immediately with any suggestions made by the government, especially when that government had committed a gross breach of faith by going back on its word over the extra meetings. Dissatisfaction with the situation led to the formation of a new pressure group, the Thoroughbred Breeders Association, under the presidency of Lord D'Abernon. However, the Jockey Club had not thrown the breeders to the wolves. Having complied with the government's request to abandon racing, the stewards felt it equally their duty to outline the consequences of abandonment.

Thoroughbred horse-breeding, they pointed out, was no longer conducted merely by a few rich owners for the sake of developing horses for their own racing. It was now an important industry, making a contribution to the country's balance of payments and to its defence. But, they argued, racing was indissolubly connected with the industry:

> Firstly, the general admission acknowledged in all parts of the world that the thoroughbred is indispensable to any scheme of light horse breeding;
> Secondly, the fact that the thoroughbred is produced and maintained in this country almost entirely by private enterprise, and could not be so produced were it not for the added value given to the breed by racing; and
> Thirdly, that the racecourse is the only test which can be applied to prove that certain animals of the breed possess those qualities of speed, soundness, and stamina which constitute the value of the thoroughbred in the general scheme of national horse breeding.[6]

The reduction in racing, abroad and at home, had led to a 60 per cent fall in the price of yearlings, thus producing a very low rate of return on the investment in the industry, some seven to eight million pounds in bloodstock alone. Abolition of racing, concluded the stewards, would bring disaster to industry.

The government was convinced. On 4 July 1917, the President of the Board of Trade wrote to the Jockey Club to sanction forty days racing in view of 'the national importance of horse-breeding'. Moreover, this racing was not to be restricted to Newmarket but could take place elsewhere subject to the approval of the War Office, the Board of Trade, and the Ministry of Munitions. By now it was becoming accepted that, far from distracting workers, occasional race meetings might rejuvenate them and contribute to increased productivity; no doubt this explains the sanctioning of meetings at Manchester, Stockton, and Ayr.

For the 1918 season, eighty days of racing were approved, half of them at Newmarket and the rest distributed among fourteen courses, with liberal allowance to the munitions areas. After 31 May, however, racing was again restricted to

Newmarket, but this was because of acute strain on railway facilities, not because of any attack on the sport. The importance of racing had been acknowledged: it was to be curtailed not suspended.

Once the war ended, racing lost its shackles. All restrictions were withdrawn from 19 December 1918 and in the immediate ensuing seasons the public, starved of sport during the wartime famine, flocked to race meetings. Despite the interruptions brought about by mining and transport strikes, racing boomed. At the completion of the first post-war season, a leading commentator on the racing scene declared that 'never in the long history of the British turf have such enormous crowds attended race meetings as those seen during the past season'.[7] Similar remarks were also made after the following year's racing. But this happy situation was not to last. By mid-1921 the postwar boom in racing, as in the economy, had spent itself and many racecourse executives had cause to echo the words of Professor Tawney that 'in April 1920 all was right with the world; in April 1921 all was wrong'.[8]

Racing was bound to be influenced by the state of the economy. In times of depression owners were less likely to have the funds to pursue what could be a very expensive hobby, but for the course executives the real worry in such times was whether the spectators would be able to pay for their pleasure. Some recent studies have suggested that the interwar years were not as economically depressed as many contemporaries believed, but none can gainsay the fact that there were times of intense economic crisis and that throughout the period there lurked the monster of unemployment, consuming at least one in ten of the nation's work force.[9] Although unemployment provided more free time, the dole and poor relief did not allow for such luxuries as racegoing. Even if they had the funds, it is arguable whether or not the unemployed would have gone racing, for those who become cut off from the normal work-leisure rhythm of the industrial economy often find that their capacity to enjoy leisure is seriously undermined.[10] Cases in point are the retired, the shift workers, and, especially, the unemployed.[11] What about those in work; could they afford to go racing? If they wished to, then probably they could, for, despite periods when real wages

and earnings fell below previous peaks, over the entire period
1920–38 average annual real earnings rose 27 per cent and
average annual real wage earnings 18 per cent.[12] Although the
wretchedness of the poor dominates the social history of the
interwar years, poverty did not exist for everyone or indeed for
the majority of the population: the inescapable fact is that during
this period the great bulk of the British population enjoyed an
advance, albeit sometimes a modest one, in their spending
power.

The cyclical fluctuations of the economy were reflected in the
attendance receipts of the race-courses, but one cannot make a
simple correlation between the state of the economy and the
state of the racing, for the turf continually faced competition
from other leisure activities. Among the new entertainment
industries which began to challenge for the working man's
money in the interwar years were 'the talkies', speedway and
greyhound racing. Some turf fans may have preferred the cinder
track to the racing circuit, or the excitement of the screen to that
of the straight, but the greatest threat to horse racing lay in
'the dogs'.

Greyhound racing, using a mechanical hare, was introduced
on a commercial basis at Belle Vue, Manchester in 1926.[13]
Others soon followed, for it proved an instant success. Dog-
racing had much to offer the working man: meetings were held
in the evenings after his work was over; the tracks were within
walking distance or a short bus ride of tens of thousands of
people; and the excitement was perhaps more intense than in
horse racing as races were held every quarter of an hour or so.
Nevertheless, after two years of expansion many observers
thought that greyhound racing had reached its peak. They were
wrong. It continued to gain in popularity and by December 1932
there were 187 tracks in operation. Stagnation had been
averted by innovation, viz., the introduction of totalizator
betting facilities. In horse racing the tote was adopted as a
means of raising funds with which to assist the horse breeding
industry and improve race-course facilities,* but in greyhound
racing the totalizator was purely a commercial speculation.
First utilized at Carntyne, Glasgow, in 1929 it spread rapidly to

* See below, Chapter 15.

other tracks;* indeed so lucrative was the tote to its operators that at some tracks admission charges were reduced and at others free admission was offered in an effort to attract even more customers to the betting facilities.

Yet another outlet for the betting man that developed in the interwar years was the football pools; at times, ten million people a week were sending a total of £700,000 to the promoters of such schemes.[14] An Act of 1920 had made cash pools betting illegal, but whereas the working man found it difficult to obtain credit for his bets on the races,† the pools companies successfully operated on a credit basis. If the stake was not sent the following week, then all the companies agreed to blacklist the offender, a much easier task for the relatively few pools promoters than for the myriad legal and illegal bookmakers. And in practice the general view of the punter was that if he was sending in his postal order he might as well enclose next week's coupon as well.[15] Nevertheless, it is doubtful if the football coupon really hit at racecourse attendances. Many families who would never have contemplated going racing spent an evening round the fireside collectively deciding upon their pools entry; indeed many felt that filling in a coupon was akin to buying a raffle ticket and 'that wasn't really gambling – was it?'[16]

Betting was important to most racing men and many of them felt that during the late 1920s their sport was over-burdened by a tax on betting turnover of 2 per cent on course wagers and 3½ per cent on office transactions.‡ Racing opinion was not unanimous in its condemnation of the tax: indeed the Thoroughbred Breeders Association hoped that the revenue would be used in furtherance of the horse breeding industry. Most racecourse executives, however, shared the view of the Jockey Club and believed that the tax was the prime cause of a 16 per cent fall in attendances between 1925 and 1927, though they admitted that it was difficult to disentangle the various influences of bad weather, industrial stoppages, and greyhound racing from those

* At one stage such totes were deemed illegal at English tracks; they obtained definite legal status in 1934.

† See below, Chapter 13.

‡ Initially a 5 per cent tax had been planned, but it was reduced following a revision of estimated betting turnover. The tax was first applied towards the close of the 1926 flat racing season.

of tax itself. It is worth noting that betting on the dogs bore the same tax apparently without adverse effects. The most vocal protests naturally came from the bookmakers, the men who were directly liable to pay the betting duty. They claimed that their clients objected to them passing on the tax, especially on losing bets, so that they either had to stand the tax themselves or lose custom to the dishonest or illegal bookmaker. What also rankled was that although they *had* to pay the tax, the law did not allow them to press their clients for the settlement of gambling debts. The initial reaction of the bookmakers was to threaten to strike. They actually did so at Windsor in November 1926, but this, of course, merely reduced their income even more. After that essay in self-inflicted wounds, they contented themselves with vituperative placards and the formation of a Betting Duty Reform Association. Winston Churchill, the Chancellor of the Exchequer, listened to their arguments but insisted that the tax be given a fair trial of at least one full racing season. However, in 1928 he reduced the respective duties to 1 per cent and 2 per cent and eventually abandoned it altogether. Less than a third of the estimated revenue had been raised – the whole structure of the tax was honeycombed with evasion – and, as Churchill finally acknowledged, the duty 'had been a fiasco and obviously had caused more trouble than it was worth'.[17] Instead he substituted a turnover tax on tote betting and a fixed sum tax on bookmakers' telephones, but both these were dropped when Labour came to power in 1929.

By this time too, the totalizator was being adopted on many racecourses, not merely to provide an alternative betting mechanism for the racing public, but also with the intention of utilizing a proportion of the turnover for improving the amenities available to racegoers.* There was much to improve. In his Gimcrack Dinner speech of 1927, Lord Hamilton of Dalzell, a progressive member of the Jockey Club, had voiced his dissatisfaction at the facilities offered by most racecourse executives; in doing this he was merely reiterating the views he had advanced eight years before in a report commissioned by the Club. Then he had suggested that facilities could be improved by using the savings consequent upon course amalgamation. The

---

* See below, Chapter 15.

Dalzell Report had been a shock to those who criticized the Jockey Club as being a hopelessly conservative body; but commissioning reports was one thing, acting on them quite another. The Club refused to impose amalgamation and left the initiative to the course executives. If they brought a scheme forward then the Club promised to consider it, but even then it declared it would be with due regard to local opinion and tradition. The result was that nothing was done. Nor was much done as regards spectator facilities: for many of the crowd, conditions in the iron-railed, asphalt enclosures were no better than the cattle markets which they closely resembled. Initially little could be done because 'luxury' building was prohibited in the immediate post-war years, but even after restrictions were removed little continued to be done. If, as most executives claimed, finance was the problem, then the totalizator offered assistance; though not immediately, for unforeseen technical, economic, and accounting problems severely limited the initial volume of surplus funds. Between 1936 and 1938, however, over £76,000 was allocated for race-course amenities and improvements.[18] Unfortunately a decision was taken to distribute the money to courses in proportion to their tote turnover and number of days racing rather than concentrating the spending on one or two courses. This drastically diluted the impact of the assistance.[19]

In the late nineteenth century the widespread adoption of gate-money racing had led to an improvement in spectator facilities. But standards are relative: what was modern in 1889 was old-fashioned by 1939. With some exceptions, racecourse amenities in the interwar years could rightly be considered inadequate and, in a few cases, downright primitive.[20] The first enclosed courses had sought their returns by actively attracting spectators; now raising revenue appeared to take second place to reducing costs. Too many racecourse executives seemed uninterested in cultivating new spectators and content with the appearance of perennial attenders, no doubt ones of the hardier varieties. As an official Jockey Club inquiry commented:

> There is little doubt that in attractiveness, from the point of view of the general public as distinct from the regular race-goer, racing in England has fallen far behind that in countries

in which it is of more recent origin. Racecourse executives, with few exceptions, have shown little disposition to cater for the individual man or woman outside the fringe of those directly concerned with the business of racing.[21]

Control:
The Morality of Racing ⌉

It is to the residence of our nobility in their ancient
halls, and to the races and magnificent hunting
establishments they maintain or largely contribute
to, we are chiefly indebted for that excellent
tone which pervades the English character, the good
effects of which are visible in every class, from the
peer to the peasant.

J. C. Whyte, *History of the British Turf* (1840)

I do not say that all those who go racing are
rogues and vagabonds, but I do say that all
rogues and vagabonds seem to go racing.

Sir Abe Bailey, Gimcrack Dinner Speech

A wealthy industrialist, having failed yet again to secure election to the august ruling body of racing, is reputed to have declared that 'to become a member of the Jockey Club you have to be a relative of God – and a close one at that!'. He was wrong. In the interwar years even God himself, in the portly shape of the Aga Khan, could not obtain the necessary support. The apocryphal tale and the historical fact serve to underline the exclusive nature of the Jockey Club. No official list of members was published till 1835, but, judging from the names attached to entries in Jockey Club Plates and to the resolutions published in the *Racing Calendar*, it seems clear that from the beginning the membership was predominantly aristocratic. Little had changed by 1835. Upper-class turf supporters remained the backbone of the Jockey Club and also made up much of the rest of its anatomy. Throughout its history the policy of the Jockey Club has been to elect 'its own members from those who are interested in racing and *whom members consider suitable* to exercise authority and jurisdiction in such matters'.[1] Two black balls from a minimum of nine votes, were sufficient to exclude any aspiring member and ensure that the composition of the Club veered towards a preservation of the *status quo*.[2] The Earl of Glasgow used to blackball a certain Colonel Forester with unfailing regularity, once hiring a special train from Scotland so as to arrive in time to perform his self-appointed duty.[3] The result of the election policy was that even at the end of the nineteenth century the governing body of racing remained very much an association of peers and esquires. New owners, representatives of industry and commerce, came on to the turf but not into the Jockey Club. In 1870 Sir Joseph Hawley and Lord Durham raised the issue of extending the basis of the Club to render it more representative of racing interests, but they

* The title of the Club was not the misnomer it might appear. Until the beginning of the nineteenth century the word 'jockey' denoted an owner as much as a rider; in his diaries for the 1830s Greville still used the word in this context. In any case at the time of its founding many members of the Jockey Club were accustomed to riding their horses in matches.

gained little support from their brethren.[4] Even when the leisured class was no longer the ruling class it remained so in horse racing. Little altered with the twentieth century. Writing in 1957, one historian of racing's parliament noted that 'almost alone the Jockey Club stands out as a fortress of the old order that the forms of democracy have not so much failed to capture as chosen to by-pass'.[5] But is this completely true? Had this self-elected, rule-making body been allowed to govern by common consent; or did it seize power and then so consolidate its position as to render usurpation impossible?

Rules were necessitated by competition and gambling. Bets and wagers, either for money or purely to satisfy the competitive instinct, were best made on the basis of known hazards. Without rules there was bound to be confusion, irritation, and dispute. As racing spread, rules and discipline became increasingly important: if owners were to send their horses to different meetings some consistency in the procedure and practice of events made things easier for all concerned. True enough, but there were rules of racing before there was a Jockey Club. Not only did certain Acts of Parliament contain laws relating to the conduct of horse racing, but a body of 'rules concerning racing in general' had been published in *Ponds Kalendar* of 1751. Most likely this collection of rules emerged from articles drawn up for individual matches; a similar explanation has been offered for the development of a body of rules in cricket, cockfighting, and pugilism.[6] What really has to be explained is not so much why rules developed, but more how a power group emerged to set the rules that its members wanted.

Initially, or so it has been argued, the Jockey Club was no more than in informal dining club of gentlemen with an interest in horse racing at Newmarket. Admittedly there is no evidence that when the Jockey Club was founded its members had any intention of governing the affairs of the turf, but this is hardly conclusive as there is very little evidence at all about the Club at this time. It is not even known when exactly it was founded, though it was probably in 1751 or 1752. The first mention in print is in the *Sporting Kalendar* for 1752 which noted 'a Contribution Free Plate' run at Newmarket in April 'by horses the property of the noblemen and gentlemen of the Jockey Club at the Star and Garter in Pall Mall'. Roger Mortimer, a knowledgeable turf writer, maintains that the character and habits of many of the original members were such as to render ridiculous any suggestion that they might wish to govern racing.[7] This is unacceptable. Certainly the Jockey Club included rakes and profligates, but it also ranked among its members some of the richest and most influential men in the country, not that these were necessarily different individuals: since when has a lust for flesh precluded a lust for power? These men were used to power: elected (but remember this was not an age of mass suffrage) and hereditary political legislators dominated the Jockey Club. If they governed Britain, surely they would not be averse to governing its national sport. It is clear from *Cheyney's Calendar* (1727–51) that, in the years preceding the formation of the Jockey Club, there was already a tendency to regard Newmarket as the headquarters of racing and as a court of appeal for disputes. This latter function, it can be suggested, was deliberately taken on by the Jockey Club.

When the Club began to control racing at Newmarket is unclear. For several years there is no mention of Jockey Club legislative activity, but 'control' and 'legislation' are not synonymous: one can be in charge and not wish to do anything. The first recorded reform came in 1756 when heats were abolished in Jockey Club Plates, but these were races solely for horses owned by Club members. By 1758, however, the Club felt powerful enough to issue an authoritative order concerning the weighing-in of jockeys at Newmarket. By this time the regulation of Newmarket racing was entirely in the hands of the Club, and of course racing here was dominated by Jockey Club members. Nevertheless, the Club's influence was also stretching beyond the Heath. In 1757 a dispute at the Curragh was referred to the Jockey Club for arbitration and other cases followed.[8] These appeals to the Club perhaps stemmed from the social nature of horse racing. Local stewards might be reluctant to offend local patrons and would welcome the opportunity to pass on the awkward decisions. That Jockey Club members were keen supporters of racing in their own localities as well as at Newmarket could have encouraged this procedure, especially where they were respected locally as honest and unprejudiced men.

Towards the end of the eighteenth century an incident involving the Prince of Wales's horse, *Escape*, did much to establish a public image of the Jockey Club as being composed of such trustworthy individuals.[9] On 20 October 1791, *Escape*, a short-priced favourite, finished last of four in a two-mile race at Newmarket. Next day, however, *Escape* beat a well-backed favourite and four other horses, including *Skylark* and *Pipater* who had finished ahead of *Escape* the previous day. The result was not popular. Now *Escape* was an inconsistent horse and perhaps had needed a gallop to prepare him for the winning race. Moreover, the second race had been over four miles, twice the distance run the day before, and the going was softer. Against this, it must be remembered that most races, no matter what length, were generally run at a slow pace and only gathered speed in the final furlongs. Whatever the reason, Sir Charles Bunbury, virtual perpetual senior steward of the Jockey Club, had decided that the fault lay with Sam Chifney, the rider of *Escape*. Bunbury led the deputation which made it clear to the Prince that if Chifney ever rode one of his horses again 'no gentleman would start against him'. The Prince stood by his man, settled an annuity of 200 guineas on Chifney, and never raced again at Newmarket. The opinion within the Jockey Club was by no means unanimous. Some members blamed Lake, the trainer, rather than the jockey. Maybe Bunbury had been waiting to have a go at Chifney. No record of the reasoning exists, only the action and its aftermath. That the Club was clearly no respecter of persons when sharp practice was suspected increased its prestige and stimulated further provincial appeals to the central court.

Although it is a matter of conjecture whether or not the Jockey Club actively sought to extend its influence beyond the Heath in the eighteenth century, there is no doubt that it made a bid for power in the next. Only three years into the nineteenth century, Sir Charles Bunbury, still the prominent Club official, authorized the publication of the Jockey Club's own rules of racing. Then, in 1807, the *Racing Calendar*,* the official journal

---

* First published by James Weatherby (see p. 120) in 1773, the *Racing Calendar* soon became the official organ of the Jockey Club. It contained records of races run since previous issues, programmes of races to come, notices and orders of the Jockey Club, lists of licensed jockeys etc., the forfeit lists, and details of any other matters which the Club desired to make known.

of the Jockey Club, began to publish the results of cases judged by the Jockey Club. Although these were intended as a guide to local stewards, they also served to draw attention to this function of the Club and perhaps encouraged the sending of disputes to it for judgment. Nine years later a deliberate attempt was made to cast wider the net of influence. An announcement in the *Racing Calendar* stated that 'persons who may be inclined to submit any matter in dispute to the decision of the senior steward of the Jockey Club were at liberty to do so', provided that certain conditions were observed: the parties involved must have agreed on the written statement of the case and must be willing to abide by the decision made; the local stewards must have given permission for the approach to the Club; and, except in cases at Newmarket, the Jockey Club refused to give opinions on such matters as foul riding which it believed were best decided on the spot. Power was being sought. For the first time the Jockey Club had volunteered to intervene when requested.

In the meantime, and perhaps not unconnected with the bid for power, the Club had attempted to raise the prestige of Newmarket racing by sponsoring the 2,000 Guineas (1809) and 1,000 Guineas (1814) as counter classics to the well-established St Leger (1776), Oaks (1779) and Derby (1780). A recent comparative study of the role of the Jockey Club and the Pugilistic Club in re-organizing their respective sports maintains that the Jockey Club established all five classic races.[10] It did not. The founders of the Oaks, Derby, and St Leger were Jockey Club members, but they devised the races for their locally patronized courses, not for Newmarket. The St Leger took its name from one of its three founders, Colonel Anthony St Leger, who resided at Park Hill near Doncaster; the Derby was named after the twelfth Earl of Derby, and the Oaks after his country residence in Banstead.[11] At the time of founding, neither Colonel Anthony St Leger nor the Earl of Derby probably envisaged the great popularity and esteem that their offspring would attain. Perhaps the Jockey Club did not appreciate this either; though it certainly did so thirty years later. It did not seem right to the members that Doncaster and Epsom should monopolize such major events when the headquarters of racing was supposed to be at Newmarket.

The Doncaster executive in fact openly acknowledged the Jockey Club's authority in 1819 when it asked the Club to adjudicate in a dispute over that year's St Leger. Several horses had not got away at the off and the local stewards had declared that the race should be re-run. It was, but the original winner, *Antonio*, was not sent to the post. After protests, the matter was referred to the Jockey Club who decided that there had not been a false start and that the Doncaster stewards should not have sanctioned a second race. The verdict was accepted and *Antonio* took his place in the turf history books.[12]

Steps were also taken to tighten the grip that the Jockey Club had on the reins at Newmarket. From 1808 the Club began to acquire the racing grounds and within roughly a decade was almost master of the Heath.[13] Some individual proprietors remained. One of these was the Duke of Portland who improved his part of the Heath at his own expense so as to support the actions of the Jockey Club, of which, naturally, he was a member.[14] After consolidating its proprietary rights by purchase, the Club then imposed a tax of one guinea on all horses either racing at Newmarket or training on Jockey Club grounds. The money raised was spent in improving the gallops in order to attract more horses to the Heath. This policy began in 1819. Next, the Club established its right to warn off malefactors. In 1821 a tout named William Taylor was not sufficiently sharp-eyes to spot the approaching Jockey Club posse. He and his telescope were ejected from the Heath and told not to return. He went quietly enough, unlike George Hawkins, some six years later, who refused to accept a Jockey Club decision that he was liable for a bet made at his instigation but in someone else's name. He was warned off after taking umbrage at this decision and cursing Lord Wharncliffe, the senior Club steward, both loudly and vehemently. Hawkins contested this action of the Jockey Club equally vociferously, both vocally and in print. Eventually an action had to be raised at the Cambridge assizes where the Club's right to warn off was upheld.[15] Now anyone venturing on the Heath after being warned off could be summoned for trespass – no light offence in a nation ruled by land owners.

In the 1830s the Jockey Club really went on the offensive. The decade opened with a petty piece of class influence, when the

Ascot executive was persuaded to restrict entry to the Gold Cup to owners who were members of either the Jockey Club itself or one of the exclusive London clubs whose membership was so obviously self-selecting as to render ballots unnecessary.[16] The aim was simply to stop John Gully collecting the major trophy at racing's social event of the year. Gully was the son of the landlord at the Crown Inn, Wick near Bath. His first job was as a butcher's assistant, but he gained his initial fame by chopping at human carcases in the prizering, and is reputed to have been brought from a debtor's prison for his title fight with the 'Game Chicken' in 1808. Later, like many prizefighters, he became a publican, taking the Plough Inn in Carey Street. He did not stop there. Almost inevitably a prizefighter running a public house became involved in betting, but, unlike most fighters, Gully developed into a trusted turf commissioner, made a lot of money, established himself as a professional backer and owner of horses, made even more money, invested it in collieries and in 1832 was elected M.P. for Pontefract.[17] After this election, the first following the Reform Act which disposed of pocket boroughs, Greville, a racing man and diarist of high society, wrote: 'some very bad characters have been returned; among the worst – Gully, Pontefract'. He continued, 'there appears no reasons why the suffrage of the blackguards of Pontefract should place him in different social relations towards us than those in which we mutually stood before'.[18] The members of the Jockey Club could tolerate Gully's prizefighting past; indeed many of them had patronized the prizering as enthusiastically as they supported the turf. They could accept his gambling, even though he often won at their expense. What rankled was that this ex-butcher boy, the son of a publican, had become a successful race horse owner. The prizering and the betting ring could accommodate both high- and low-born, but the winner's enclosure at Ascot was not so welcoming: there, the owners, as well as their horses, had to be thoroughbred.

More important things followed. The *Racing Calendar* of 1832 carried a Jockey Club statement that because of the

uncertainty [that] had prevailed with regard to the operation of the rules and orders of the Jockey Club . . . it was thought proper to declare that they apply to all races run at, and engagements made for Newmarket only; the Jockey Club having no authority to extend their rules and orders to any other place, although they have for the sake of greater uniformity and certainty, recommended the adoption of the same rules to the stewards of other races.

To assist the doubtful to make up their minds, a clause was added stating that the Club would not receive any disputes referred to it from other meetings unless the Newmarket rules were in operation there. Any disputes were to be settled by the three stewards of the Jockey Club, though the parties concerned in the dispute could each send along a referee, providing that he also was a Jockey Club member. The Club was out to bring all race meetings under a unified control. The next move was to declare that from 1 January 1834 the age of all horses running at Newmarket was to be taken from New Year's Day not May Day. It was left to 'other places' to adopt this policy if they wanted. Then in 1835 came another assault on the uncommitted. For the first time the Jockey Club published a membership list. The eighty or so members knew each other well enough. Clearly this was an attempt to increase the Club's control by overawing the provincial executives.

Nonetheless, the Jockey Club did limit its political ambitions. All that it desired was to control flat racing; steeplechasing was left well alone. The steeplechase, which began in an organized form in the 1830s, was perhaps too new at this time to attract the Club's attention, but even later it was considered an illegitimate sport by the Jockey Club whose stewards refused to take cognizance of it.[19] A recent work on national hunt racing suggests that disputes were referred to Admiral Rous, a long-serving Jockey Club steward; if so, it was in a private capacity.[20] No authoritative body existed to govern non-flat racing till the formation of the National Hunt Committee in 1866. Most of its members also belonged to the Jockey Club, but the two ruling bodies were separate entities.

In general the local racing executives yielded to the overtures and pressure of the Jockey Club. By 1851 the Club felt confident enough to omit the reference to 'other places' in the regulation concerning the age of horses. Why had the local meetings given way before the Jockey Club attack? There may have been a continuing element of the socially-based buck-passing of awkward decisions; more likely it was to do with a growing acknowledgement within racing circles that something was rotten in the state of racing.

Some members of the racing fraternity had realized this earlier than others. Charles Apperly ('Nimrod'), for one, was convinced as early as 1833 that a tight hand of control was needed if the English turf was not to decline.[21] Others continued to wear blinkers, dismissing criticism as prejudiced outbursts either from outsiders who did not really know the sport or from racing men who refused to accept defeat graciously. Eventually, however, even their eyes were opened: if not by the Jockey Club stewards' resolution of 1838 which declared their 'extreme disapprobation of horses being started for races without the intention on the part of their owners of trying to win', then surely by the unforgettable Derby of 1844.[22] Although this Epsom classic was the supreme test of three-year-old horses, two of the runners in that year were later discovered to be four years old! Not surprisingly, one of these more mature specimens won the race. This was nominally *Running Rein*, in reality *Maccabeus*, the property of a rascally Jew, Abraham Goodman; was ever a person so misnamed? Not only owners were misbehaving: the favourite, *Ugly-Buck*, lost its chance because of foul riding, and Sam Rogers, the jockey on the well-fancied *Ratan*, pulled his mount because he had backed another horse. * A mere fortnight after the Derby there was a scandal at Ascot when *Bloodstone*, winner of the Two-Year-Old New Stakes, was revealed to be a three-year-old. That such deception was taking place at Ascot and Epsom was a cause for concern. If fraud was

* Another fraud is alleged to have been associated with the 1844 Derby. William Crockford, the famous gaming-house owner, took substantial bets from a syndicate who were wise about the *Running Rein* substitution. His death in the small hours of Derby Day should have rendered the bets null and void. However, or so it is claimed, the conspiratorial group concealed his death by dressing the corpse and placing it in the window so that passers-by would merely observe an old man asleep in a chair. They then reported that he had died that night, presumably of shock following *Running Rein*'s victory. P. R. Chalmers, *Racing England*, 1939, p. 89. However, in his *Mirror of the Turf*, 1892, p. 259, L. H. Curzon, despite his strong criticisms of turf morality, flatly denies the story.

being practised at two of the top race meetings in the country what on earth was happening elsewhere? Clearly the conduct of racing had to improve if the sport was not to follow prize-fighting on the path to extinction.

According to John Ford's recent history of that sport a plethora of fixed fights in the early 1820s led to a withdrawal of disgusted upper-class patrons. Corruption spiralled as lower-class entrepreneurs increasingly replaced gentlemen as fight promoters; the heyday of the prizering was over.[23] Yet why should the upper classes have been so dismayed at what was happening? Ford never makes it clear who first started the fixing. In racing, however, the nobility and landed gentry seemed as open to corruption as anyone so why should the situation be any different in prizefighting? Another interpretation of the decline of prizefighting can be suggested in the light of the experience of twentieth-century American wrestling. Here too, corruption got out of hand, and an excessive number of fixed fights resulted in the abandonment of the sport by the gambling interest: if odds no longer reflected probability then betting was too risky.[24] Perhaps this also occurred in the British prizering.

Pierce Egan, possibly the best contemporary commentator on prizefighting, predicted that it might happen. After the abominable contest between Sharp and Reid at Moulsey Hurst in 1824 he despairingly wrote that

> the Beaks will have little if any more trouble to interrupt it; and the Judges likewise have no further occasion to deprecate the system from the Bench. THE THING WILL STOP OF ITSELF. Who will make any more matches? Who will bet a single half penny after the display of Reid?'[25]

It is arguable that the growing unpredictability of fights was a weightier factor than any moral revulsion in the withdrawal of the upper classes. Unfortunately for prizefighting the withdrawal came at a time when a host of enemies were arraigned against the sport. It had been declared illegal in 1750 because of crowd behaviour, but enforcement of the law depended very much on the attitude of the local magistrates. Venues of fights were not openly advertised, though judging from the size of the crowds it must have been easy to find the location.[26] Thus the law could have been enforced if the magistrates had pursued the matter energetically. Many J.P.s, however, were reluctant to prosecute the law with vigour while the upper classes looked favourably on the noble art; indeed many magistrates secretly shared this aristocratic pleasure.[27] The decline of upper-class patronage coincided with a mounting attack on brutal sports in general: the way was open for prizefighting to be hounded into extinction. Falling support and increasing opposition produced inevitable decline. It lingered on till the 1860s as a financial prop of the underworld, increasingly being conducted by delinquents for delinquents.[28]

Cricket too had its share of corruption. 'It's not cricket' as a cry against unfair play is a product of the late not the early nineteenth century. As with boxing and horse racing the root of the trouble lay in gambling. In prizefighting the Pugilistic Club did nothing to rectify the situation, but in cricket the M.C.C. exerted its influence and made its attitude towards gambling very clear: in 1825 betting was banned at Lords, and, slightly before this, William Lambert, one of the great professionals, had been forced to leave the game after palpably throwing a match at Nottingham. Gambling continued to play a part in the promotion of cricket, but, thanks to the positive approach of the M.C.C., it was never again the problem or the force that it had been.[29] If the Pugilistic Club had taken the initiative and banned, or even frowned on gambling, prizefighting would have died from lack of support earlier than its eventual demise; so how was cricket able to survive? Basically it was to do with their respective legal status. Cricket, like prizefighting, had raised social problems, but it had never been made illegal, so it could count on attracting a non-gambling, more respectable, sport-loving audience who had nothing to fear from vigilant law-enforcement officers.

Firm action on gambling by the ruling body of cricket did much to improve the conduct of that game. Would the Jockey Club do the same for racing? If it followed the line of the Pugilistic Club and did nothing, racing might collapse from the loss of gambling support; yet if it adopted the approach of the M.C.C. and severely cut down on gambling the same result could well follow. But the latter option was not really open. Racing was much more expensive than cricket and, with the generally low level of prize-money, many owners looked to gambling for a contribution towards covering costs. Nonetheless, given the wealth of some owners, the sport could have continued without gambling, though at a lower level of participation. The essential point, however, is that too many Jockey Club members were too interested in gambling to contemplate such a situation. This was very much the case with Lord William George Frederick Cavendish Bentinck, the man who took on the Herculean task of cleansing the racing stables. His trainer reckoned that Lord George 'was apt on all occasions to bet too much rather than too little'.[30] His cousin and one-time racing partner, Charles Greville, argued that Lord George 'desired to win money, not so much for the money, as because it was the test and trophy of success; he counted the thousands he won after a great race as a general would count his prisoners and his cannon after a great victory'.[31]

Since the death of Sir Charles Bunbury in 1821 the Jockey Club had been without a strong and forceful leader. Fortunately for racing Lord George proved more than willing to pick up Bunbury's discarded mantle. He had taken an early interest in racing, perhaps because his father, the fourth Duke of Portland, was a fervent follower of the turf, and he gained his first plate at Goodwood, aged twenty-two. By 1826, the year in which he lost £27,000 on a St Leger bet, Lord George had decided to devote most of his time to the turf, even thought he had succeeded his brother as M.P. for the borough of King's Lynn. In 1827 his elder brothers, Lord Titchfield and Lord Henry Bentinck, guaranteed him £300,000 with which to start a stable. But he could not refrain from gambling, or rather at this time from losing at gambling, and his father, a true sportsman who never bet, begged him to quit racing. Lord George agreed, but only nominally, for he continued to race horses in other owner's names and not always with their permission; the Duke of Richmond was once incensed when he discovered a Derby entry made in his name. Later Lord George raced again under his own colours, but the action he had taken showed that he was not a straightforward individual.[32] Was this devious, high-staking gambler really the man to reform racing?

Lord George pursued his attack on two fronts: one was concerned with improving racing for the spectators; the other involved a determined drive against crooks and defaulters. In the first sphere he insisted on order and regulation, culminating in a stringent code of rules published in the *Racing Calendar* for 1844. He introduced the dual flag* system of starting which cut down time wasted on false starts. Moreover, if races did not start on time the clerk of the course was fined 10s. for each minute the race was delayed. Boards had to be displayed showing the numbers of the horses and the names of the jockeys, who had to wear 'silk, velvet or satin jackets' so that they could be identified easily. At Goodwood, with the financial assistance of the Duke of Richmond, he transformed the course, making it a spectators' delight. Here he also insisted that horses be saddled in a paddock in view of the crowd instead of anywhere on the course which had been the traditional pattern.[33] His major efforts, however, were concentrated against turf corruption and defaulting. As an inveterate gambler he hated defaulters and insisted that they be posted and warned off not only Newmarket but all courses where the Jockey Club had influence or authority. He even pursued them beyond the race track. Once, when dining out, he intercepted a defaulter's bill and, in a deliberately raised voice, warned the offender off a different type of course, by declaring that 'before Sir . . . orders such expensive dishes, he should pay his debts of honour'.[34] Gambling debts, of course, were not recoverable at law. Lord George was equally hard on those who transgressed the Jockey Club's code of conduct. Till his time dishonesty at one course did not necessarily debar the offender from competing elsewhere; Lord George, however, insisted that the punishment be universal. This and items such as his efforts to ban presents to judges helped create an image of Bentinck the improver. But his reputation as a reformer was really made by the *Running Rein* affair.[35]

Running Rein's age had already been the subject of an objection even before he 'won' the Derby. Following a victory in a two-year-old Plate at Newmarket, the Duke of Rutland,

* See below, pp. 116–17.

owner of the second horse, claimed that the winner was a year too old, but he could not substantiate his allegation and the stewards dismissed the objection. However, Lord George's noble nostrils had sniffed an unpleasant odour. He made further inquiries and the more he poked his nose in, the greater became the stink. A few days before the 1844 Derby, Lord George, John Bowes, and the famous trainer, John Scott, sent a joint letter to the Epsom stewards asking them to make the owner of *Running Rein* prove the age and identity of his horse. Lord Maidstone sent a similar letter querying the eligibility of *Leander*, the entry of the brothers Lichtwald, who made their living exporting horses to Germany. The Epsom stewards did not accede to the requests; instead they accepted the advice of Captain Rous, brother of Lord Stradbroke, one of the stewards, that, as the owners of the two suspect horses had fulfilled the normal articles of entry, any enquiry would best be held *after* the race should one of these horses win it. If *Running Rein* had not won would the affair have been hushed up? *Running Rein* did win, however, and after the race Colonel Peel, owner of the second-placed *Orlando* lodged the inevitable appeal; inevitable because Lord George got to him immediately the race was over. The stewards ordered the stakeholder to withhold the prize-money pending a Jockey Club inquiry, but whether this would have revealed much is debatable since the Club could not compel the attendance of witnesses nor punish them for perjury. In the event it was not necessary because Colonel Peel, again at the instigation of Lord George, obtained a more thorough investigation by bringing a civil action against Alexander Wood, an Epsom corn chandler and nominal owner of *Running Rein*. Lord George once more played bloodhound and tracked down the evidence, even discovering the hairdresser who had sold Abraham Goodman, the instigator of the substitution, the dye with which to disguise the horse's legs. With Lord George's work to hand Peel's counsel tore the opposition apart; though Wood's attorney was hardly able to fight back since his client steadfastly refused to produce the horse.

In his class-conscious summing up of the case the judge, Baron Alderson made very clear what he felt lay at the root of turf corruption:

Since the opening of this case a most atrocious fraud has been proved to have been practised; and I have seen with great regret, gentlemen associating themselves with persons much below them in station. If gentlemen would associate with gentlemen, and race with gentlemen, we should have no such practices. But if gentlemen will condescend to race with black-guards, they must expect to be cheated.[36]

He was only partly correct. Nobles and gentlemen as a group may have been less corrupt than the lower elements of racing society, but individually some of them were less averse than others to straying from the paths of righteousness.

The *Running Rein* incident and its publicity-blazoned aftermath woke many honest racing men to a real appreciation of the state of turf affairs and to an acceptance that something had to be done. The time was ripe for turf reform and for order to be imposed on British racing. Lord George made sure that the Jockey Club seized the opportunity. Abraham Goodman, villain of the affair, and the Lichtwald brothers, owners of *Leander*,* were warned off *sine die* and the Club decided that in future cases of this kind not only would the offending parties be disqualified for life but they would also be prosecuted. Under Lord George's leadership the Club agreed to tighten up racing's regulations and declare war on the criminals of the turf. Race-course executives, aware that the future of racing might be in the balance, rallied to the flag. At Epsom, the scene of the Derby scandals, the stewards of the Jockey Club were appointed *ex-officio* stewards;† elsewhere the executives acknowledged the supreme authority of the Club by generally adopting the stricter code of conduct emanating from Newmarket. Lord George had done his job well.

His reward for trying to clean up the turf was twofold. A public subscription to thank him for his efforts raised over £3,000. He appreciated the action as the public had appreciated his, but he had no need of the money so he handed it over to the

---

* Poor *Leander* had been kicked by another horse – ironically probably *Running Rein* – and was so severely injured that he had to be destroyed. His jaws were cut off in an attempt to disguise his age, but eventually it was proved that he was a four-year-old.
† Royal Ascot followed suit in 1857 and Goodwood in 1881.

Jockey Club to form the nucleus of a fund, the Bentinck Provident Fund, for the assistance of distressed jockeys and their dependents.[37] Less welcome were the *Qui Tam* actions of 1843. Under Acts passed during the reign of Queen Anne, anyone could make money by informing on people who had made bets of more than £10.* If successful prosecutions followed the informant could obtain up to three times the amount involved. The Acts were virtually a dead letter, but a proportion of the undesirable element whom Lord George had caused to be warned off decided to use them to elicit revenge. Sixty-eight writs were issued against Lord George and other racing notables with total potential penalties of over half a million pounds. Only one action reached court. This was at Guildford Assizes where the chief instigator, a man named Russell, tried to obtain £12,000 from Lord George. The action was lost on a legal technicality, and, before the other actions could be commenced, the law was changed when the Duke of Richmond successfully introduced a Bill into the House of Commons, by which the statutes were repealed and their penalties abolished.[38]

Lord George did much to rid the turf of abuses and abusers, but his influence for the good of racing was tempered by his own actions. He held other Jockey Club members in contempt: writing to John Bowes in 1843 he declared that: 'I know so well the selfishness of mankind and above all that portion of it which constitutes the Jockey Club'.[39] This attitude may well have limited the influence he had within the Club. Moreover, Charles Greville reckoned that he made for himself a peculiar code of morality and honour and 'the same man who crusaded against the tricks and villanies of others did not scruple to do things quite as bad as the worst of the misdeeds which he so vigorously and unrelentingly attacked'.[40] In 1844 he acted as starter for the Chester Cup which was won by his own horse, and at Newmarket in 1841 his two-year-old, *Tripoli*, nominally carrying a 'featherweight' actually had nearly eight stone on its back, Lord George taking advantage of the fact that at that time jockeys riding at such a theoretical light weight need not use the scales.[41] He did not break the rules of racing though he frequently sailed close to the wind. If this somewhat arrogant

* For a survey of British betting legislation see below, Chapter 13.

individual had been more straightforward and upright in his own turf dealings, perhaps the conduct of British racing would have improved even more than it did.

Nonetheless, racing was worse off for his retirement from the turf. In 1846, to the astonishment of all who knew him, he decided to sell his racing establishment and concentrate on politics, particularly the issue of protection which Peel, the leader of his party, was choosing to abandon. To his later sorrow, *Surplice*, one of the horses he sold, went on to win the Derby. The day after the Epsom classic Disraeli met Lord George who groaned: 'All my life I have been trying for this, and for what have I sacrificed it? . . . You do not know what the Derby is.' 'Yes I do,' replied Disraeli, 'it is the Blue Riband of the Turf.' Lord George merely repeated the words: 'it is the Blue Riband of the Turf', and, sitting down at a table, he buried himself in a folio of statistics. Not even the £11,000 he won in bets could console him.[42]

Admiral Rous,* the man who replaced Lord George as dictator of the turf, was a much more honourable and straightforward individual; though he acknowledged that gambling was vital to racing, unlike Lord George he did not favour heavy betting, believing that 'the extravagant rate at which it had been carried on [was] one of the reasons of the decline of the turf'.[43] He retired from the Navy in 1836, after twenty-eight years service, and devoted his life to the turf.[44] In 1840 the Duke of Bedford invited him to take charge of his private stable at Newmarket; he arranged many matches for the Duke's horses, always standing in for a quarter of the stake, and in twenty years could always rely on at least £1,500 per annum from this source.[45] His lucrative years as a match-maker stood him in good stead when he was invited to become public handicapper in 1855. He was elected to the Jockey Club in 1821 and first became a steward in 1838. In 1856 he was asked to take charge of the Jockey Club's finances; there had been a deficit of some £5,000 the previous year. The Admiral steered the

---

* The Captain Rous who was an Epsom steward at the time of the *Running Rein* affair. He became Rear Admiral in 1852 and full Admiral in 1864, both positions being on the Reserve List. T. H. Bird, *Admiral Rous and the English Turf*, 1939, p. 133.

accounts into the black and by the 1870s the Club had £18,000 per annum at its disposal.[46] From 1859 to 1875 continuous re-election ensured his position as virtual president of the Jockey Club.[47]

Yet Lord George had retired from the turf in 1846 and Rous did not attain a dominant position till the mid 1850s. In the meantime the good work of Lord George was eroded: a decade without a real leader had undermined the authority of the Club so much that the turf was again becoming rotten with corruption. Fraud was a common occurrence at some of the smaller meetings. In a letter to *Bell's Life* in 1855 Rous cited an incident at Waltham Abbey where a hot favourite bolted the wrong way, but the two other runners waited till he could be brought under control and trotted past them to victory.[48] The Club could not even keep its own house in order; it was also in 1855 that a steward of the Club fled the country as a defaulter.*

Rous determined to rectify the situation. He had already proved his courage in the Navy; in 1835 he had piloted his rudderless command, H.M.S. *Pique*, across the Atlantic from Labrador.[49] Now he was going to take on those who would destroy the turf. It could not be done by banning gambling; he firmly believed that if betting was abolished four-fifths of race-courses would have to be ploughed up.[50] The solution was to attack the corruption that followed in the wake of gambling. This he did. The rules of racing were recast into a more workable code of laws and he insisted that the rules be enforced. Various amendments were made at his instigation such as giving stewards the power to suspend jockeys and not just to fine them, and limiting payments to judges solely to the local executive or to the Jockey Club itself. Blunt, vigorous, with a quarterdeck manner, Rous was something of a martinet, but till his death in 1877 he strove, with some success, to ensure that the laws of racing were honoured; perhaps he was listened to because he was relatively disinterested, caring more for racing than for winning.

In 1870 Rous was instrumental in obtaining the ruling that neither the programme nor the result of any flat race meeting in Britain should be published in the *Racing Calendar* unless the

* See below, p. 105.

meeting was advertised as being subject to Jockey Club rules. The Club went on to impose the penalty of disqualification on any owner, trainer, jockey or official who took part in such unrecognized meetings. Potentially this distinction between recognized and unrecognized courses was a powerful weapon in the hands of the Jockey Club, providing, of course, that executives wished their meetings to be recognized. In fact the first major attempt to employ this sanction backfired for this very reason. This was in 1878 when the Club passed a resolution that all recognized meetings must provide at least 300 sovereigns added money for prizes on each day of racing they had. The legislation was aimed principally at several meetings on the fringe of London which were speculative ventures organized by publicans and bookmakers, partly for the entrance money (when the spectators could be persuaded to pay), but mainly to attract customers for their respective wares. If this was not enough to annoy the gentlemen of Newmarket, there was also the criticism that 'many of the races run at these suburban saturnalia of rogues and roughs were utter shams', the winner frequently being decided in advance of the race.[51] Crowd disturbances, riots, and vandalism were almost a built-in feature of these meetings, attractive as they were to the criminal fraternity of the metropolis. The waving of the Jockey Club's big stick made very little difference to these suburban speculations: owners racing their £30 nags had no Ascot aspirations, and sufficient failed jockeys could be found to ride the decrepit creatures. Eventually Parliamentary legislation was needed to put an end to the events.* The Jockey Club resolution, however, had unintended consequences. It put paid to many of the traditional meetings which had no ambitions to join the racing circuit and had continued as predominantly local social events. The executives here had never offered substantial prizes and the race fund could never hope to stretch to the level of added money required by the Jockey Club. Unlike the participants at the metropolitan meetings, the owners and jockeys who frequented these courses were not prepared to defy the Club; they wished to race elsewhere.†

---

* See below, p. 99.
† This is discussed more fully above; see pp. 45-6.

The distinction between approved and unapproved race-courses proved more useful with the development of the enclosed, gate-money meeting. Founded in response to rising working-class incomes, the first enclosed courses soon forced others to follow suit and adopt a policy of charging most spectators entrance money. Initially the Jockey Club feared abuse of this innovation and legislated accordingly by setting a limit to the number of courses it would recognize. The reason given for this decision of 1883 was the difficulty of fitting new fixtures into an already congested racing calendar. This was hardly valid considering that in the period 1875–82 sixty-three meetings ceased and only fourteen new ones were founded. The real reason became apparent with another resolution which limited the dividends of new courses to 10 per cent and insisted, as a condition of obtaining a licence, that their accounts and financial arrangements be subject to Jockey Club inspection. The Club need not have worried; the enclosed course had revolutionized racing and racecourse executives were no longer willing to turn a blind eye to malpractice. The paying customer had become the focal point of racing and the honesty of turf affairs was seen as a key feature in attracting large crowds. Turnstiles clicked more frequently with the promise of good racing and good horses, and this could only be guaranteed by giving owners a fair deal. Even as early as 1885, it could be observed by a critic of racing that, although there was still room for improvement, 'the morality of the Turf is perhaps at this moment purer than it has been during the last fifty years'.[52] The rules of racing were being honoured thanks to the paying spectator. When the working class entered racing through the turnstile, the authority of the Jockey Club became much more firmly established.

Those transgressors who deliberately flouted Jockey Club rules may not have been challenging the authority of the Club, but merely hoping that they would not be found out. Yet there were several attempts during the nineteenth century to force the Jockey Club to take certain lines of action and indeed, on a couple of occasions, to usurp its authority altogether and take action whether or not the Club was in favour. In general these attempts were unsuccessful; the dissentient had little chance.

The discipline of publicity was a favourite device, if not a recreation, of the mid Victorians. They have been likened to vigilantes, though pursuing their offending victim with pen and printing press rather than with rope or gun.[53] If they were unhappy about the moral state of the nation or its inhabitants, pen was put to paper and out came a pamphlet or at least a letter to the press. The affairs of racing were no exception to this attempted rule. Throughout the century, the correspondence columns of all types of papers carried criticisms of the turf and its administrators. Admiral Rous, himself, was a frequent contributor to *The Times* and to *Bell's Life*. However, as a leading Jockey Club member, his letters had more chance of influencing Club policy than had those of most writers. In general, press publicity served only to close Jockey Club ranks and there was a sturdy refusal to even comment on external criticism: the Jockey Club knew that it was right. Formal pressure groups do not appear to have existed in nineteenth-century racing outside the Jockey Club itself, though towards the end of the century, the annual Gimcrack dinners, at which the subscribers to this York race stood dinner to the Jockey Club stewards and other leading sportsmen, became regarded as occasions on which racing reform and legislation could be discussed informally between leading owners and Jockey Club representatives. Airing turf grievances was no guarantee that they would be remedied. The call for stipendiary stewards was an almost annual appeal, but nothing was done; and it has been suggested that putting forward radical views cost at least one speaker his chance of election to the Club where he might have been able to do something.[54]

Appeals to law over Club decisions were rarely made and were even more rarely successful.[55] It simply was not feasible to challenge the Jockey Club in the law courts. By the 1870s the Club had so tightened its grip over racing that jockeys, trainers, and executives could obtain licences only by accepting that the licence could be withdrawn at any time without a reason having to be given. It was not that natural justice had no place at Newmarket, but to give reasons was to risk libel actions in courts where judge and jury could be totally ignorant of racing matters. Anyone associated with banned personnel was liable to suffer the same fate, and to participate in an unrecognized meeting was to cast oneself into the wilderness. Agreements were made with the ruling bodies of national hunt and pony racing and with most foreign Jockey Clubs for the universal application of warnings off and a reasonably common policy regarding the rules of racing.[56]

Perhaps the only way to beat the Jockey Club was to go over its head to a greater ruling body. Parliament had intervened in the sporting world to put down bull- and bear-baiting in the 1830s and to ban cockfighting in 1849, but racing was never regarded as cruel, except by a faddist minority. The government taxed racing and subsidized it, but made few attempts to control it. On only two occasions was a real effort made to legislate on racing matters, both times in face of determined opposition from the Jockey Club.

In 1860 Lord Redesdale introduced his Light Weight Racing Bill into the House of Lords by which no horse would be allowed to race if it carried less than seven stones. He was giving voice to the opinion that the ridiculously low weights assigned in some handicap races were detrimental to the breed of horses; if a horse could not carry seven stones then he could not conceive how its existence could serve any legitimate purpose of racing. The Earl of Derby presented a Jockey Club petition protesting that the regulation of racing was best left to the Club, who were in fact considering the issue. Lord Redesdale cogently argued that the Club was more concerned with objecting to interference in what they regarded as a divine right to rule than in remedying what he felt was a great evil. He received some support from those who feared that child jockeys were being exploited; if seven stones was the minimum weight, more mature riders would probably be employed. He lowered his sights to six stones after receiving a letter of support from a group of Newmarket trainers. Lord Derby then promised that the Jockey Club would most likely bring in legislation setting five and a half stones as the minimum weight. Lord Redesdale did not force the issue and withdrew his bill.[57]

Whether he could have got his bill through is a matter for conjecture. If the backwoodsmen had turned up in force to defend their right to rule the turf his success would have been doubtful. In the late 1870s, however, the Jockey Club was unable to persuade the lower Chamber that it was able to remedy a turf abuse without outside intervention. The issue was more controversial, the promoter of the bill less yielding, and the Jockey Club representation less prominent than in 1860. On this occasion a Glasgow M.P., Mr Anderson, described by his opponents as a dour, sport-hating, Sabbatarian Scot, successfully brought in a bill which required all racecourses within ten miles of Charing Cross to obtain a licence from the local magistrates. These were the suburban speculative meetings which he and his supporters felt were being held too frequently, served no legitimate purpose, and were 'resorted to by the dregs of the population for a very different purpose from that of amusement'. The Jockey Club was aware of the abuses and brought in the added money rule which ended several of the meetings though not all of them. It was not regular racing men who frequented the survivors; and the promoters and owners active there did not give a damn for the Jockey Club or its regulations. When given an assurance that the Club would take cognizance of abuses brought to their knowledge, Mr Anderson agreed to wait a year, but as nothing seemed to be done, he reintroduced his bill in the 1879 session, and, with the support of those who would have banned all racing, he carried the day.[58] Apart from this isolated incident, by the last decades of the nineteenth century, and especially after the development of the enclosed course, the Jockey Club was the undisputed authority in horse racing. The seams of power had been very effectively sewn up.

Unfortunately the Club's efforts to gain sole control of racing were not matched by its performance when in power. Sir Charles Bunbury, Lord George Bentinck, and Admiral Rous were talented administrators, though it must be stressed that their emergence as dictators of the turf lay as much with a lack of ability and concern elsewhere in the Club. Membership of the Club was a jealously guarded family heirloom: social position determined election to the Club not administrative ability. The Fourth Marquis of Hastings was elected soon after he came of age, even though he had made a mockery of the Quorn when he was its master of hounds: his sole concern seemed to be to get home before lunch so as to leave the afternoon free for cards.[59] The Jockey Club, like the magistrate's bench, was not for the industrialist or businessman: top flight men of the economic world had the Club doors firmly shut against them, though they surely had much to contribute to the government of racing. Most Club members showed no distinction in Parliament, in local government, or in turf administration. It is a sad reflection on the Jockey Club that a business meeting of this ruling body rarely attracted more than fifteen to twenty attenders out of a membership of about one hundred.[60] This is hardly comparable with the low participation at trade union branch meetings or in local government elections where the voter is much further away from the real decision-making process than were Jockey Club members who were actually in the seat of power. Too many Club members were too old and too tired to bother with the obligations of membership; to be an active member meant too great a sacrifice of leisure time. Perhaps Bunbury, Bentinck, and Rous regarded administration as leisure; maybe they enjoyed the hard work of power; whatever the reason, the way was open for leading personalities to emerge without too much of a struggle.

Moreover these turf dictators could have done more than they did do. Even Rous, the most open of them, had his blind spots.[61] He hated tobacco, heavy betting, and jockeys. Sir Joseph Hawley smoked, on at least three occasions won over £70,000 in bets, and frequently gave the prize-money to his winning riders. There was thus a natural antipathy between the two men, not helped by Sir Joseph's manner: he possessed no tact and even less patience. It is arguable that Rous opposed several suggested reforms simply because the proposals emanated from Sir Joseph. The Jockey Club followed Rous, partly because he argued rationally against Sir Joseph, but also, one suspects, because he was more straightforward. Sir Joseph had temporary periods when he castigated heavy betters, but he had a racing career studded with spasms of heavy plunging; he demanded the curtailment of two-year-old racing, but ran his own two-year-olds when he felt they could win; and a suspicion of sharp practice still lingered following the race for the Doncaster Cup in 1851. He ran both *The Ban*, the eventual winner, and *Vatican*, though Rule 40 stated that 'no person can enter and run either in his own name or in the name of any other person, two horses of which he is wholly or partly the owner, for any plate'. However, the Jockey Club stewards accepted his explanation that he had sold *Vatican* shortly before the race. Others did not, and so unfavourable were the rumours and whispers in racing circles that Sir Joseph temporarily retired from the turf.[62]

In 1869 Sir Joseph brought forward a set of resolutions designed to restrict two-year-old racing. He believed that the British thoroughbred was being weakened by the volume of such racing which had encouraged the development of quick maturing stock without much stamina. Rous argued that if the Jockey Club adopted Sir Joseph's proposals it would ruin Newmarket because owners would race elsewhere at courses which did not follow the Club's line.[63] Can Rous seriously have believed that the Jockey Club could not have imposed its policy on British racing? Next year a further set of proposals emanated from Sir Joseph, including one for a committee to consider the present position of the turf which he felt was being run too much for the benefit of gamblers. Rous at once delivered his customary broadside via *The Times*. His most telling point was that one of his friends had won £75,000 on a single race and another friend £115,000; the 'friends' were Sir Joseph Hawley and Henry Chaplin, one of Sir Joseph's principal supporters![64]

More support would have been given to Sir Joseph had he been willing to drop from his proposals everything connected with betting, a subject of which the Jockey Club professed to take no official cognizance. This policy stemmed from events following the 1841 Derby, when a Mr Gurney paid only five shillings in the pound on his losing bets but demanded full poundage on money owed to him. A Mr Thornton, believing that Gurney could afford to pay his debts in full, refused to hand over his own losses; instead he donated the money to Christ's Hospital. Gurney appealed to the Jockey Club who supported his plea, warned off Thornton, and had him posted as a defaulter. A libel action ensued in which Thornton was awarded damages, one of the rare occasions on which the Club lost a battle in the courts. It seemed that making decisions on betting disputes could prove expensive and, considering the growing volume of such disputes that were being referred to it, the Club elected to wash its hands of them. A statement was issued to the effect that no more cognizance would be taken of betting.[65] The Club was burying its head in the sand: most turf transgressions were a direct product of gambling and the worst ones certainly so. The ostrich was also hypocritical: rules 'respecting stakes, forfeits and bets' continued to be printed in the *Racing Calendar*; the Club catered for gambling by publishing the handicaps for the Cesarewitch and the Cambridgeshire by the time of the St Leger, even though they were not run till mid or late October; and the anti-tout legislation, and the warnings off for those guilty of the high crime of watching a trial, existed only because owners wanted the best odds for their horses.

The apathy of many of its members perhaps reflected the inertia of the Jockey Club itself. In the early 1860s, Squire Osbaldeston, soured by gambling losses of over £200,000, complained of jockeys owning horses and making bets, a practice which had ruined many gentlemen, but which 'those at the head of affairs don't exert themselves to put down'.[66] It was not until the 1880s that the Club passed the requisite legislation. Some time earlier the passivity of the Jockey Club in the face of a flagrant case of disgraceful fraud stirred one of its leading members to action. A court case of 1857 revealed that a certain James Adkins, a well-known race horse owner, was also the proprietor of a crooked gambling house where he had fleeced a young man, albeit a foolish youth, of over £25,000 by the use of loaded dice.[67] Yet, despite the revelations of the lawsuit, the Jockey Club took no steps to prevent Adkins participating in racing. This did little for the image of the sport and it spurred Lord Derby to action. In identical letters to *The Times* and the Jockey Club stewards he noted:

> It has become a subject of general observation and regret, that the number of men of station and fortune who support the Turf is gradually diminishing, and that an increasing proportion of horses in training is in the hands of persons in an inferior position, who keep them not for the purposes of sport but for the purposes of gambling. I am aware that it is

not in your lordships' power to apply a remedy to this acknowledged evil; but I conceive that there are occasions on which it is within your power; and if so I venture to think that is your duty as stewards of the Jockey Club, to exercise a wholesome influence upon the character and respectability of the Turf.

You cannot debar any man, whatever his position in society, from keeping race horses, nor do I recommend a wholesale and inquisitorial scrutiny into the character and conduct of those who do so; but when among their number are found those against whom flagrant cases of disgraceful fraud, and dishonesty, have been legally established, it appears to me clearly within your preserve to stamp them with your reprobation; and to exclude them from association on an equal footing with the more honourable supporters of the Turf.

He felt that the late trial of Adkins had raised such a case for intervention and that it concerned 'the honour of the Jockey Club not to pass [it] over in silence'.[68] The letter prodded the stewards into action; Adkins was warned off and for a time the flood of turf pollution was stemmed. Yet it is easy to believe that, without Lord Derby's spurring, the Club would have continued to turn a blind eye, at least till Rous became senior steward two years later.

Perhaps the greatest instance of Jockey Club inertia was on the question of doping. Admittedly Dan Dawson had received the ultimate warning off in 1812 when he was hanged for poisoning horses at Newmarket.[69] His was a crime punishable by death under a statute of George I. Not till 1904, however, was the giving of stimulants or depressants to a horse made a turf offence by the Jockey Club. It is impossible to assess how much 'nobbling' or speeding-up of horses took place before this legislation, though actual *doping*, as contrasted with a debilitating bucketful of water or a stimulating nip of whisky or bottle of port, was very much a product of the American invasion. In the United States racing often took place at one course for eight or nine days at a time. With horses running several times at one meeting, it frequently became a case of the survival of the fittest, but it was discovered that racing Darwinism could be thwarted by a dose of cocaine to the jaded. When they crossed the Atlantic the Americans brought their knowledge and practice of doping with them. In 1896 doping in British racing was in its infancy; by 1900 it was a serious menace, though it must be stressed that the Americans, and their less knowledgeable British imitators, were acting within their rights.[70] Despite the outcry, the Jockey Club stewards refused to act. They believed that the situation was not as serious as was made out and they feared that instant legislation might merely become a dead letter.[71] Eventually the eyes of the triumvirate – the 'Three Blind Mice' as they were being irreverently called – were opened by the actions of the Hon. George Lambton, the trainer brother of Lord Durham. He told his brother, a leading Club member, what he was going to do and then doped five of his own rogue horses, creatures that had shown no form at all, but which, running under the influence of drugs, gained four first places and a second.[72] Obviously if the practice became widespread horses and gamblers would be ruined and the fate of both was important to racing. Doped horses were 'wrecked by the end of the season',[73] and in any case were not necessarily the horses from which to breed; and men would not bet if they had to gamble not only on the horse's ability, but also on the effectiveness of different drugs and the practitioner's chemical expertise. Yet improving the breed was the official rationale of racing, and gambling its actual reason for existence. So in 1904, following Lambton's demonstration, the Jockey Club made doping a horse a racing crime. Thereafter open doping ceased: no doubt covert doping continued but it too must have lessened after the development of the saliva test in 1910.[74]*

The legislation against doping was based on expediency rather than on justice. It was simply too difficult to catch the culprits, so that assumption was made that either the trainer or someone in his stable must have been involved. To some extent this was reasonable because, to be successful, a stimulant must be given within a few hours of the race, and it was argued that security during this period was the trainer's responsibility.

---

* Doping did not end. Even today it is admitted 'that doping of racehorses cannot be entirely eliminated'. *Report of the Paton Committee on the Scheme for the Suppression of Doping*, 1971, para. 78.

Nevertheless, it was not always his fault if someone got at his horse and the earning capacity of the innocent could be adversely affected if owners unquestioningly accepted the Club's verdict on his involvement.[75]

Not only did Jockey Club members wish to exercise power without exercising themselves; some even refused to adhere to their own rules. Ever since William Taylor had been caught in 1821 the Club had set its official face against touts; such industrial espionage was not to be tolerated. Spying, however, could prove lucrative both to the tout and his employer, and not infrequently the noble men of the Jockey Club allowed monetary considerations to outweigh their official principles. The most famous case was in 1869 when, after being assaulted by a trainer, a tout named Bray brought an action to court during which it was revealed that his employer was the Earl of Stamford, a prominent Jockey Club member.[76] Defaulting too was considered a serious offence by the Club: Lord George Bentinck had campaigned unceasingly against those who did not pay their bets and eventually the Club had agreed to post all defaulters. This was done to the Hon. Francis Villiers when he fled the country in 1855 owing at least £100,000 in gambling debts. Yet at the time Villiers was a Jockey Club steward and had been due to become senior steward the next year![77] Towards the end of the century there was another scandal involving a leading Jockey Club member. It was common racecourse gossip throughout 1887 that the jockey, Charles Wood, was pulling some of his mounts, and doing so with the knowledge of Sir George Chetwynd. At the Gimcrack Dinner in December of that year Lord Durham scathingly commented on the in and out running of horses from a certain stable, and added that if *he* was the owner of the horses concerned, he would have insisted on an inquiry into the conduct of the jockey. It was generally accepted that he was referring to Sherrard's stables at Newmarket; Sherrard was trainer for Sir George Chetwynd. Sir George sued for libel. He and Lord Durham appeared before their peers; by mutual agreement the case was referred to the Jockey Club for arbitration because the nature of the dispute necessitated a knowledge of racing on the part of the jurors. The arbitrating Jockey Club stewards were shocked by the revelation of an extraordinary relationship between Wood and Sir George, by which the latter had assisted the jockey to flout the rules of racing regarding jockeys owning horses. Moreover, the proceedings made it apparent that Sir George, although once judged fit to be a Jockey Club steward, was nothing more than a professional punter. The allegations levied by Lord Durham were not proved and Sir George won his case, but was awarded only a farthing's damages. So disgusted was he at this decision that he resigned immediately from both the Jockey Club and the turf.[78] Undoubtedly Chetwynd and Villiers were guilty of hypocrisy, by saying one thing – indeed actively legislating for it – but doing another. Other Club members who broke the rules were perhaps less guilty of this charge, for most did not bother to attend Club meetings and vote on policy decisions. Nevertheless, their actions as much as those of Chetwynd and Villiers, almost certainly encouraged imitation from those outwith the charmed circle.

Throughout the nineteenth century the conduct of racing left much to be desired. Nonetheless, Sir F. Sullivan, a critic of racing's conduct, went too far when he claimed that among racing men 'roguery is dismissed with a smile, rascality with a shrug'.[79] The Jockey Club made positive attempts to set the racing world in order, though it took action only when bad behaviour was pushed under its nose and it could not help but notice what was going on. Perhaps gentlemen were not expected to seek loopholes in the laws of racing, but some did; and more money in racing meant proportionally less gentlemen. Moreover the deterrent effect of the punishments meted out by the Jockey Club is open to question. Sentences, save for short-term suspensions given to jockeys, were indeterminate, though those warned off were at liberty to apply for reinstatement. Generally minor figures were cast permanently into the wilderness, whereas all too frequently those with influence or influential friends found their way back.[80] The Earl of Ellesmere, sometime Jockey Club steward, made it clear that great pressure was often exerted on the stewards to reinstate malefactors.[81] This was particularly true where jockeys were concerned, for their employers were reluctant to lose them. Several attempts were made to get Charley Wood reinstated after he was warned off following the

Chetwynd affair.[82] Eventually in 1897 the Jockey Club relented and allowed him back on the turf. Lord Durham, a Club steward and the man virtually responsible for having Wood warned off, wrote to him to bury the hatchet:

> If you are going to ride at Lincoln I should be pleased to give you your first mount and would put in a horse for you to ride in the Trial Stakes – you would thereby have public proof that I feel confident that you will do your best to reinstate yourself as a jockey.[83]

Wood had in fact learned his lesson and he became a successful and honest jockey, but other jockeys who were let back again incurred suspicion.[84] Clearly the deterrent effect of a warning off was diluted by forgiving sinners their trespasses: calculating the odds of being found out and comparing the rewards of transgression with the penalty of temporary disqualification may in some quarters have become as much a part of racing as calculating the odds on the horses.

However, at least by the end of the nineteenth century most racing men seem to have accepted the authority of the Jockey Club. This was a product of events in racing, particularly the coming of the enclosed, gate-money course, which put a premium on a code of morality, and the genuine concern for racing of the Jockey Club, the suppliers of that code. A more vigilant press may also have played a role. By the end of the century flagrant disregard of the Club as in *Running Rein's* Derby or at the metropolitan saturnalia was less observable; remember doping was allowed. It may be, of course, that roguery was merely pushed underground; that racing changed only from being overtly disreputable to being covertly disreputable. This was the firm opinion of L. H. Curzon, a severe critic of racing morality. Writing in the 1890s, he declared that

> today racing rogueries are too numerous, too varied, too much a matter of course to attract much attention [though] there almost never fails nowadays to be chronicled any vulgar or pronounced frauds – these seldom become public [for] what is being done is being accomplished in a manner so refined, and at the same time is so quietly done, that the public outside have no chance of detecting it.[85]

Yet if this was true why did racing not collapse? Even if the public remained ignorant surely those in racing would suspect what was happening; and if they suspected widespread malpractice, surely racing would not have expanded as it did? There was some debate in turf circles as to the degree of misconduct, but most racing men agreed with Alfred Watson, a leading writer on turf affairs, that 'a few rogues are still to the fore, sometimes in prominent places, and not a few others have conveniently elastic consciences, together with excessively liberal ideas of what is permissible, but I do believe that there is far less rascality on the turf than there used to be'.[86] Racing was and will always be susceptible to corruption: gambling will see to that. But, façade or not, and one suspects not, the image of the sport at the turn of the century was certainly less tarnished than at earlier points in time.

Just after the First World War, it was reported that a new body was to be set up, representative of owners, breeders, racecourse executives, trainers, bookmakers, and the racing press.[87] Whether it was to replace, advise, or exhort the Jockey Club was not made clear, but nothing concrete emerged from the proposals, 'those within the Club felt no loss of their customary standing; those outside it were submissive and content as ever'.[88] Pressure groups did develop in racing in the twentieth century, but invariably they bowed to Jockey Club authority.[89] Chief of these was the Thoroughbred Breeders Association which, though the Jockey Club always denied it, may have catalysed several of its inquiries into racing reforms. However, the Association was adamant that it had no designs on Jockey Club power; its role was that of pacemaker, it had no ambitions to breast the tape.[90]

The exclusive nature of the Jockey Club diminished a little after the First World War, but only a little. Some industrialists and businessmen managed to secure election, though usually only after they had secured honours and belated acceptance into society, and generally years after they could have made an impact as turf administrators.[91] Yet these were only minor chinks in the otherwise impenetrable armour of the Jockey Club, only slight exceptions to the age-old, prescribed channels for its recruits. A few ageing industrialists might gain entry, but the small owner or press representative found the door firmly shut.

Nonetheless, Jockey Club authority was universally accepted and even Sidney Galtry, racing correspondent and stern critic of the Club, freely conceded that the Club had done wonders since the war: 'the old Tory spirit has been moved to heed the restlessness of the age and the necessity of trimming sails to the passing breeze while maintaining ancient authority'.[92] The Club abandoned its stubborn resistance to dipping its bucket into betting's stream of gold and accepted the totalizator and its financial contribution to racing.* Misconduct was dealt with severely; legal proceedings being instituted in the worst cases. This had been the declared policy since the *Running Rein* affair, but it had never been pursued with enthusiasm, partly because of the cost.[93] After the First World War, however, there was no such reluctance: policy and practice were made clear in 1920 when the substitution of horses at Stockton led to imprisonment for those responsible.[94] Perhaps the new, forceful attitude acted as a greater deterrent for, although malpractice did not cease, there was certainly less complaint about the conduct of racing in the interwar years. It was the conduct of the crowd, or rather certain sections of it, that excited publicity at this time and even though this was really the responsibility of local executives rather than of the Jockey Club, the Club took positive action to counteract the problem.†

Writing in the 1930s, one rational turf observer commented that 'it is generally conceded that the English Turf today, if not altogether immaculate in its many phases, is as clean an institution as one could reasonably wish to find it. The system of control was never tighter. Acute misdemeanours are few and far between.'[95] This could not have been written a century previously.

---

* See below, Chapter 15.   † See below, p. 142.

7

Racing Officials]

Two reliable writers on turf affairs swear as to the truth of the following tale about racing in the early 1850s, the era between Bentinck and Rous.[1] At this time it was not uncommon for clerks of the course at lesser provincial meetings to double up on other functions, either to save money for the race committee or to increase their own incomes, the yield from the sparse entries satisfying neither's pecuniary ambitions. One such jack-of-all-trades was a past-master at making money. His plan was simple: he acted both as handicapper and stakeholder and in return for not having to hand over the stakes he virtually allowed owners to nominate their own weights. One winning owner, however, was ignorant of the etiquette of the situation and asked for the prize-money. The clerk-cum-handicapper-cum-stakeholder was aggrieved:

'Was that the weight you wished to carry?'
'Yes'
'Did you back him?'
'Yes'
'Well I'll pay you this time, but take care you never make such a mistake again.'

An equally blatant case of official venality occurred at Doncaster in 1827.[2] John Gully, the prizefighting publican turned colliery and racehorse owner, had successfully offered 4,000 guineas to Lord Jersey for *Mameluke*, already the winner of the Derby. This was a good deal of money to pay for horse-flesh, but Gully, a heavy better, was supremely confident that the animal could win the St Leger and more than recoup his high outlay. Others shared Gully's confidence but not his bets. Their money was on Mr Petre's *Granby* which offered better odds. *Mameluke* had to be stopped, but how? Stable security excluded nobbling and Chifney, the jockey, was not to be bought. The starter, however, was amenable to financial persuasion; and if the horse could be upset at the starting post it might reduce its chances of catching the judge's eye. The conspirators almost got a non-runner for their money. Seven false starts and a two-hour delay played havoc with the nerves of *Mameluke*, never the epitome of equine equanimity, and when the race finally got under way, Gully's horse was facing the wrong way.[3] Nevertheless, despite being left almost a hundred yards, *Mameluke* almost pulled it off, being beaten by only half a length. It is pleasing to note that though Gully lost, so did the schemers for, although Petre became the winning owner, it was not with *Granby* but with his stable companion *Matilda*.

Impartial officials were vital to the long-term success of race meetings: if racing was to retain its support, then owners and gamblers had to be convinced that odds fairly reflected chances and that horses could win on merit. Imagine a race meeting without officials, where jockeys chose their own weights, decided when to start, who had won a close finish, and whether objections for foul riding should be over-ruled or sustained! Rule makers and rule enforcers were obviously necessary to prevent a meeting degenerating into a succession of disputes, possibly resolved more by might than right. In itself the provision of officials was still insufficient. They had to be seen to be acting in an unprejudiced manner: starters should ensure equal opportunity at the commencement of a race; handicappers should attempt to give an equal chance to all horses; impartial judges should decide which horse reached the post first; and independent stewards should consider if there had been fair play during the race itself.

Unfortunately, for much of the nineteenth century there was no national supervision of turf officialdom and this absence of control led, almost inevitably, to venality and abuse. Each clerk of the course, or whoever was in charge of the meeting, was generally at liberty to appoint whoever he wished to officiate. This freedom did not guarantee good officials. If the race fund was depleted (a not infrequent occurrence prior to the enclosed, gate-money course), then cost rather than ability could determine the appointments. Moreover, those offering their services cheaply might have ulterior motives for obtaining the posts. Others simply proved too obsequious for the employment. Lord Chesterfield, chief patron at his local meeting, eventually ceased to run his horses there because he felt that they were unduly favoured by both the starter and the judge.[3] The annual races for gentlemen riders at Heaton Park, seat of the Earl of Wilton, were similarly abused by the appointed officials. Each year the handicapper was a guest at his Lordship's mansion and coincidently the weights assigned usually gave little chance to any horse not belonging to the Earl or his associates. On one occasion, however, Lord Wilton had ridden in four or five races without success and was apparently beaten yet again in his next race. To the consternation of the betting men, the judge, a Mancunian by the name of Orton, awarded the race to the Earl – he was threatened with a ducking, and worse, in the betting rooms of Manchester, though what a racing official was doing in such premises one hesitates to think.[4] If such a palpable manipulation had been widespread, it could have destroyed racing; happily, for various reasons outlined below, similar incidents occurred less frequently as the century progressed: the corrupt and inefficient were weeded out and by the early twentieth century, the morality of British turf officialdom was beyond question.

The overall responsibility for the organization of a meeting usually lay with the clerk of the course: although he was appointed by the race committee, or whoever was guarantor of the added money, he was generally left to get on with his job without interference. In many instances the position became a family possession to be passed on from one generation to another. W. J. Ford and his three sons officiated at Nottingham for over four decades and Epsom was ruled by the Dorling family for most of the nineteenth and well into the twentieth century; though in the latter case the Dorlings were also dominant on the race committee and thus appointed themselves.[5] The clerk's functions were numerous. He had to ensure that the necessary facilities were available for all participants: the provision of weighing-room, parade ring, police, catering and stabling were all within his province; he was responsible for seeing that the course was measured accurately and that it was in proper order; he had to draw up the programme, check that the conditions were foolproof, and complete the racecard. His prime concern was the running of the meeting rather than of the races, though at lesser gatherings he often performed other tasks directly associated with the race such as clerk of the scales, and even starter. Clerks acting as starters were quite common in the 1830s; and even at Ascot in 1857 Edward Hibburd, who had succeeded William Hibburd as clerk of the course in 1852, acted as starter when his brother Henry, the official starter, fell ill.[6] In general, however, the clerk or the race committee appointed others to do these duties. This was a vital function: if they were lax in the standards they applied to applicants then corruption and inefficiency could wax.

The clerk of the course was not merely a salaried manager. Frequently his income was partly dependent on his entrepreneurial ability, for in addition to the fee from the race committee he generally – at least from the 1860s when the system was initiated by John Frail, clerk at Shrewsbury – obtained an entry fee from each owner.[7] So did the clerk of the scales and the stakeholder, positions often taken on by the clerk of the course in order to maximize the return on his efforts to attract entrants.[*] This duplication of functions continued throughout the century, but in 1897 the Jockey Club forbade doubling up between clerk of the course and handicappers. The position was not being wildly or widely abused, but it was felt that specialist handicappers would be above suspicion. Other regulations concerned efficiency rather than honesty: from time to time the Jockey Club made it plain that if a course hoped to retain its licence improvements would have to be made.[8] Some courses had been nothing short of a scandal: Northallerton was so narrow that the horses had to be started in rows, and at many others the run-in was not fully fenced off, thus allowing dogs and people to stray on to the course and possibly interfere with the finish.[9] In 1907, on the suggestion of Viscount Downe, the office of Inspector of Race-courses was created with the right to suggest alterations in track width, gradients, drainage, contours, and fencing. Spectator facilities, however, were left entirely to the discretion of the clerk and the race committee. Many clerks

---

[*] At most meetings the clerk of the course obtained 2s. 6d. from each entrant, the clerk of the scales 2s. 6d. from each runner, and the stakeholder 1 per cent of the stakes. 'The Expenses of Racing', *Badminton Magazine*, vol. 38, February 1914, p. 175.

became specialists undertaking the function at several different meetings: the I'Ansons ranged from Doncaster to Scotland; the Ford family covered meetings in the midlands and the north of England; and the Frails worked at several of the southern courses. Specialization was not new – in the 1840s Henry Dorling had acted at Brighton as well as at Epsom – but the development of the enclosed course had led to competition for experienced racecourse managers to ensure success in the drive to attract spectators. By the late nineteenth century most clerks at authorized meetings found themselves in 'not unprofitable berths',* though they had to work for their money.[10] The added money rule of the 1870s and the racing revolution brought about by the enclosed course had put paid to many fixtures whose supervision lay in the hands of local men of little reputation or experience.† A few country meetings, complete with long wine-imbibing luncheons, continued to offer a sinecure, but generally clerks at authorized meetings were compelled to be efficient by both Jockey Club regulation and the pressure of competition.

In 1839 the races at Goodwood started three-quarters of an hour late, yet this was 'designated as great punctuality by the entire sporting press'.[11] It seemed an almost indispensable feature of the day's amusements to prolong the entertainment and keep the spectators in suspense as long as possible. This reflected a social atmosphere in which lunch took precedence over racing; there would be a race or two in the morning and more racing after lunch, though the advertised starting time of the later races frequently fell victim to the quality and quantity of the fare provided for the owners and officials. However, even when the horses reached the starting post wearisome delays occurred due to the incompetence or dishonesty of starters and jockeys. Big races were not immune. The 1827 St Leger fiasco has already been mentioned, but such débâcles were not rare in the St Leger, though usually they were unplanned. In 1819, *Antonio's* year, several horses were left at the start and in 1823, after three false starts, twenty-three of the twenty-seven runners broke away

---

* I have been unable to trace any actual figures.
† See above, pp. 45–6.

and completed a void race.[12] One authority believed the troubles were due to a combination of the antagonism between northern and southern jockeys and the sending of half-trained animals to the post merely to win bets as to the number of runners.[13] At Epsom in 1840 Victoria and Albert witnessed sixteen false starts to the Oaks, a similar number to the Derby eight years previously.[14] There were also ten false starts in the Derbys of 1817 and 1830.[15] The signal for the off at most meetings was a shout of 'go' from the starter: it did not help to have an official with a stutter who so spluttered over 'no' and 'go' that his starts at Goodwood in 1830 were a combination of bedlam and burlesque.[16] At some meetings noble patrons occasionally assumed the starter's duties: Lord Derby at Prescot and Liverpool; the first Marquis of Westminster at Holywell; the fifth Earl of Glasgow at Catterick Bridge; and Lord George Bentinck virtually anywhere he chose to, including Chester where in 1842 he started the Chester Cup in which not only was his own horse running, but where he also had a large stake on the eventual winner, *Red Deer*. It has been alleged that he placed his own horse, the heavily backed *Bramble* next to *Red Deer* with orders for his own jockey to let the other horse through as soon as the flag fell.[17] To allow such owners and gamblers to act as starters was an expression of faith in the concept of honour, but inevitably, no matter how honestly the function was performed, some losers used different expressions as to the integrity of noble officialdom. At least these aristocrats stood no nonsense from the working class: jockeys got away with much less than when more timid individuals were in charge. Without doubt, jockeys were responsible for most of the delay at the starts. It was a common device deliberately to false start in order to upset a fancied horse, particularly as the horses often ran some distance before they could be recalled. In many instances unfair starts occurred simply because the starter lost patience.

Unless corruption was blatant, no one seemed prepared to rectify the situation. Perhaps good starts were not considered too important when races were generally of relatively long distances and had few runners; and, of course, with heats a horse always had a second chance. Reforms became essential when shorter distances increased the importance of a good start and also as the expansion of the railway system increased both the number of horses running and the number of races on the card, for more runners meant greater complications at the start, especially in the days before a draw was made for places, and more races meant less time to spare for delay.[18]

The first major attempt to reform came from Lord George Bentinck, who, as part of his campaign to cut turf chicanery and improve racing for the spectator, devised the dual flag system of starting. The starter, armed with a small red flag, stood at the post; his assistant, with a much larger white flag, was posted some fifty or sixty yards down the course in the centre of the track. When the horses came under orders the white flag was raised; after the roll call the red flag too was raised, to be dropped as the starter shouted 'go'. Simultaneously, the white flag was lowered so that all the jockeys would know that the race was under way; if the start was false the white flag could quickly be raised again before the horses went too far. Relative punctuality at Goodwood, where Lord George dominated the proceedings, led to imitation elsewhere and for a while the innovation was successful; but once Lord George retired from the turf, his influence waned. Too many starters were weak and too many jockeys were uncontrollable for the reform to become decisive; it could not prevent false starts if the jockeys were determined to risk them. The giving of presents to the starter – in 1859 the official starter at Newmarket received over £1,000 from winning owners[19] – had not helped matters. It made jockeys suspect that someone in the race had bought an advantage and tempted them to offset this by unfair tactics of their own.[20] What was required was the power to suspend jockeys: most meetings allowed for jockeys to be fined, but this was no real deterrent since the fines were regarded as a small price to pay for an advantageous start.[21] Given his low opinion of jockeys, one suspects that Admiral Rous would have suspended them all from time to time as a matter of principle, and it is no surprise that the requisite legislation to suspend jockeys for causing trouble at the start came during his stewardship; in 1863 to be exact, by which time the Jockey Club was becoming strong enough to have its regulations generally accepted. However, the authority to suspend was vested in the local stewards;

not till the twentieth century were starters even allowed to fine the jockeys. Stewards were gentlemen, often aristocrats, and could be trusted not to abuse their authority; starters could not, at least not unless they were appointed by the Jockey Club and subject to its discipline.[22] Initially even the employment of the Jockey Club starter did not guarantee perfection. After the 1862 Derby, McGeorge, the starter, was severely reprimanded by the Epsom stewards and threatened with dismissal for starting the horses in advance of the post and leaving some behind.[23] But such instances were rare and in the last quarter of the nineteenth century the Jockey Club starter and his deputies found increasing employment outside Newmarket. The abominable starting at many country meetings could not be tolerated at the enclosed courses where the drive to attract spectators put a premium on starting on time; so those officials with the Jockey Club seal of approval found themselves in great demand.

Improved technique perhaps did most to improve starting. Merely shouting 'go' gave way to the dual flag system and at the end of the century this bowed to modern technology in the form of the starting gate. First used in Britain in 1897, it was made compulsory by the Jockey Club within half a decade.* Yet the gate had many detractors. Racehorses were valuable animals and there was a twofold risk of injury at the gate: it was more difficult to get away from the attentions of a fractious horse because runners were wedged closer together than with the flag start; and there was danger from the apparatus itself with horses liable to tangle themselves in the tapes or be catapulted back from them.[24] The latter risk was reduced by giving starters the discretion to over-rule the draw and place excitable horses where they wished in the line.[25] The former was cut by experience; in effect jockeys stopped trying to beat the gate because it hurt, physically and financially. Starters were also given permission to start the race behind the line.[26] Some horses did not get a fair break from the gate: many refused to approach the contraption at all, others bolted the wrong way when the webbing flew up.[27] However, although animals could not be expected to behave like machines, trainers could be

* In 1900 it was used for all two-year-old races; in 1901 for all three-year-old events; and it was in general use by 1902.

expected to accustom their horses to the workings of a machine: what trainers objected to was not the gate but the extra work it necessitated.

A few really excitable horses never got used to the gate, but their loss must be weighed against the advantages that the machine brought to racing as a whole. It put jockeys on more even terms and gave inexperienced boys a vastly better chance than did the flag. With the flag, wily jockeys would not go until they were ready and they were never ready till they thought they had the best of it. Hanging back at the start became a fine art and a well-rewarded one if done successfully, for to be on the move, even fractionally, is a tremendous advantage in a short race. The gate method of starting, at least in its early days, virtually forced them to be in line and standing still.[28] Experienced jockeys could still anticipate the starter's actions by looking for a movement of his head or shoulders, though it was less easy than in the days of the flag. The greatest advantage of the gate was the considerable reduction it brought about in the delay at the start. At a Croydon meeting in June 1871, one race was delayed at the post for over an hour, another for forty-five minutes, and finally, after waiting till eight o'clock to start the last race, the starter threw down his flag in disgust and declared the race void.[29] This was extreme, but even in the 1890s it could fairly be stated that 'any unprejudiced person who has been in the habit of going down to the start is always prepared for a long delay'.[30] Tedious waits of up to half an hour were common. The gate changed all this: it did not eliminate delay – fractious horses saw to that – but it drastically cut it. At one Epsom meeting in 1906 the last race on Tuesday was only two minutes late, on Wednesday three minutes, and on Thursday and Friday five minutes.[31] It is unfair to compare this best practice with the Croydon incident, but there is no doubt that practice in general was much improved.

The classics are the true test of thoroughbred race horses; in these races the competitors meet with similar weights or at weight for sex so, other things being equal, the winner should be the best horse in the field. Weight for age races also test the best. However, racing also needs handicaps; not so much to promote bloodstock breeding, though the high-class events do serve this purpose, but to encourage gambling and ownership, the mainstays of racing. The very fact that horses carry different weights tempts the gambling fraternity to criticize the handicapper's work; in addition handicaps maintain the interest of all owners by giving even poor-quality horses a chance to win. Handicaps allowed more racing than would otherwise be possible; good handicaps encouraged more runners and close finishes, both an attraction for spectators.

In the first half of the nineteenth century handicappers were not above suspicion. Sharp practice was suspected at one west country meeting where the Danebury stable swept almost everything before it.[32] But there was a built-in semi-safeguard against corruption; the success of a meeting depended on the number of horses it attracted, so if a handicapper was too blatant in his favours there might be too few acceptances to satisfy his employers. Really the basic problem was incompetence rather than dishonesty. Too many provincial meetings were handicapped on a one-off basis by men out of touch with racing form: to be effective a handicapper must be in constant contact with racing, cognizant of the form of hundreds of horses. A good handicapper must constantly practise his trade, even if not in employment, or he will lose the thread of public form. This means regular attendance at race meetings in order to assess what conditions were like and how well horses had run. Recorded distances were no substitute for personal observation; a short head victory by a tired horse means something very different from a similar win by a horse with plenty in hand. However, experience could be expensive; travelling was costly, especially when race meetings encouraged famine prices at hotels, so many small-time handicappers were tempted to stay at home and rely on newspaper reports. If a handicapper could be guaranteed employment he might be more willing to do his job properly. Moreover, there were economies of scale to be had if the knowledge of a competent individual could be used to handicap several meetings. Good handicapping could thus beget further good handicapping.

The Jockey Club took the lead. After several disputes had been referred to them, the stewards decided to appoint a public handicapper, whom they recommended to all provincial meetings. The first appointment, in 1855, was Admiral Rous, aged sixty with a lifetime of equine match-making behind him. It was the Admiral who had allotted the weights for the great match between *Voltigeur* and *Flying Dutchman*. Rous had already published his own recipe for a public handicapper: he 'should be a man of independent circumstances, in every sense of the word, and beyond suspicions of accepting illicit compensation for favours'.[33] Rous was universally recognized as incorruptible; perhaps this was why no one really took issue at him letting a gambling friend, George Hodgman, assist him occasionally. This collaboration once saved Rous from a serious blunder. He was persuaded to allot 7 st. 13 lb. to *Gridiron* for the 1861 Cesarewitch instead of the 6 st. 4 lb. he had contemplated. Even with the heavier handicap the horse ran extremely well.[34] Rous exhibited neither favour nor vindictiveness;* even his old enemy, Sir Joseph Hawley, could never complain about the weights assigned to his horses.

On the death of Rous in 1877, professional handicappers took over; gentlemen of independent means prepared to sit up half the night to have form at their fingertips, as Rous did, were difficult to find. The first replacement was Messrs Weatherby. They had a long-standing association with the Jockey Club beginning in 1773 when James Weatherby first published the *Racing Calendar*. Over time the Weatherbys became secretaries to the Jockey Club, taking responsibility for receiving entries to races, registering owners' colours, and accepting horses for the *Stud Book*. They also acted as agents for many owners, dealing with entries, forfeits, winnings, and payments to jockeys.[35] The Weatherbys undertook the onerous duties of official handicapper till 1886 when Major Egerton took over. By this time so many meetings were requesting the services of the official handicapper that an assistant, R. K. Mainwaring, was ap-

---

* A letter from W. Read to J. Bowes (5 August 1863, D/St. Box 162, Durham County Record Office) does claim otherwise: 'With regard to the handicapping of your horses, there can be no mistake but that ill-feeling towards Scott's stable exists in Rous' heart – he has never forgotten the apology he had to make to J. Scott (over an allegation of not running a horse to win).' However, in the particular issue which raised this outburst, the Free Nursery Handicap, though no expert, the author felt that the weights allotted by Rous were quite justified.

pointed; he succeeded Egerton in 1898. In addition the Jockey Club certificated other handicappers to act at meetings where quasi-private handicapping was preferred.[36]

In most other spheres of racing officialdom, the enclosed course forced an improvement in standards: with handicapping, however, the immediate reaction was in the wrong direction. Many clerks of the course who handicapped their own meetings found that they had too much work on their hands simply stage managing these new theatres of racing and could not devote sufficient time to handicap efficiently. Others felt the necessity of attracting as many runners as possible and handicapped accordingly, alloting all the entrants much lower weights than they could normally have anticipated in the hope that owners might confuse relative with absolute handicaps.[37] The same purpose was served by soliciting the entry of a horse a class above the rest; one clerk kept his own horse specifically to meet this need.[38] Fortunately some clerks recognized their responsibility to racing and requested the services of the Jockey Club handicapper. This created excessive pressure of work on Major Egerton and, in the opinion of Sir George Chetwynd, caused him to make too many mistakes.[39] The appointment of deputy handicappers eased the burden, but many observers still felt that the Jockey Club officials undertook too many commitments to do justice to them all. The Jockey Club eventually accepted this argument and in 1897 limited the volume of work that a handicapper could do by restricting his efforts to one meeting a week which he must either attend in person or to which he must send a licensed deputy. Special permission from the Club stewards was required if extra work was to be accepted. At the same time further legislation increased the problem of efficient handicapping by preventing a handicapper from holding another office at any meeting for which he had allocated the weights. This forced several competent clerks of the course to give up the job of handicapping, though, naturally, it also removed the inefficient ones. However, their replacements were not necessarily any better. The best solution was more official handicappers but in the short run good ones were difficult to find.

The employment of specialist handicappers raised problems of subjective judgement. A starter or a judge would hardly deliberately ruin the chances of a horse, but a handicapper could, though not with evil intent. If he rated a horse higher than perhaps he should have, then he would weight it out of a race; and if he officiated at many meetings there was a danger of the horse being constantly shut out of the prize money. A variety of handicappers would give it a chance somewhere. This was the theory behind the Jockey Club's decision in the early twentieth century to use the three official handicappers as a committee, each drawing up a separate handicap and then arriving at a consensus.[40] However, this triplication of effort was a waste of scarce talent and after 1912 the triumvirate was disbanded: it was hoped that the employment of several handicappers would give owners sufficient choice of races to compensate for the possibility of bias.

The handicapper was perhaps more sinned against than sinning. Admiral Rous was adamant that 'every great handicap offers a premium to fraud, for horses are constantly started without any intentions of winning, merely to hoodwink the handicapper . . . the honest fair trader who always starts to win, has a very indifferent chance of getting his horses fairly weighted against such competitors'.[41] Rous had his own way of assessing form and ensuring that it was realistic.[42] He attended every major race meeting, usually watching the race from the top of the stand through the telescope he had formerly used at sea. Before each race he made a thorough inspection of the horses in the paddock and afterwards he would check to see which runners were blowing most. All matters of interest were consigned immediately to his notebook. At Newmarket he watched the races on horseback, usually from a spot where he felt non-triers could be picked out; if he saw a flagrant case he would roar at the jockey to get a move on. When he could not attend meetings he asked the clerks there to let him know of 'horses (that) have been run out of condition, or with too severe a curb'. His observations were not confined to race meetings. Most mornings he was out on the Heath, field glass in hand, watching to see if work was being shirked in an attempt to run an unfit horse. If any other handicapper had done this he would have faced a mutiny; Rous, however, was a law unto himself.

Later handicappers had to rely basically on form, on the

weight-for-age scale (devised by Rous himself), and on personal observation of races supplemented by the comments of other officials and trustworthy jockeys or trainers. They could not play a hunch that a horse had been pulled; if stewards had seen nothing wrong, who was the handicapper to insist that malpractice had occurred? Unless owners, trainers, and jockeys were to be handicapped alongside the horse there was little that could be done. One handicapper explained that, as any aggrieved owner could call the handicapper before the stewards to explain his work, he preferred to avoid libel actions and stick to the safety of book form.[43] Unlike Rous, later handicappers could not 'make it a standing rule never to answer any man who thinks he had a right to question the justice of a weight'.[44] Nevertheless, the same critic who in 1899 complained that 'some of the handicapping during the year has been simply preposterous', willingly conceded that the handicappers 'diligently do their level best without fear or favour, and without the vaguest shadow of suspicion as to their absolute integrity'.[45] Many things were completely beyond the control of the handicapper: the state of the going, the choice of jockey, the intentions of the owner, the behaviour of other horses in the race, and interference from stray dogs and the occasional suffragette were hardly within his jurisdiction.

TABLE 7. A TEST OF HANDICAPPING

	Percentage of handicaps won by neck, head or dead heats	Percentage of handicaps won by favourites
1865–9	23	40
1897–1902	30	31

Source: calculated from *Racing Calendar* (*Races Past*)

The employment of specialist, professional handicappers did much to improve the state of the art. Of course some owners were never satisfied; the discontented Duchess of Montrose frequently accused the corpulent Major Egerton of handicapping in the hope of securing mounts for himself![46] However, there is some evidence as to the improved standards. If the aim of the handicappers was to get close finishes and open races, then, as is shown in Table 7, they were more successful in achieving this at the end of the century than before the development of the enclosed course; more races were won by a neck or a head and the betting market found winners less easy to predict.

Five minutes' work on the day was all a judge needed to do in order to draw his salary; he had to observe the finish of perhaps six races and write a report for the stewards. Good judges, of course, did more. They familiarized themselves with the colours, checked the runners against their lists, and noted which horses were likely to contest the finish. The work was hardly arduous, but it was vital: thousands of pounds could depend on the judge's eyesight and quickness of decision. Unlike in the law courts, in racing the judge's verdict was inviolate; owners and jockeys could appeal to the stewards about events during the race itself, but the order in which the judge said the horses reached the line was not open to question.* Unless the judge admitted that he had erred it was hard luck on a misplaced horse. Judges did make mistakes: C. E. Robinson once fell asleep during the Steward's Cup (fortunately an observant policeman woke him up); judge Clark once left the box before the race finished in the mistaken belief that all the horses had fallen; and it was said that the same judge had a blind spot for horses running close to the chair.[47] Yet errors were rare considering the difficulty of the job. Decisions had to be instantaneous. This was easy when horses trailed each other home, but not when there was a close finish in bad weather with indistinguishable, rain-soaked liveries flashing by the post, perhaps at different sides of the track.† In the 1830s it must have been even more difficult as at many courses the stewards acted as multiple judges. Nor were matters helped by the practice of owners, trainers, and spectators riding in with the horses: on one famous occasion the judge, frustrated by

---

* Here a common fallacy can be corrected: it is first *at* the post, not first *past* the post.

† The photo-finish was not introduced till 1947. It was first used at the Epsom Spring Meeting.

the charge of the mounted gentry, declared that the first horse home was ridden 'by a tall gentleman in a white coat', none other than Lord George Bentinck.[48] In 1838 the Jockey Club eased matters by passing a rule 'that any Member of a Racing Club riding in with the leading horses in a race shall be fined to the amount of 25 sovereigns, and all other persons to the amount of 5 sovereigns'.

Judges were the earliest professional Jockey Club officials. Following a dispute in 1776 between stewards who were acting as judges, the Club decided to employ John Hilton to officiate at Newmarket. In 1805 the Clark family took over: first was John Clark; then in 1822 his son, John Francis Clark; followed by his son John Clark who served from 1852 to 1889 when the post went to C. E. Robinson, his son-in-law. As with other official posts further work came their way simply because they were employed at Newmarket. But they could not be everywhere; and by 1900 in order to ease the pressure of demand, the Jockey Club had licensed ten officials to act as judges at authorized meetings. They were all honest and straightforward men. Perhaps there were too many eyes concentrated on the finish for overt dishonesty to occur; whatever the reason there were few complaints about corrupt judges. Indeed, an article published in 1880 which was critical of many aspects of turf morality exempted judges from rebuke, acknowledging that they were men of integrity.[49] Nevertheless, the Jockey Club took no chances: having the best judges that money could buy was not to have a double meaning. Over the years the custom had developed of winning owners in important races being obliged to give presents to the judge. In 1848 the Jockey Club decided that this practice was objectionable in principle and that instead a fixed sum should be paid out of certain large stakes and the judge precluded from receiving any presents whatever. In 1866 they went further and resolved that the judge should be paid only by the Jockey Club or the executive of the particular meeting and that there should be no requirement on winners to pay any sum towards the expenses of the meeting. Later regulations prevented judges from owning racehorses or having any financial interest in any race in which they adjudicated.

At the beginning of the twentieth century it could justifiably be written that 'complete confidence in our salaried officials is held by the racing world'.[50] The morality of British racing officialdom was unquestionable. Errors still occurred but never wilfully: and incompetence and inefficiency, while not things of the past, were far rarer than fifty years previously. The reason for this improvement was the emergence of specialist, professional officials. The demand for better officials was part of the desire for improved turf morality and organization as a whole, both of which were boosted by the development and extension of the enclosed, gate-money meetings and their competitive drive to attract owners and spectators. The existence of a railway network enabled the best officials to respond to this demand and accept employment all over the country. Nevertheless, the Jockey Club played an important role in influencing the market; both by example in employing specialist professionals and by regulation in the form of licences, rules on payment, and legislation to enforce standards of competence.*

There was one important exception to the professionalization of officialdom. Significantly this concerned the ultimate decision makers at any meeting, the stewards: here the amateurs reigned supreme. Throughout the nineteenth century the stewards tended to be selected from the local aristocracy and gentry, a hangover from the pre-railway era when local patronage was vital to the success of a meeting. As a writer in the *Sporting Magazine* for 1839 pointed out, it was also an acknowledgement of the worthy's social position:

> It is a post of honour which cannot fail to afford considerable gratification. Viewed as one of very great responsibility the nomination carries with it a very high compliment . . . it frequently occurs that gentlemen of property and influence, on account of their known integrity and zeal for the welfare of their neighbours and property of the county in which they reside, are called on to accept the undertaking . . .[51]

Three major criticisms were levied against these amateur

---

* In 1937 the Club went a stage further and decided to appoint all licensed officials to meetings rather than allowing course executives discretion in the choice of men for the jobs.

officials. First, that many of them accepted the honour but not the responsibility that went with it. The author of the *Badminton Library* volume on racing, no less a personage than the Earl of Suffolk, complained of the lack of attendance by appointed stewards; and in 1903 a further commentator asserted that, because many of the named stewards would not turn up 'it may be taken as certain that a large majority of race meetings are less well-managed from a racing point of view, and less closely looked after, than the names of their sponsors upon their race-cards lead me to expect'.[52] Secondly, although other officials were not allowed to bet on races in which they were involved, no such restriction applied to stewards. Gentlemen by definition were honourable and deemed incorruptible. The very great majority probably were, but to take this for granted was to show a gross ignorance of racing history.* Thirdly, it was argued that when they did attend they were ineffective and per-formed their duties in a perfunctory manner. Apart from the implication of incorruptibility, there was no good reason why title or position should make any person suitable to be a steward. No doubt inherited wealth allowed some both the time and the money to become thoroughly acquainted with the sport, but unfortunately too many of the gentlemen stewards were ignorant of the rules of racing. At York in 1888 the stewards were unable to explain the conditions of one of the races: Charles Morton the trainer asked what weight *Althorp* should carry in the Ebor as the penalty clauses seemed am-biguous, but the stewards would not offer an opinion.[53] Most stewards also exhibited a marked reluctance to go down the course to the points where horses would be pulled.

Stewards were better at the end of the nineteenth century than at the beginning. The Ascot stewards in 1900 would never have consulted *spectators* before disqualifying a horse as their predecessors did after the Gold Cup of 1833. Nevertheless, numerous observers felt there was much room for improvement. In the opinion of many racing men justice would be better done, and seen to be done, if stipendiary stewards were appointed, either to replace or assist the local honorary officials.[54] These stewards, by travelling the country and attending race meetings

* e.g. see above, Chapter 6, passim.

regularly, could have form and the rules of racing at their fingertips and be aware of inconsistent running. There was little response.

However, ignorance of racing among stewards became less of a problem. Writing in the 1920s one commentator considered that stewards were in the main drawn from the ranks of those who knew racing backwards.[55] But there are ranks and other ranks: the selection of stewards on social grounds went on as before. However, they did begin to go down the course and also to use a crow's nest for watching the race. And stewards began to act on their own initiative rather than wait for the owner, trainer, or jockey to lodge an objection. The credit for stewards beginning to do this goes to Lord Hamilton of Dalzell. He was acting as steward at Sandown when a horse lost a race because of bumping, but no objection was raised. He thought that as stewards were there to see fair play they should have stepped in and done something. Nothing was done in this instance, but his views led to a discussion in influential quarters as to the precise nature of the duties of stewards and eventually to the acceptance of his policy.[56] An outstanding example of the policy in action was the 1913 Derby. This was a dramatic race in more ways than one. Just after the horses rounded Tattenham Corner, Emily Davison, a militant suffragette,* ran on to the course, caught the reins of *Anmer*, the King's horse, and brought it down; neither the horse nor the jockey was seriously injured, but poor Emily died from a fractured skull. Sensation followed sensation. The 'All Right' flag had been hoisted and the bookmakers had begun to pay out when it was announced that the stewards had taken it on themselves to object to the winner. After an enquiry they disqualified *Craganour* for bumping and awarded the race to *Aboyeur*, a 100 to 1 outsider.

Despite these improvements the situation regarding stewards was far from perfect. In the 1930s Sidney Galtrey, the racing correspondent of the *Daily Telegraph* could still criticize stewards 'who have grown old, with their faculties impaired

---

* The suffragettes also attempted to burn down grandstands, successfully at Ayr and Birmingham, and unsuccessfully at Cardiff and Kelso. Interference with horse racing was an attack on the sport of politicians, a crack at a bastion of male privilege, and a guarantee of publicity.

through age', but who expected to officiate until they died, stewards who were notorious backers, and stewards who entertained a few favoured owners and trainers in the luncheon rooms at the expense of the racecourse shareholders.[57] In 1931 Lord Rosebery instituted a discussion which led, three years later, to the Jockey Club agreeing to appoint secretaries to assist the local stewards if the Racecourse Betting Control Board (R.B.C.B.)* would finance their employment. This commenced in 1936. But really the problem had never been a financial one; it had been the refusal of the Jockey Club to accept that men of high social position were not necessarily equipped to perform the task of stewardship effectively.

* For details of the R.B.C.B. see chapter 15.

8

The Crowd]

Racing men, and particularly the more privileged of them, were fond of claiming that their sport was not a class-ridden one, appealing as it did to both high- and low-born. Admiral Rous, a holder of firm views on all racing matters, maintained that 'there is at least one amusement in which all classes participate, one point of contact between all parties and one source of enjoyment to individuals of every rank – namely horse racing'.[1] And a Select Committee in the 1840s was persuaded to report that racing 'is in accordance with a long-established national taste, because it serves to bring together for a common object, vast bodies of people in the different parts of the country, and to promote intercourse between different classes of society'.[2]

Certainly racing was an activity involving all ranks of society, but was it the social unifying force which its supporters frequently claimed it was? It is difficult to see how it broke down class barriers when the upper ranks of society generally viewed the scene from the safe confines of private stands and carriages, or later the club enclosures, well segregated from the lower elements. There was a greater physical mingling of the classes in at least two other sports, hunting and prizefighting.[3] Hunting men were proud to boast that their sport was open to all. And indeed it was: it had to be, otherwise those excluded from the hunt might retaliate by excluding the hunt from their farms or by destroying foxes as vermin rather than preserving them for sport. Nevertheless, hunting was no social leveller: fraternization did not lead to equality. During the heat of the chase tenant farmer and lord of the manor may have ridden as equals, but afterwards conversation was along conventional, ritualized lines and was recognized as such by all parties: pleasantries might be exchanged, visiting cards never. The fixed location of the prizering necessitated a greater concentration of the crowd than in racing, but perhaps this too would have been more segregated had it not been for the illegal nature of the sport. Venues might have to be switched at a moment's notice, hence seating, an easy way to discriminate between spectators, could not always be arranged. Moreover, ringside seats, today's privileged positions, were not so advantageous when the magistrates and constabulary were liable to arrive: ease of escape took precedence over viewing facilities. And any inter-class contact was solely for the duration of the event. After the fight all but the most rakish of the Fancy's privileged members went their own way, not to renew their low acquaintanceships till the next fight, or, for the more dedicated, at the training gymnasium. In this respect racing was no different. Although a few jockeys, perhaps atypical representatives of their class in more than just size, entertained and were entertained by the aristocracy, generally any social intercourse between the classes was limited to the racecourse. Contact anyway tended to be economic rather than social: gypsies selling lucky heather, tipsters vending information, and bookmakers taking bets all met their social superiors, but both sides were well aware of their place in the social hierarchy.

Even if the opinions of contemporaries on the unifying role of horse racing are rejected, it is likely that they were correct in depicting the varied social backgrounds of racegoers. Unfortunately empirical data on the racecourse crowd is not readily available: there were no disasters comparable to the Ibrox football catastrophy, and anyway, if the crowd was segregated, the victims of a collapsing stand or exit crush would not be representative of the spectrum of attendance; arrests too were unlikely to be random samples. Nevertheless, it is possible to speculate that racing might cut across class barriers, for the sport is more than a mere contest between animals. It has many characteristics; some, as we shall see, have a specific class appeal, others, such as a regard for the aesthetic and athletic prowess of the thoroughbred horse, the excitement of gambling, and the catharsis of escaping from worldly cares, knowing no class boundaries.

No doubt many members of nineteenth-century leisured society enjoyed watching a tense struggle for supremacy between highly bred and highly strung horseflesh, but for them racing also served important social functions. It enabled them to reinforce their position in the social hierarchy; attendance at the local meeting reminded the community who was at its head.

Some meetings had more than local significance: in the south, Goodwood, Ascot and perhaps Epsom, and in the north, Doncaster and later York, were part of a wider social calendar. Indeed, Ascot was one of society's greatest gatherings: entry to the Royal Enclosure was the true certificate of social standing. Both York and Doncaster, however, lost their fashionable importance once a national railway network made it easier for northern ladies to participate in the metropolitan social scene.[4] The railways also cut down on the balls and dinner parties which traditionally had been part of upper-class racegoing;[5] getting home became easier so it was no longer necessary to take lodgings for a week and hence to seek such time-filling leisure activities. By the end of the nineteenth century genteel high jinks were no longer a regular accompaniment of racing.[6] The racecourse also had a political function, for it was here that prospective parliamentarians, especially those from the social élite, were paraded before their constituents.* For others the racetrack was a refuge from the political arena. Charles Greville for one, 'while on these racing expeditions never knew anything of politics'.[7] He was not alone: at the Oaks in 1833

> it was curious to see Stanley. Who would believe they beheld the orator and statesman, only second, if second, to Peel in the House of Commons, and on whom the destiny of the country perhaps depends? There he was, as if he had no thoughts but for the turf, full of horses, interest on the lottery, eager, blunt, noisy, good-humoured . . . at night equally devoted to the play, as if his future depended on it.[8]

* So much were politics and racing intertwined that political squibs in the form of racecards were a common form of political propaganda. One in the York Racing Museum deals with an election fought on the issue of slavery:

> May 20, 1807   York Spring Meeting
> To Start for the County Plate
> Earl F—W—M's chestnut colt INDEPENDENCE by ROCKINGHAM:
> rode by a Yorkshire clothier in white and gold.
> Lord H—W—D's black horse BARBADOES by SLAVERY:
> rode by a Leeds merchant in deep Mourning.
> Mr W—B—E's piebald gelding TRIM by CANT:
> rode by the owner in a cloak.
> 5 to 1 on the Chestnut Colt, on account of the rider.

In fact the result of the election was Wilberforce 11,808; Milton (Fitzwilliam) 11,117; and Lascelles (Harewood) 10,990.

There is no hard evidence that the middle class attended race meetings. Certainly the respectable middle class would not go racing. These members of Victorian society had a horror of the misuse of leisure time: indeed some felt that any leisure was morally dangerous. That racing appealed to the idle rich and the idle poor would be sufficient reason for them to condemn it, but, worse than this, racing broke their cardinal rule that recreation should be serious not sensual. That racing provided employment for myriads of decent folk – farmers, saddlers, blacksmiths, corn dealers, etc. – was by the way. Their image of racing was of indulgence, of rowdyism, of drunkenness, of gambling, and of vulgarity ranging from bawdy songs to public copulation: racing did not merely misuse leisure time, it abused it. A pamphlet by the Revd Power against the introduction of racing to Worthing is a fair illustration of respectable opposition to the turf: in it he argued that the establishment of a race meeting would 'bring into the town bad characters of various kinds' who would 'foster a spirit of gambling in the young men of Worthing' and subject them 'to the temptations of prostitutes of every degree'.[9] It is possible that Queen Victoria's alleged views on the sport of kings influenced respectable opinion. In the early 1840s many observers felt that she disliked racing and towards the end of her reign she made it quite clear that she frowned on her son's racing activities.[10] Yet she was appallingly ignorant of the sport: when Lord Rosebery won his second Derby, the classic race for three-year-olds, she asked him if it was with the same horse![11] This poses the unanswerable question as to what degree the respectable middle-class image of racing was similarly based on ignorance, on hearsay rather than on observation. How much did rumour and prejudiced gossip magnify 'the great rioting and drunkenness in the booths on the racecourse' complained of by the middle-class opposition to racing at Darlington?[12] Clearly some of the critics writing in the grave weeklies and monthlies did not fully comprehend racing and its nuances. Nevertheless, even devoted followers of the turf sometimes felt that their sport was shameful. The famous trainer William Day, objected to 'drinking [being] carried to excess followed by dancing in semi-darkness'.[13] He was castigating others; George Greville shamed himself:

All last week at Epsom, and now, thank God, these races
are over. I have had all the trouble and excitement and worry,
and have neither won nor lost; nothing but the hope of gain
would induce me to go through this demoralizing drudgery,
which I am conscious reduces me to the level of all that is
most disreputable and despicable, for my thoughts are
entirely absorbed by it. Jockeys, trainers, and blacklegs are
my constant companions, and it is like dram-drinking; having
once entered upon it, I cannot leave it off, though I am disgusted with the occupation all the time.[14]

My life is spent in the alternations of excitement from the
amusement and speculation of the turf and of remorse and
shame at the pursuit itself.[15]

Whatever their source of information, the more respectable
elements of society had no intention of risking their reputations
by frequenting race meetings. They believed racing was not
respectable and, partly because they did not attend, their image
of the sport became reality.

Some members of the middle class were racegoers: respectability was not all pervading, otherwise how do we explain the
middle-class embezzler and the middle-class clientele of some
prostitutes. Thus, no doubt there were those who went racing
to escape the strait-jacket of Victorian class convention; to
sample and enjoy the drink, the gambling, and the vulgarity,
with the added attraction that their respectable neighbours
would not know what they had been doing. Others, however,
wanted everyone to know that they had gone racing: and with
whom. For these, the chance of mixing with the aristocracy and
landed gentry outweighed any reservations over the disreputable nature of the sport: they went wearing their social blinkers,
not seeing the baser turf follower, but focusing on those
attenders with whom they wished to be identified.

The bulk of the crowd came from the lower ranks of society.
Of course the respectable working man did not attend: he
shared his middle-class counterpart's distaste for uninhibited
leisure. But other working men did come. Traditionally racing
had been associated with local holidays and for many this continued well into the nineteenth century. The Manchester

Whitsuntide meeting, for example, always coincided with a general holiday in the Lancashire manufacturing districts.[16] But the epitome of the holiday race meeting was Epsom on Derby Day: many local workers, particularly those in agriculture, had this holiday stipulated in their hiring agreements, but others came from all over England.[17] Derby Day was a national carnival-cum-public-saturnalia, a holiday spectacle, an opportunity for play and display, a licence for behaviour that would not be tolerated elsewhere. Indeed, most attenders came for the raciness not for the racing: thousands flocked 'to the Downs, in the hope or on the pretence of seeing a race which not one man in fifty ever really sees, nor one in twenty cares about seeing'.[18] In the north, things were different. Racing folklore makes much of the northerner's love of horses and knowledge of racing matters. Not for them the frivolities of Epsom, the false noses, paper decorations, and discordant noises: no, in the north they appreciated racing for its own sake.[19] In strict contrast to the Derby there were 'relatively few men who went professedly to see the Leger without really desiring to see it', and most spectators at the Doncaster classic knew 'something, probably not a little, of the animals engaged in it'.[20] So much did Yorkshiremen love horses that it is alleged there was a noticeable increase in the Tyke population following the abolition of the death penalty for horse stealing! Nevertheless, northerners still enjoyed the ancillary activities of the racecourse. No doubt the words of 'Blaydon Races' were rooted in fact:

> Thor was spice stalls an' munky shows,
> an' oad wives selling ciders
> An' a chep wi' a Ha'penny roondeboot shoutin'
> 'Noo me lads for riders.' *

For most of the century it remained true that 'racing acted like a loadstone on the masses and furnished the never-failing nucleus of an English holiday'.[21] Holidays boosted attendances but there was also a number of regular working-class racegoers,

---

* Incidentally Blaydon Races was not a traditional northern air, but a Victorian pantomime song containing a blatant commercial for Geordie Ridley's show at the Mechanic's Hall. P. A. White, *Portrait of County Durham*, 1967, p. 77.

particularly around London where the number of courses gave them ample opportunity to attend, especially on Saturday afternoons.[22]

In the later nineteenth century race crowds of 10,000 to 15,000 were not uncommon; double this could be expected at leading fixtures; and perhaps 70,000 to 80,000 at a major Bank Holiday event.[23] Such numbers put pressure on facilities and led to exorbitant prices being asked for travel, accommodation, and sustenance. Tickets for railway specials frequently cost more than the normal fare; cab rates and hotel charges often more than doubled during race weeks; and the price of food and drink rose 'to an awful height'.[24]

Racegoers were prey to more than commercial vultures; the criminal fraternity also found easy pickings at the racetrack. An observer at Epsom in 1826 noted that 'the vicious and unprincipled form a tolerable proportion; nor is it indeed surprising where 60,000 persons are assembled to witness a horse race, that these should obtrude themselves either with the view of propagating vices or robbing the bystanders'.[25] Criminals always saw their local meetings as a potential source of income, but there was also a regular crowd of the underworld who travelled the racing circuits: in September 1829 it was reported that 'more than two hundred regular thieves had left Doncaster races' for Carlisle – 'many of them were accompanied by girls of ill-fame, whose task is to lure countrymen into the situation where they may be robbed with facility'.[26] And, of course, the coming of the railway made it much easier for them to be continually attending race meetings.[27] It was these, the thieves, the thimblemen, the coiners, the thugs, and the prostitutes, who, perhaps more than anyone else, made a career out of horse racing.

Thieving on the racecourse took many forms, ranging from pocket picking to robbery with violence. Racing meant crowds, and crowds meant pickpockets; if the spectators did not gather in sufficient numbers, decoys would be employed to attract them.[28] Other robbery was more open: the beating-up of successful bookmakers or backers; crying 'welsher' and attacking innocent punters; and welshing itself, especially on the outer fringes of the courses where escape was easy.[29] Cardsharps of all kinds, and thimblemen, with their tin cups, dried peas, and horny thumbnails, found racecourses, particularly rural ones, ideal for their trade: here they could take advantage of country fellows who probably never went to more than their local meeting from one year to the next. With the coming of the railway, the 'find the lady' brigade to some extent switched their activities from the racecourse to the race train where they could fleece their victims without fear of interruption, for corridor trains were not introduced till the late nineteenth century.[30] The race meeting, especially at holiday times, was also the perfect place to pass dud coins: the working man, freed from his machine and flushed with alcohol and excitement, was unlikely to check his change carefully; nor were the bookmakers, hurrying to take as many bets as possible, going to be all that vigilant.[31] Prostitution, too, was an inevitable concomitant of racing: the stimulation of drink, successful gambling, and the general holiday atmosphere produced a ready clientele. Like other underworld racegoers, many prostitutes travelled the racing circuits: in Scotland the Musselburgh races drew a large influx of prostitutes from Glasgow and other large towns; and those from Edinburgh went west to the Ayr meetings.[32]

Derby Day was an excuse for excess: 'every vice that could be imagined had full scope at the Derby'.[33] Nevertheless, one nineteenth-century commentator proudly proclaimed that 'a quarter of a million, including all the ruffianism that London and every racecourse in the Kingdom can produce, should assemble and disperse in so orderly a manner, with so little police restraint, is not the least curious part of the day . . . in any other European country, an army of infantry, cavalry and artillery would be called out to keep the peace'.[34] Perhaps he was right in this instance, but certainly elsewhere race meetings were frequently scenes of violence. Not all the trouble stemmed from the criminal element, for the British working classes were notoriously rowdy and aggressive. Riots occurred at many sporting events: prizefights often saw as much violence outside the ring as inside; and invasions of the soccer field were not uncommon.[35] Hangings witnessed some frightful behaviour by the crowd: the scandal of the street scenes was one reason for the abolition of public executions.*[36] Wakes, too, could be rough affairs with 'the Lancashire lads and lasses making holiday at them in the wildest possible fashions. The clog was their weapon and they considered there was nothing unmanly in kicking and biting to death.'[37] Violence seemed to be an inevitable accompaniment of any event attended by the less respectable of working men. At the racetrack, however, the situation was aggravated by the ready availability of sex, alcohol, gambling, and by the activities of the criminal fraternity. Welshing was a major cause of trouble. Gambling debts were not enforceable at law but lower-class punters had their own sanctions, usually violent ones: at Catterick welshers were tarred and feathered, at Northallerton they were horsewhipped, and at Stockton, Durham, and Wetherby they were thrown in the river.[38] The mob was not disposed to show mercy. Brutal treatment was the rule rather than the exception; whenever the cry of welsher was heard, it was 'the precursor to a scene of cruel violence and positive outrage'.[39] A welshing bookmaker caught by his pursuers was in desperate peril even on a well-policed course, for anyone bold enough to intervene was equally likely to face the fury of the mob.[40] Violence could also erupt if backers felt that they had not had a fair run for their money.† At Doncaster, for example, when *Blink Bonny* won the Park Hill Stakes in a time faster than the winner of the recent St Leger, a race in which she had finished a moderate fourth, her owner and trainer had to be rescued by pugilists.[41] It was also at Doncaster that the trainer John Scott had to be similarly rescued after *Acrobat* won the 1854 Doncaster Stakes following a poor St Leger performance.[42] Even worse was the situation when the offending parties were foreigners, particularly French: when *Fille l'Air*, nowhere in the Two Thousand Guineas despite being favourite, won the Oaks, the betting crowd, influenced by patriotic and other spirit, determined that the jockey would not

---

* It is interesting to note one commentator's view that 'we have hardly a real holiday in England. Executions and races make the nearest approach to one.' 'Holiday Times', *Household Words*, 1853, p. 329.

† This introduces the issue of perception and whether spectators 'see' what they want to see. There is an interesting study of an American football match as 'seen' by rival fans in A. H. Hastorf and H. Cantril, 'They Saw a Game: A Case Study', *Journal of Abnormal and Social Psychology*, 1954, pp. 129–34.

weigh in and he had to be protected by mounted police with drawn sabres.[43]

Before the enclosed course, disorder at a race meeting was taken for granted. At most meetings the executive would employ a few pugilists to protect the horses and other racing property, and a gateman or two to keep undesirables out of the stands. At the society events, police would also be in attendance to control the rough element with a strong hand. But, generally, as long as the masses, in their anger or exuberance, damaged only themselves and did not offend anyone who mattered, those in charge were content.*[44] A blind eye was often turned at certain overt criminal activities – indeed more than one clerk of the course charged thimblemen and cardsharps an extra admittance fee[45] – providing that the mark was not overstepped, for even the most tolerant of patrons and executives drew the line somewhere. At Doncaster in 1829 the local nobility and townsmen of influence made it clear that they intended to reduce the volume of gaming associated with the local races, as the numbers of itinerant and impoverished thimblemen was proving a menace to all and sundry, not merely the racegoers. The local yeomanry was put under arms and many special constables were enrolled. But forewarned was fore-armed: hundreds of ruffians carrying bludgeons, often the stout legs of their thimble tables, prepared to resist but, in a pitched and brutal battle, they were routed and their ringleaders arrested.[46]

Nevertheless, such incidents were rare: generally, criminal activity and crowd disorder were accepted features of racing. Perhaps they had to be. To keep the vultures of the turf away from their pickings would have required a force of policemen and most executives could not afford this. Others saw no need to, for at many meetings there was little property that could be damaged. Beer and gaming tents contributed to the crowd problem – no doubt alcohol and gambling losses provoked many a fracas – but the race fund needed the rents from the booths;

---

* It has been argued that soccer crowd hooliganism was never seen as a social problem till after the Second World War when social groups other than the working class began to patronize the game, and hence became aware of, and possibly affected by the violence. I. Taylor, ' "Football Mad": A Speculative Sociology of Football Hooliganism', in E. Dunning, *The Sociology of Sport*, 1971, pp. 352–77.

and at some meetings, particularly the London suburban ones in the 1860s, the whole object of the enterprise was to sell beer and to take bets. Ruffianism and hooliganism were thus inevitable. No wonder J. H. Peart, the right-hand man of the famous trainer, John Scott, was so impressed with racing at Chantilly where 'the arrangements on the racecourse are far beyond what they have in England. The roughs are kept in their proper place, and there was no hustle or confusion, and no fear of being robbed of your wallet.'[47]

As with many other aspects of racing, crowd behaviour changed for the better with the coming of the gate-money meeting: when racegoers paid for their pleasure, they were less tolerant of abuse. Segregation was one way of reducing trouble: it was done by differential pricing,* by vetting membership of the racing clubs, and by absolute exclusion. Traditionally segregation had been a matter of keeping the riff-raff out of the stands and other exclusive areas: the epitome was Goodwood Park 'where the privileged enclosure round the grandstand excluded all that the most fastidious would desire to exclude' and racing could be seen 'divested of all its coarse and disgusting accessories, the degraded mob, the blasphemous, greedy, obscene Bohemianism that revels on Epsom Downs and ordinary racecourses'.[48] Now, at many meetings, the lower elements of the racing world were not even to be allowed on the course; gatemen were given strict instructions to refuse entry to all undesirables. Obviously the system was not foolproof, especially with gate staff of the calibre who allowed free admittance to six self-styled judges but kept out a seventh on the grounds that there were only six races. Over time, however, their general standard improved, especially when, like jockeys, trainers, and officials, they became subject to Jockey Club licence.[49] In addition, gambling† and drinking became more stringently

* At York, for example, in the 1890s, it cost 10s. 0d. (5s. 0d. for ladies) to enter the grandstand, 5s. 0d. for the paddock, and 2s. 6d. for the second class enclosure. The policy became firmly entrenched: the Ilchester Committee in the 1940s believed that 'to make admission to the Grand Stand too cheap would be to flood it with the more noisy and undesirable elements who now confine themselves to the cheaper stands'. *Report of the Racing Re-organisation Committee*, 1943, para. 44.

† Racecourse executives began to respect and enforce the gaming laws. The Vagrancy Act Amendment Act of 1873 made it illegal to use betting machines

controlled. Booth rents were less important now that spectators were paying at the gate; and the course executives were prepared to restrict the facilities offered, both in volume and character. It was not merely beer and betting that was controlled. Itinerant entertainers, tipsters, and traders found themselves less welcome than before: indeed, the whole holiday atmosphere of racing was being dampened down. Yet the objective of the enclosed course was to attract spectators, many of whom came in expectation of a carnival. The explanation of this apparent paradox lies in the very fact that the new courses were enclosed: there was too much property at risk if the crowd got out of hand, so the executives chose to emphasize racing and cut down the ancillary activities. However, in order to encourage the racegoing public to accept the change,* racing itself was changed: spectators were offered the types of races they preferred to see; sprints and handicaps replaced weight-for-age, staying events.† At the same time as the enclosed course executives were reducing one set of possible stimuli to trouble, the Jockey Club's attack on corruption was undermining another. With less overt malpractice to anger spectators, the crowd's propensity to riot was reduced. Together the pinchers of commercialization and Jockey Club legislation took a firm grip on the crowd problem: the incentives to violence were lessened and by the end of the nineteenth century it was claimed that on some courses 'ruffianism [was] practically unknown'.[50]

Serious disorder reappeared after the First World War. The problem this time was not the crowd but racetrack gangs. Racing's post-war boom brought money to the courses and, in turn, the money attracted violent criminals. Thugs moved in to

(hence roulette and E/O tables could not be used) and earlier legislation of 1853 had made it unlawful to monopolize a place for betting purposes (this could be interpreted as outlawing gaming booths).

* How well their successors believed they had succeeded is illustrated in the Benson Committee's Report on *The Racing Industry*, 1968, para. 203: '. . . the Racecourse Association said that, in the main, the public attends for the purpose of seeing racing and betting. Bands, side shows, and other attractions tend to irritate the ardent racegoer, as he is in the main fully occupied in the intervals between races. However, in the cheaper enclosures at certain courses, and particularly wherever a holiday atmosphere prevails, other attractions may be acceptable, although it is doubtful whether they would bring out increased attendance by the paying public.'

† See above, p. 43.

operate protection rackets; to rob bookmakers, often with extreme violence; and to settle their differences using razors, knives, and even firearms. Territorial clashes between gangs put racing on to the front pages.[51] Clearly the image of the sport was again becoming tarnished.

Many racecourse executives seemed unable to cope with the problem. Bookmakers took it upon themselves to organize their own defence with the foundation of the Bookmakers Protection Association in 1921.[52] The Jockey Club was already considering action of its own, but the decision of the B.P.A. to employ thugs as bodyguards added impetus to the deliberations. It was decided to appoint officials whose duties would be to protect the public and supervise security arrangements, matters previously left to the discretion of individual racecourse managers. The new policing force began operations in 1925 and was swiftly effective: by 1926 the Jockey Club claimed that it had 'already attained in many directions the objectives for which it was formed'.[53] There was no hesitation in bringing in the police to deal with trouble-makers. But there was less trouble, for known undesirables were either excluded or expelled; and more were known by these officials who attended meetings throughout Britain than by infrequently employed, local gatemen. On the unprotected portions of the courses, such as the Downs at Epsom, unpleasant experiences were not unknown; and even in the enclosures, there were still occasional outbursts of violence, most notoriously at Lewes in 1936, but in general, if spectators were willing to pay for their racing, then they could expect it to be troublefree.[54] In the 1930s no-one could echo the nineteenth-century sentiments of a Scottish police inspector who 'cursed these race meetings. They were nothing else than carnivals of drunkenness, crime and misery. They collect from all the lowest and most degraded centres of population the worst of their elements. Debauchery and criminal pollution always follow horseracing.'[55]

Participation:
The Men of Racing ⌐

The commonest jockey-boy in this company of
mannikins can usually earn more than the
average scholar or professional man, and the whole
set receive a good deal more of adulation than
has been bestowed on any soldier, sailor, explorer,
or scientific man of our generation.

J. Runciman, *Contemporary Review* (1889)

. . . it is not so much the bad horses that trouble you
but the ingratitude of some of your employers,
who made a great fuss of you during your success
but quit you like rats from a sinking ship when
you are out of luck.

J. Porter (Trainer)

9

Jockeys[*]

Only weeks before he successfully piloted the Duke of Westminster's *Bend Or* to victory in the 1880 Derby, Fred Archer
almost lost his life when a lesser animal, *Muley Edris*, turned
savage out on the gallops at Newmarket. Archer had dis-
mounted to adjust a marker when the horse seized him, threw
him on the ground, and knelt on him. Had not the creature
slipped, frightened itself, and galloped off, turf history would
surely have traced a different course. As it was, Archer's arm
was injured so severely that it was feared he would miss his
Derby mount. Such was the importance of this ride to Archer
that he paid for the services of the eminent physician, Sir James
Paget. He could well afford the learned doctor's fee, for during
their conversation Archer revealed, to the amazement of Sir
James, that their incomes were about the same: the value placed
by the market on their relative skills was such that both earned
around £8,000 per annum, worth somewhere between £50,000
and £60,000 at 1970 prices.[1]

Clearly Archer was an outstanding artist, an individual at the
top of his chosen profession. He committed suicide before he
reached thirty, but in his short career he was champion jockey
for thirteen consecutive seasons, riding 2,748 winners, including
those of five Derbys, four Oaks, six St Legers, four Two
Thousand Guineas, and two One Thousand Guineas. Nevertheless, he was not alone among jockeys in making money.
Although for most of the nineteenth century the basic riding fee
was only five guineas for a win and three guineas otherwise,[†]
presents and retainers made the rewards, to the more successful
of these diminutive men, as large as they were small. Such

[*] All generalizations made below are based on a study of 124 jockeys, riding
between 1830 and 1930, for whom more than minimal information can be traced.
Most of these jockeys were to a degree successful. It is unfortunate that little
evidence exists concerning those that never became top class, for they were the
great majority.

[†] Extra was paid for the classics. At least five guineas could be expected for a
mount in one of these status events and by the 1860s, a custom had arisen of charging
twenty-five pounds. (The Druid, *Post and Paddock*, 1895, p. 38; H. Rous, *On The
Laws and Practice of Horse Racing*, 1866, p. 29.)

additional income to top-rank jockeys in the late nineteenth century could 'produce an annual total before which 2,000 guineas in bare riding fees shrinks into insignificance'.[2] Even an ordinary jockey, if these extraordinary characters can ever be so termed, could earn at least £1,000 a year.[3] At this time typical earnings of other skilled workers ranged from thirty-five shillings a week to a high of about a pound a day, the latter being obtained, for example, by iron puddlers sweating their way through a gruelling twelve-hour shift.[4]

No doubt, like transfer fees in present-day soccer, the value of jockeys' presents became exaggerated by both rumour and the media; nevertheless, a contrast can be drawn between those of the early nineteenth century and those of the later, highly commercialized, racing world. If successful, the early nineteenth-century riding groom, nothing more than a liveried servant, could have expected a side of bacon, a cheese, or perhaps a sack of potatoes, scarcely gifts to be appreciated by the weight-watching professional jockey.[5] Such a contracted jockey did better, especially if he won a classic race, for victory in one of these status events was always likely to bring a handsome present.[6] The £1,500 that *Birmingham*'s rider received for his success in the 1830 St Leger was extreme, but certainly John Day could consider himself unfortunate to get only twenty pounds from the Duke of Grafton for winning both the Guineas in 1826.[7] By the 1850s, it was customary for a classic-winning owner to reward his jockey with between £300 and £500; and when Wells won the 1868 Derby on *Blue Gown*, Sir Joseph Hawley presented him with the whole stake, somewhere in the region of £6,000, a gift calculated to raise the blood pressure of Admiral Rous who was never really happy that upstart jockeys had replaced subservient riding grooms.[8] It is possible to trace instances of valuable presents throughout the nineteenth century, but generally in the first two-thirds of the century they were either for classic victories or isolated examples of an individual's generosity or eccentricity. After that, however, large presents became the norm for any big race; a jockey winning any major event on the Newmarket card could anticipate a gift of up to £500.[9] The growing tendency to disburse largesse to successful jockeys was most certainly associated with the growing commercialization of racing and the greater stress laid on winning, but perhaps there was also an element of conspicuous consumption as *nouveau-riche* owners sought to impress society with their wealth. Jockeys could also anticipate presents from successful and appreciative gamblers.[10] One critic claimed that it was not uncommon for a jockey in the early 1870s to receive ten or twelve cheques a year, each for £100 or so from men who followed his mounts.[11] A less biased and more knowledgeable commentator reckoned jockeys could double their riding fees by such contributions.[12]

Retainers rose even more strikingly than presents in the later decades of the nineteenth century. Frank Butler, Sam Rogers and Jem Robinson, all leading jockeys in the 1830s and 1840s, respectively received £100 from Lord Derby, £50 from Colonel Lowther, and £25 from Mr Ross.[13] Contrast these with George Fordham's perennial £1,000 from Mr Stirling Crawfurd, Archer's £3,600 in 1881, Tod Sloan's £5,000 from Lord William Beresford in 1899, and £15,000 given to Tom Cannon for a three-year retainer in the 1880s.[14] Many of the top jockeys later in the century obtained substantial retainers for third or even fourth call on their services. Unlike presents which were paid after success, retainers were an attempt, sometimes a costly one, to ensure that success. The rising cost of retainers reflected the intensifying struggle to secure the services of top-rank jockeys; and, of course, to keep them off someone else's horses.

Even before racing came under the influence of the enclosed course, one or two jockeys made £5,000 in a season; Nat Flatman, for one, had done it as early as 1848.[15] However, in the last two decades of the nineteenth century the number of jockeys earning such money rose to at least ten.* Racing had become a highly commercialized activity; increasing prize money and rising stud fees had put an even greater premium on winning. Other things being equal, and often when they were not, it was the skill of the jockey that determined the result of the race. There was thus a high and increasing demand for the services of top-class jockeys, and since the supply of such talent

---

* Calculated on the assumptions of a retainer of around £1,000 and being awarded 5 per cent of the prize money won.

was extremely limited, the normal working of economic laws ensured high rewards to the gifted. This was why in 1910 Danny Maher obtained £8,000 in retainers from three owners, Lord Rosebery, Fairie Cox and Leopold de Rothschild and why a champion jockey in an inter-war season could make around £15,000.[16]

Not everyone was happy with a free market mechanism which produced a situation apparently incompatible with their vision of the social order. One critic voiced the outrage felt by others about this 'school of skinny dwarfs whose leaders are paid better than the greatest statesmen in Europe' and their disgust that 'the commonest jockey-boy in this company of mannikins can usually earn more than the average scholar or professional man'. These 'uneducated and promoted stable lads' had committed the cardinal sin of earning more than their betters thought was right for the working class.[17] Even within racing circles there was disquiet, again based on social distinctions. William Day opposed lavish gifts, not only because they tempted jockeys into improvidence, but because they also encouraged them to become impudent towards owners who could not or would not meet their demands.[18] However, Day was a trainer and hence not unprejudiced in his observations, for the rising economic position of jockeys undermined his authority and relationships with owners. Status and class considerations also lay behind Lord Suffolk's call for the Jockey Club to take action over 'the unwholesome system of lavishing extraordinary rewards in return for very slight services. It is impossible that jockeys can be kept in their proper position when successful members of the riding fraternity are enabled to realize fortunes of £100,000 and more, within a dozen years of their first appearance in the saddle.'[19]

Social rewards were as much part of a jockey's remuneration as the cheques he received. At one level jockeys became cult heroes: their pictures outsold those of most other personalities; their names were used in music hall jokes; and their movements were chronicled like those of royalty. The public would block a street simply to see Archer leave a hotel and take a cab; and when he married in January 1883, special trains were run to bring the cheering crowds to Newmarket and Cambridge.[20]

Champions from their own ranks were always to be fêted; jockeys had merely replaced criminals and prizefighters as objects of public idolatry. At another level, leading jockeys were allowed to mix with the best of society: they lunched with lords and ladies; noble captains accompanied them on their holidays abroad; and the favours of many high-born women were theirs for the taking. Both the adulation of the crowd and the applause of the elite were phenomena which intensified during the later nineteenth century. The development of the sporting press did much to stimulate jockey worship among the masses by quoting their opinions, reporting their activities, and creating identities for them on and off the racecourse. Riding grooms had attained proficiency but neither fame nor social prestige: not only were these jockeys rarely mentioned in race reports till the 1820s, * they were also completely subservient to their masters. In the early nineteenth century most owners also regarded professional jockeys as servants, albeit well-paid ones, wearing their employer's livery: indeed, the first Duke of Cleveland shocked his contemporaries by having the Chifney brothers stay with him at Raby Castle, and General Dyott, commenting on the 1831 Lichfield races, opined that 'Lord Wilton did not add much to the noble ranks by exhibiting himself on two occasions as a jockey in two races with the commonest members of the stable'.[21] Even in the 1840s and 1850s many owners still shared the opinion of Admiral Rous who would never have dreamed of letting a jockey share his table.[22] In the 1860s the Admiral probably had nightmares as jockeys were more frequently seen in the dining and drawing rooms of their patrons.[23] Professional sportsmen had been employed by the wealthy for many years prior to this: any sporting activity which was competitive found the upper classes sponsoring men of lower rank who possessed skills they could admire but never emulate. The rich were often willing to pay well for this vicarious athleticism; prizefighters especially obtained high economic rewards. But jockeys, or at least the leading ones, seem to be the first group, as opposed to select individuals, who gained entrée to high society. Why this developed when it did is not easy to say. Possibly it was a

---

* Even the riders of classic winners were not noted in the *Racing Calendar* till 1823.

fashion begun by a few social pacemakers and continued because the company of jockeys proved pleasurable. No doubt some were fascinated by associating with men thought not quite respectable.* Others had a genuine affection for their lower-class companions; this was probably true of Lord Hastings's friendship with Archer and Lord and Lady Rosebery's vigil at Harry Constable's death bed.[24] Yet, surely the increasing commercialization of racing played a role: on the one hand there were owners anxious to secure a star rider for their horses and, on the other, the high-born hangers-on, attracted by the free spending of the increasingly well-paid jockeys.

Relations between owners and jockeys were not merely a question of economic transaction or social intercourse; they also involved the question of power and here the jockey became the dominant partner. A minute or two's work from a jockey could make or mar months of work on the part of owner or trainer. In the early decades of the nineteenth century, the jockey rode very much to orders; by the 1860s when jockeys required 'so much money and humouring' many did not;[25] and by 1900 one authority claimed that jockeys were the masters of most of their employers.[26] Supply and demand had placed power in the hands of the jockeys; they now held the reins in more senses than one. Unhappily in too many instances the jockey became 'the spoiled child of the turf, and spoiled children are the same in every walk of life'.[27] Races lost through carelessness, false ideas of social standing, and impudence to their employers, were all tolerated simply because 'the supply of men between 7 stone and 8 stone possessed of the needful skill and experience [was] extremely limited, and people think it diplomatic in consequence to put up with this, that or the other'.[28] Not all owners were tolerant. In 1885 rumours reached the Duke of Portland that Archer might be contemplating setting up a racing establishment with Abington Baird, the *enfant terrible* of the racing world. The Duke sent for Archer and told him bluntly that no jockey of his was to associate with this brash son of a Scottish ironmaster who

---

* Show business personalities exude a similar fascination. In the nineteenth century they were certainly thought not respectable and even today their unusual working hours, by closing many normal avenues of recreation, encourage them to develop deviant lifestyles.

was doing his best to outride and cuckold British racing society. Archer was not to be browbeaten: no-one was going to tell him how to run his life. He sent back his cap and jacket along with the balance of his retainer. Significantly, when the Duke tried to persuade Lord Hastings, his partner in Archer's retainer, to follow his line, Hastings refused, possibly because he now had first claim on Archer's services.[29] As with economic rewards, and for the same reason, this power relationship continued into the twentieth century. However, when one racing writer in the 1920s complained of it being 'an age of grovelling, almost toadying, sycophantic jockey laudation and admiration', he was not referring to the public at large.[30] Racegoers might still cheer the leading jockeys, but for the general public new idols had arisen: other sports had given talented members of the working class the opportunity to seize fame, and the silver screen, though still silent, was beginning to create its own heroes.

The good jockey could taste the fruits of success early in life. Young men could burst almost overnight from poverty and obscurity into wealth and popularity. John Wells was a household name before he was out of his teens; Luke Snowden died of typhus aged only twenty-two but already he had two St Legers and an Oaks under his silken belt; Martin, the tiny boy who won the Cesarewitch on *Don Juan*, was rewarded with £1,000; and in the early twentieth century Frank Wootton retired, still a minor, having amassed £30,000.[31] Such enticing examples tempted many boys into becoming lads.

Almost without exception the recruits for the racing stables came from the working class, and, with slightly more exceptions, had a minimum of formal education, though of course, the institution of compulsory schooling in the 1870s raised the general standard of jockeys' education.[32] The lack of middle-class participation may probably be explained by the fact that, although the rewards to some jockeys could be high, they were much less certain than in conventional middle-class occupations. Perhaps this was also why the sample contained no sons of craftsmen. And there is, of course, the question of the respectability of the profession. The great majority of those aspiring jockeys whose backgrounds can be traced, alas only a fraction of the total, came from a rural environment. No doubt geography influenced the catchment area: inevitably racing stables were located in the countryside and poor families in the vicinity were glad to embrace the opportunity of putting their children to work there, where they would be better fed and have a chance of rising in the world.* Others came from families already associated with racing. This was to be expected. Jockeys had to be small, and size is to some extent determined by heredity. Furthermore the family background itself would, in many cases, incline children to favour racing as a career. It must be emphasized that these children would be making their decision at an age when they would be very much influenced by their parents. If father was a success no doubt his reputation would open closed stable doors; if he had not made the grade there could well be pressure to succeed where he had failed. In some cases the question of a life in racing might produce family strife, but the extent of inter-marriage within the racing fraternity would keep this to a minimum. And of course not all families need favour their sons entering racing for a significant number to do so. Some budding jockeys did come from urban areas: in the nineteenth century John Osborne, the great Middleham trainer and former jockey, frequently recruited from the Manchester district—Tom Chalenor was one of his discoveries – and in the twentieth century Stanley Wootton, best remembered for his training of apprentices rather than of horses, had a penchant for giving opportunities to working-class cockneys.[33] But, like other trainers, Wootton and Osborne often found that the small stature of many of these boys had owed more to nurture than to nature: a few months of fresh air and good food soon ruined their chances of becoming jockeys. Not all failed to make the grade; among the more successful urban recruits were Tommy Weston, Charlie Smirke, and the charming, if wayward, Steve Donaghue.

Apprentices entered the stables at an early age not just because they were young men in a hurry; trainers too preferred to get them young as it provided them with a steady

---

* This was as true of the 1820s as of the 1920s. C. J. Apperley, 'The Turf,' *Quarterly Review*, vol. 49, July 1833, p. 405; J. Fairfax-Blakeborough, *The Analysis of the Turf*, 1927, p. 102.

stream of lightweight jockeys. In the early and even mid-nineteenth century mere children were apprenticed specifically for this purpose. The official weight of little Kitchener when he won the Chester Cup in 1844 was a feather (nominally four stones), but his actual body weight has been alleged as 2 st. 12 lb., or even less, though most likely it was 3 st. 4 lb.[34] Low weights implied less strength but this would not be vital if the course was straight, especially in the days before the monkey-on-a-stick-style, though if a horse proved troublesome there was little his diminutive rider could do; in the Goodwood Stakes of 1856 *Chevy Chase* could not be controlled by his jockey, a little boy named Hearden, and he brought down seven other horses and put two jockeys in hospital for several weeks.[35] In 1860 Lord Redesdale proposed that Parliament legislate a minimum weight of seven stones for all horse races: his prime motive was to preserve the quality of the British thoroughbred, but, indirectly, of course, it would hit at this exploitation of child riders.[36] Although children could still have been employed, the horse would have carried too much dead weight for the liking of most trainers; in any case, if a skilled jockey could make the weight he was to be preferred. In the end Redesdale withdrew his Bill after the Jockey Club compromised and themselves set a minimum of 5 st. 7 lb., later raised to six stones. *
The crushing blow, however, was delivered by the higher authority with the Education Acts of the 1870s. These effectively ended the use of infants: very young children were unlikely to be employed in racing stables if they had to attend school regularly as they would 'inevitably be marked down in their goings to and fro, and persecuted for information by all the touts of the neighbourhood'.[37] In 1903 Mr Brassey, a leading owner, asked the Jockey Club to devise a system in which formal education and stable instruction could be harnessed together. Nothing practical emerged.[38]

Young apprentices possibly also made for easier discipline. The moral welfare of his lads was left to the trainer, and possibly his wife. He had reason to do something, for an indolent or corrupt boy could ruin a stable's fortunes. Generally he relied on

* In the 1920s it was raised to seven stones; by this time, however, the Jockey Club had instituted the apprentice allowance and also special apprentice races.

a combination of physical violence and Christian virtue. Daily prayers with Church and bible readings on a Sunday were a feature of most stables; but woe betide any apprentice who fell asleep while Old John Day was preaching that 'God is Love'.[39] John Smith, trainer for the Marquis of Queensberry and later the Duke of Cleveland, was very severe on his lads, though with good intent: 'thou'lt come to me in ten years' time, and thank me on thy knees for saving thee from the gallows' was his constant claim to the chastised youths.[40] Many nineteenth-century apprentices learned their trade at the end of the trainer's stick, but by the close of the century corporal punishment was much less in evidence.[41] At Newmarket the trainers were given some assistance in their task as moral guardians by the opening of an institute in the early 1890s for the use of the 1,500 or so men and boys employed in the local racing studs and stables.[42] Although the institute kept many of them from the contaminating influence of alcohol and street corner society, the 'amelioration of a stable boy's moral condition [was] a slow process due to a lack of desire to be ameliorated'.[43] Racing was a corrupt sport and boys whose lives revolved around the stables and the course were hard put not to become tainted by what went on; if their reference groups were all associated with the turf and its immorality, almost inevitably they came to accept the values and attitudes pertaining to the sport.

Life in the stables was not hard; the hours were long but the work was scarcely arduous.[44] Indeed most industrial apprenticeships were probably far tougher. Those fortunate enough to be apprenticed to John Porter at Kingsclere enjoyed reasonable living conditions. Unlike some stables where the boys had to wash in a bucket, Kingsclere had bathrooms and lavatories. Each boy there had his own bed; elsewhere two or even three to a bed was not unknown, though sleeping with a horse grew much rarer as the century progressed. The first few weeks in the stable were the worst. The new apprentice, probably away from home for the first time, had to perform the most demeaning tasks in the stables. This he might accept for boys everywhere were expected to do the dirty, menial jobs. What would be galling to this aspiring champion jockey was that initially he would not be allowed to ride, only watch and work. Soon, however, his chance would come; he would be given a leg up on a quiet horse under the eye and instruction of the head lad, or even the trainer. After that it was up to the apprentice to show his worth. If a boy did not like the life there was little he could do about it, at least not after he was indentured. In the first half of the nineteenth century, the apprentice was for most practical purposes his master's property; indeed little Kitchener was virtually sold as a chattel along with his employer's horses and when Bell, the boy wonder, ran away, his master got him back by offering a £10 reward, more in fact than he paid in a year to the boy.[45] Not all trainers of the time treated their apprentices so inhumanly, but none would take on a runaway or redundant boy till his late master had been consulted:[46] stable discipline simply could not tolerate boys changing their employers at whim. Eventually the Jockey Club formalized this practice and barred from Newmarket any trainer who took on a boy who had run away from another stable.[47] Although this policy was later relaxed, trainers continued to exercise restraint in adopting strays; Charlie Elliot, for example, was very fortunate that his enthusiasm for racing had not been dampened by his harsh first master, for it was this that persuaded Jack Jarvis to give him a trial and then have his indentures transferred.[48]

Apprentices made very little money. Archer's indentures with Matthew Dawson gave him nine guineas per annum in his first year, rising to thirteen guineas in his fourth and fifth years.[49] By the 1920s, apprentice finances had taken a turn for the better: Reginald Scott, in his third year with Fred Darling, was on a shilling a day;[50] nevertheless, this was still a striking contrast to the value of the bloodstock he helped care for. Moreover, if an apprentice showed promise as a jockey the fees for any rides he obtained could be pocketed by his master. All indentures carried a clause allowing trainers to do this, supposedly as a reward for teaching the boy to ride; John Porter took only half, others appropriated the whole lot.*[51] Trainers can be found in both the nineteenth and twentieth centuries whose views on apprenticeship were dominated by financial considerations: Tom Jennings practically established a racing school so as to make

---

* By the 1950s taking only half was standard practice. E. Rickman, *Come Racing With Me*, 1951, p. 112.

money in this way and Major Sneyd, a first-rate if hard teacher (from whose Sparsholt stables graduated Doug and Eph Smith, and Joe Mercer) regarded a successful apprentice as a good means of supplementing his income.[52] Happily, some owners would put something in the bank for a winning apprentice;[53] enough perhaps to whet the boy's appetite for what the future might hold.

But most apprentices would never make the grade. Table 8 shows this for the twentieth century; the data does not exist for the nineteenth.* What happened to those who were unsuccessful? Most curbed their disappointment and remained in the stables simply because they loved racing and racehorses: many so-called lads had their grandchildren working alongside them.

TABLE 8. SUCCESS RATES AMONG APPRENTICES

	Number of apprentices	Apprentices who became jockeys		Jockeys for more than one season		Jockeys for more than three seasons	
		No.	%	No.	%	No.	%
1900	187	75	40	48	26	23	12
1910	230	92	40	59	26	24	10
1920	196	90	46	60	31	32	16
1930	175	77	44	56	32	28	16

Source: calculated from data in *Racing Calendar*

Of course the rewards were far less than if they had become jockeys: in the 1890s they got their 'keep and a sovereign a week';[54] in the early 1900s they could receive up to twenty-five shillings if they were lucky (as a leading jockey remarked: 'the most ordinary jockey would think that chaos had come again if he did not earn a great deal more than as many pounds');[55] but by 1937 when the Transport and General Workers Union was recognized by the Newmarket Trainers' Federation, they could expect forty-eight shillings a week plus eight days' paid holidays a year and one Sunday off in three.[56] In addition, there was the

* Whether the proportions are high or low relative to other apprenticeships is, in the absence of comparable data, a matter for conjecture.

possibility of presents for 'doing' a winning horse. In general
lads could keep riding till aged fifty or sixty, although some who
got knocked about too much might have to seek casual employment or turn to the Poor Law authorities, for there was no
Jockey Club provision along the lines of the Bentinck Fund.
However, most lads who chose to remain in the stables could
anticipate staying there for the rest of their working lives,
though if they wished, lads from the stables of respected and
reputable trainers could often obtain employment with the
horses of a gentleman's family.[57] A few, though only a few,
could rise to the exalted position of head lad, a job which in a
leading stable could pay up to £500 a year in the 1890s, not the
princely sum earned by top jockeys but no mean income.[58] This
liberal remuneration was justified by the responsibility; trainers
had to spend considerable time away from their stables and they
had to be confident that things would run smoothly in their
absence.

Putting on too much weight ended the riding careers of many
apprentices; for others the trouble was not being too big but
being too small. The raising of the minimum weight, while
protecting children from exploitation, rebounded in that it
limited the number of rides offered to apprentices; so much so
that in the late nineteenth century complaints abounded as to the
dearth of experienced jockeys, especially when the Americans
began to carry all before them.* There were two schools of
thought on the minimum weight issue, each championed by a
reputable trainer. William Day wanted a seven stone minimum
because he felt that young boys in the saddle were dangerous,
whereas John Porter would have preferred only four and a half
stones so as to give apprentices more chances of riding.[59] The
Jockey Club's compromise was to keep the six stones minimum
but to institute an apprentice allowance in certain races and to
encourage races specifically for apprentices. Although many
critics felt that the allowance system ruined some races by
nullifying the handicapper's work, it undoubtedly gave many
youngsters opportunities that would not otherwise have come
their way.[60] In 1905 Elijah Wheatly rode 124 winners, thus

* For the influence of the Americans on British jockeyship, see above, pp.
54–7.

heading the jockeys' championship while still an apprentice.*
Nevertheless, despite the obvious advantage of employing
stable apprentices who were riding their horses daily and getting
to know them thoroughly, too many owners remained reluctant
to give the apprentice a chance to show what he could do. In
astonishment that the high financial rewards had not brought
forward more capable jockeys, one Jockey Club handicapper
suggested that in racing 'the law of supply and demand does not
appear to work'.[61] But he was looking at the supply side only;
the demand for jockeys was for top flight jockeys, and, more
than that, it was for existing jockeys of rank not potential ones.[62]

Even when his chance came the apprentice might not be able
to seize it. Some boys, quite competent horsemen on the gallops,
never learned how to ride a race. Others, no matter how keen
and educable, lacked that certain inborn quality which separated
the men from the lads. Jockeys required 'hands' and 'head'.
Hands, the ability to control and encourage a horse independently of one's physical strength, was almost entirely a
natural gift; head, the capacity to note circumstances during a
race and without hesitation to see what is the right thing to do,
was partly instinctive but could no doubt be picked up by
practice, experience, and observation. In addition to these
qualities the truly outstanding jockeys possessed distinctive
attributes of their own: cases in point are Sam Chifney's rush,
Fordham's 'kid', Tom Cannon's delicate touch, and Archer's
unscrupulous determination – on one occasion he even put his
own brother over the rails!

It was difficult to make the transition from apprentice to
jockey: it was equally difficult to emerge from the ruck and
become a successful jockey. One author, writing in the 1880s,
described the hierarchy: there are 'some half-dozen artists at
the head of the profession, and perhaps a score of second-class
performers, followed *longo intervallo* by a host of cut-and-thrust
stableboys stuffed into boots and breeches'.[63] As can be seen in
Table 9 the situation changed little over time. Relatively few

---

* It should be pointed out that there was no organized jockeys' championship; it
was merely a press publicity device. If there was, the percentage of winners ridden
would surely be a better guide than the absolute number of winners (cf. batting
averages in first class cricket).

TABLE 9. SUCCESS RATE AMONG JOCKEYS

	Number of riders		Number of riders winning						Percentage of all races won by the twelve leading jockeys
	Jockeys	Appren-tices	0 races*	1–4 races	5–9 races	10–19 races	20–29 races	30 or more races	
1879	?	?	?	71	20	12	10	14	55
1889	?	?	?	54	10	10	5	16	61
1899	252	170	306	71	14	9	8	14	62
1909	212	207	309	50	18	12	13	17	49
1929	242	196	306	67	19	16	13	17	47
1938	180	209	263	65	14	20	6	21	50

* Some may not have ridden in any races.

Source: calculated from data in the *Racing Calendar*

jockeys rode ten or more winners in a season and the leading dozen jockeys, perhaps 3 per cent of the total registered riders, consistently rode around half of the total winners.* Those critics who complained about jockeys earning more than bishops probably never considered the relative odds of reaching the top doing God's work or assisting man's play. The high rewards paid to the top jockeys no doubt stimulated recruitment into the profession and thus possibly led to falling average rewards for the run-of-the-mill jockey. The English football authorities used such an argument to defend the maximum wage system prior to 1961.[64] This would only be true, however, if there was a limited wages fund and about this one cannot be positive. We do not know if the new owners coming into racing were enlarging the supply of money available to jockeys or merely replenishing it. When he reached the pinnacle of his profession the jockey could entrench himself: success brought offers of more mounts and thus the opportunity to reinforce that success. Providing that his skill did not desert him, injury befall him, or calories thicken his waistline, the eminent jockey probably found it easier to remain at the top than to get there in the first place.

All jockeys could count one blessing: unlike their counterparts in national hunt racing they did not have to fear the loss of income because of successful gentlemen riders. In many nineteenth-century sports the amateur excelled and could frequently beat the professional because he was a full-time amateur, with many hours of leisure in which to practise. But generally this was not true of flat-racing, especially once heavy weights stopped being carried.† To compete successfully and regularly against the professional jockeys would have involved

---

* The discontinuity which comes with the twentieth century is due to the institution of the apprentice allowance.

† C. J. Apperley ('The Turf', *Quarterly Review*, vol. 49, July 1833, p. 437) listed several gentlemen riders with good riding records. However, a check showed they rode mainly at private meetings where professional jockeys were excluded. Why lighter weights replaced the eleven stones or more common in the early eighteenth century is not clear. Possibly it has something to do with the general move away from brutality in sports involving animals; more likely it was associated with the development of handicap races and the racing of immature horses. What is certain is that the setting of low weights put an artificial restriction on the supply of jockeys.

too great a sacrifice of the good life. Professionals could be well paid for starving themselves, but most potential gentleman riders were wealthy enough anyway: in fact those who did compete successfully probably did so for social or psychological rewards rather than monetary ones. Indeed one of the most outstanding gentleman riders of the late nineteenth century, George Alexander 'Abington' Baird, had no need of money since his father, a Scots ironmaster, had left him over three million pounds. By hard work, dedication, and wasting he made himself into an excellent jockey. His proudest moment was when he beat Archer and Charlie Wood in a close finish at Nottingham. He was perhaps driven to transfer his ambitions from the drawing rooms to the racetrack by the rebuffs he received from high society which made him very conscious of his origins.[65] Gentleman riders had to be good even to be allowed to take part, for unskilled riders, no matter how enthusiastic, were simply too dangerous; and racing bloodstock was far too valuable to be put at risk by bungling amateurs. From 1879 the Jockey Club controlled the efforts of gentleman riders by insisting that if they wished to ride alongside professionals they must be similarly licensed, a privilege not granted readily. Gentlemen, along with farmers and soldiers concentrated more on point to point racing which perhaps became the social event, at least for the participants, which flat-racing had been in the eighteenth century.

Very few gentlemen could give the professionals a real run: 'a small percentage do end by [becoming] very fair fourth-class jockeys over long distances [but], there are not half a dozen gentlemen in a generation who can ride a five-furlong race'.[66] Indeed a commentator in the *Sporting Magazine* for 1831 argued that when gentlemen raced 'you see nothing but waving arms and yellow leather breeches in convulsions!', and suggested that 'if gentlemen will, in silk jackets, mount racers, there really ought to be an Act of Parliament passed to put them down'.[67] Rather than the amateurs taking money out of the pockets of the professionals, it was more the latter who frequently spoiled the sport of the gentlemen. The term 'gentleman rider' covered a multitude of sinners and many races supposedly for the exclusive amusement of the leisured class 'too frequently [found] noblemen and gentlemen riding in the same race with those who they would not or could not acknowledge as equals anywhere else'.[68] At a North Yorkshire meeting in 1836 one 'gentleman' rider had no doubts as to his eligibility: 'I subscribes to a pack o' dogs. I hunts three days a week. I drinks wine to my dinner. And I keeps a mistress!'[69] Even without making such claims, lesser professionals were able to supplement their incomes for much of the nineteenth century by exploiting the elasticity of the definition.

Some jockeys made good money, some did not; but none had an easy working life. Work was not simply a matter of the jockey getting on a horse for a few minutes and then collecting his money. Many jockeys had to ride horses in trials and training gallops; no doubt at two guineas a time they were grateful for the money, but it meant a very early rise if there was a race meeting the same day. Because of the decentralized nature of British racing much time was spent in travelling. Before the advent of the railways jockeys had either to ride from meeting to meeting or endure the discomforts of the stage coach. Some remarkable feats of travelling were accomplished: the New-market jockey, Wakefield, travelled 500 miles between Monday and Friday, three nights and two days of which were spent on the outside of a coach; Galloway journeyed from Doncaster to Shrewsbury and back to Doncaster in three successive days; and Tommy Lye of Middleham rode two winners at Musselburgh on a Wednesday and a third the following day at Northallerton, 170 miles away.[70] The coming of the railway, and later the car, and, for a few, the aeroplane, eased travelling problems, but a proportion of the time saved had to be spent in exercise; at least when riding around the country the jockey could lose weight en route. Travelling and racing had to be done in all weathers, for owners and trainers seemed willing to turn bloodstock out in conditions that would have daunted Arthurian knights. Nor could jockeys afford the luxury of illness: not riding meant no pay – it certainly meant no winning bonuses – unless they held a retainer, but to miss races was to risk its renewal.*[71] Fear of

---

* Gordon Richards was a notable exception. He missed the 1926 season with a patch on his lung but his retainers were still paid; perhaps because he had been champion jockey the previous season. In 1927 the faith of his patrons was rewarded as he was again champion. (G. Richards, *My Story*, 1955, p. 32.)

being ill was not the jockeys' only worry. Professional sportsmen, especially in sports which emphasize physical prowess, are often over the hill long before the average worker thinks of retirement. Jockeys were lucky in that age in itself did not end their careers. Nevertheless the occupation was an insecure one: the twin spectres of serious accidents and increasing weight were an ever present anxiety.

Jockeys lose their livings if they put on weight: pushing down the scales too far ended more careers than anything else. In his study of modern American racing Marvin Scott has hypothesized that increasing weight generally *follows* rather than precedes the closing of career opportunities. He suggests that it becomes a face-saving device for those who see little future for themselves in racing.[72] There may be something in this as regards apprentices and jockeys who never made the breakthrough into regular employment; eventually they may have seen no point in not having a second slice of bread or an extra helping of potatoes. But Scott's thesis certainly does not apply to jockeys who had made the grade; they literally starved themselves in order to keep on earning the money they had become accustomed to. For them masochism was a professional necessity. Apart from a few blessed with natural lightness, all jockeys had to waste. Every season there was the problem of shedding the pounds put on by good living during the winter months. Most jockeys had to lose a stone, many two stones, and others even more; Archer frequently rode at below 8 st. 7 lb. but his winter weight was around 11 st.[73] During the season there was the constant temptation to take that extra ride a pound or so below their normal racing weight; and getting even ounces off a fit man is never easy. The basic method of reducing was a combination of sweating and diet. Tramping across country wearing heavy clothes was a favoured device; those who couldn't face pedestrian exercise had the option of the Turkish bath, but this tended to sap their strength. Nineteenth-century diets were not scientifically worked out as the nutritional knowledge simply was not available: the result was that jockeys virtually starved themselves. George Barrett did eat well but after his meals he stuck his fingers down his throat.[74] Most jockeys, however, relied on eating very little and combatting even that with doses of purgative medicines. Archer's standard fare was warm castor oil, an occasional strip of dry toast, and half a glass of champagne or half a cup of tea with a drop of gin in it.[75] In his autobiography Tommy Weston wrote lovingly of the joy of Saturday night when he could eat a meal knowing that he had an extra day in which to offset its effect.[76]

Considering the nagging insecurity of their working lives and the constant, tortuous slimming process, it is not surprising that many jockeys took their calories in the form of alcohol. Liquor was a curse of the old school of jockeys and ruined many careers. Jem Snowden had his successes but eventually years of drinking caught up with him and he died in poverty. This was the man who once turned up a week late for Chester races and on another occasion at Catterick refused blinkers for his horse on the grounds that 'bleend horse *and* bleend jockey will never do'. Lifting his elbow too much on the eve of the 1873 Derby cost Snowden a winning mount and the money that would have followed.[77] Twenty-seven years before, drink also cost Bill Scott a Derby: credible evidence suggests that he was so drunk as to be too busy arguing with the starter to realize that the race had begun.[78] Scott claimed that he had never spent a sober night since attaining his majority, but as he won four Derbys, three Oaks, and, dearer to his Yorkshire heart, nine St Legers, he at least appears to have thrived on inebriation.[79]

Most jockeys who managed to keep their weight down were unable to enjoy life to the full during the racing season. Not till October or November could revenge be taken on the sporting Lent to which they conformed so piously. They might inhabit fine rooms and wear elegant clothes, but they had to pursue a sensible mode of living; so although they could afford to eat well they dare not do so. Self-discipline was vital; if the mark was overstepped it was soon reflected at the scales. Those who failed to control their weight either retired or died. Archer's appalling end came during delirium brought on by excessive wasting. He had been riding at 9 st. 4 lb. in Ireland and had to get down to 8 stone 6 lb. for *St Mirren* in the Cambridgeshire, the only major race he never won. Despite starvation and devastating doses of purgatives he still put up a pound overweight. His weakness laid him open to a chill and later typhoid.

On the anniversary of his wife's death he shot himself, a victim of wasting, illness, and melancholy.* Other hard-wasting jockeys killed themselves just as surely as if they too had put a revolver to their head. Attempting to stave off, or starve off, the inevitable so weakened their constitutions that they became easily susceptible to illness: indeed tuberculosis was almost an occupational disease.[80]

To a degree wasting can be controlled, but not so crashes. Racing was a dangerous sport and serious accidents were a prevalent risk. Moreover, there was no easy way to learn the trade: bloodstock had no formula junior on which to practise. Apprentices were thrown in the deep-end – thrown frequently being the appropriate word. Unlike national hunt racing there was generally no indication that a fall was imminent and coming down at thirty miles an hour must have been far from pleasant, especially when horses were bunched together as they tended to be in flat-racing, Rough riding added to the hazards, particularly when northern and southern jockeys were in opposition, their natural geographical antipathy being further aggravated by a feeling of a divine right to the prizes on their own particular circuits.[81] Fortunately this antagonism was lessened by the development of the railways which eroded parochialism. It was also subjugated by tighter official supervision which enforced sanctions against riding too hard. Accidents meant loss of earnings as well as bodily injuries.† The Workmen's Compensation Act, instituted in 1897 and enlarged in scope nine years later, did not apply to jockeys on several counts: many earned above £250 a year; they worked on premises not under the control or management of the person who employed them; and most were casually employed for a purpose not connected with their patron's trade or business.[82] There was, of course, the Bentinck Benevolent Fund, created by Lord George Bentinck in

---

* By one of those macabre coincidences, Archer's record total of winners in a season was equalled by Gordon Richards on the anniversary of Archer's last ride, and beaten on the anniversary of his death.

† What is surprising in view of the risk to both body and purse is the number of jockeys whose winter amusements included hunting. Were they courageous or foolhardy? As skilled horsemen they perhaps felt they could control most situations, but their general attitude towards the future, as illustrated in their style of life and provision for retirement (see below, pp. 171–2) suggests either an irrational optimism or a refusal to consider the possible consequences.

the 1840s from money given to him by admirers of his campaign to clean up the turf.* This was later supplemented by the Rous Memorial Fund. However, the restricted resources of both funds meant that only small pensions could be given to distressed jockeys. Not till 1923 was a compulsory insurance scheme introduced.

The insecurity of jockeyship led jockeys to attempt to make as much money as possible while they could. For successful jockeys there was an additional reason for maximizing short-term income; mixing with their upper class patrons gave them a taste for the good life, but the style of living they adopted could only be financed by constant and immediate success. They dare not relax. During the season they took as many mounts as they could: more rides increased the chances of winning and wins produced presents and even more offers of mounts.† Winning big races served the same function. Steve Donaghue, who once refused to become the King's jockey because there were not enough potential winners in the royal stables, was so determined to win the Derby, and the money it would bring, that he sacrificed several retainers by preferring to ride horses other than his patrons' in the race. In 1921 he won on *Humorist* though he should have ridden Lord Derby's *Glorioso*; this led to him being replaced as stable jockey by Ted Gardner. In 1922 Vic Smyth was 'jocked off' *Captain Cuttle* to give Steve another victory and a present of £5,000. For 1923 he had a handsome retainer from Lord Woolavington, but refused to ride either of that owner's two Derby entries as he had made up his mind to ride *Papyrus* and secure his third consecutive victory. This he did, but henceforth Fred Darling, principal trainer to Lord Woolavington, refused to accept him as stable jockey.[83] As a member of the jockey elite he probably believed that he would be able to secure another retainer easily enough. For a while he

* See above, pp. 91–2. In 1837 the proprietor of the Bayswater Hippodrome racecourse had proposed setting up such a fund which would be financed out of owners' prize money, but there had been no response. J. C. Whyte, *History of the British Turf*, 1840, pp. 582–5.

† Times have not changed. Willie Carson who had 829 mounts in 1972 commented 'There were times when I felt like saying "Damn it" – but you've got to go on. You can't afford an off-day. There's too much at stake.' Quoted in J. Wilson, 'Willie Carson – Long Term Champion', in T. Cosgrove (ed.), *William Hill Racing Year Book*, 1973, p. 61.

was, but eventually no owner would trust him to honour a contract. Short-term considerations thus cost him dearly in the longer run.

Nevertheless immediate income was what concerned most jockeys. A common means by which they attempted to maximize this was gambling, but it must be emphasized that this was a most uncertain course. In the 1840s Admiral Rous, then a captain, maintained that 'any man who follows the advice of his jockey is sure to be ruined'.[84] Many jockeys gambled away much of the money they had earned, but others still continued to bet. Hopes of making money and a belief that as insiders they knew what should win drove them on. Up to the 1880s it seemed to be taken for granted that virtually all the leading jockeys gambled; Archer always claimed that his presents were reduced by owners who thought he would have taken care of himself in the betting market.[85] It was not just the elite who gambled; indeed many lesser lights claimed that they were forced to bet because owners refused to pay their riding fees.[86] Although the money was recoverable at law, no jockey was willing to risk his career by taking an owner to court. Nor do jockeys ever seem to have considered unionism: the occupation was far too competitive.* Unless a jockey was good enough and lucky enough to hold a retainer then he had to join the demoralizing, and often degrading, struggle to secure mounts. Rarely were there more than a score of runners in a race but there were twenty times this number of jockeys and apprentices seeking the rides. Moreover, most owners with whom they negotiated would be from a section of society who, at least in the nineteenth century, would not have tolerated trade union activities on the part of their employees. It was thus left to the Jockey Club to put the owners' house in order. In 1880 a rule was passed enforcing the deposit of all riding fees with the stakeholder or clerk of the course before the race took place. However, gambling by jockeys did not cease and, annoyed at the lack of response and angered by rumours of jockeys fixing races, the Jockey Club

---

* No organization emerged till 1966 when the Flat Race Jockeys Association of Great Britain Ltd was incorporated as a non-profit-making limited liability company. The competition is still fierce but attitudes towards organization have changed, as they have in society at large.

showed its teeth.* From 1884 betting by jockeys became a turf misdemeanour, punishable by suspension of licence. Henceforth jockeys who gambled risked both their money and their livelihood. On several occasions jockeys were unable to get their licences renewed. That this occurred indicated that betting did not stop: indeed one of the disciplined jockeys excused himself on the grounds that all jockeys gambled.[87] It is impossible to ascertain the extent of this illicit gambling, but it can be conjectured, given the Jockey Club's difficulty in obtaining hard evidence,† that those who were found out were probably the tip of the iceberg.

The Jockey Club's concern with jockeys who gambled was not to save these individuals from their own folly, but to protect racing from corruption. Instances of jockeys maintaining their integrity by winning races on horses they had bet against have become part of racing's folklore. Nevertheless, too frequently gambling and dishonesty went hand in glove. Even without betting themselves jockeys could fall prey to a temptation to make quick money. For apprentices there might be little option: if they wanted mounts, and what apprentice did not, then they had to ride to orders and these were not always to win.[88] Young jockeys, whose basic work was seeking work, might also have to lose or starve. Others, less desperate for rides, chose to be dishonest. Not all were like Harry Edwards who it was claimed would rather nobble for fifty pounds than obtain a hundred honestly, but it is noticeable that honest is a rare word in racing parlance.[89] It was used deliberately about jockeys such as Flatman, Osborne, Lye, Bullock, Maher, and Fordham with the implicit assumption that it was not applicable to the bulk of jockeys. John Gully said he had known only three inflexibly

---

* It was strongly rumoured that there was a jockeys' ring in existence, but the truth was that Archer was acting as adviser to a betting syndicate, using his talent and experience to select horses which he thought would win if he rode them. It may be that the syndicate then approached other owners suggesting that all would profit if Archer's mount won, but Archer was merely utilizing his expertise to assess possible winners. Earl of Suffolk, *Racing and Steeplechasing*, 1886, p. 106; J. Welcome, *Fred Archer: His Life and Times*, 1967, pp. 142–9.

† It was, for example, common knowledge that Steve Donaghue gambled, sometimes heavily, but the Jockey Club was never able to obtain the evidence to disqualify him. Q. Gilbey, *Champions All*, 1971, p. 34; T. Weston, *My Racing Life* 1952, p. 117.

honest jockeys.[90] He, of course, raced at a time when the conduct of the sport was nothing short of a scandal. Yet even in the early 1860s another owner's racing *confidant* was claiming: 'it is no use going on as you have done, you have been robbed out of many races by the jockeys. It is all very well for them to say the horse could not have, when we know to the contrary and how are we to pin anything against the jockey – it gets worse and worse everyday.'[91] Nevertheless there is a strong suspicion that jockeys were sometimes unfairly castigated. Even Rous, no jockey lover, was prepared to acknowledge that on occasions jockeys were made scapegoats for the misdeeds or incompetence of owners and trainers.[92] George Fordham, as straight as they came, refused to be blamed for someone else's shortcomings and when William Day excused *Happy Land*'s defeat in the Two Thousand Guineas on the grounds that Fordham had not tried to win, the jockey put the matter before the Jockey Club stewards who severely reprimanded the trainer for his unwarranted insinuation.[93] Whether jockeys as a whole became less dishonest as racing became more controlled and less corrupt is difficult to say, but contemporary commentators thought so. Rice, writing in the late 1870s, believed that jockeys in his day were more honest than in the past, and, a decade or so later, L. H. Curzon, a stern critic of racing's morality, acknowledged that the great majority of modern jockeys were 'beyond suspicion'.[94] Rising earnings for some may have lessened the temptation to do wrong, but for the bulk of jockeys it remained true that 'money [was] to be made with greater certainty by foul means than by fair'.[95] If fewer jockeys took such ill-gotten gains it was probably associated with the Jockey Club gaining control over most of British racing and instituting a licensing system in 1879 for all jockeys who wished to participate.

A limited study, the results of which are shown in Table 10, suggests that the typical jockey's career was relatively short. Some died; some retired because of increasing weight or injury; and some gave up in desperation at too few rides or too many losers. Others were spoiled by success. Young lads from poor homes were too easily swayed after they won a few races. They gained false ideas of their own importance and began to think they were as good as Archer, Donaghue, or Richards. If they did not price themselves out of the market by excessive demands, they lost mounts by offending potential patrons who may have accepted impudence from a champion jockey but certainly not from a recent graduate of the stables. The presents they had received were quickly dissipated: as small in intellect as in stature, they could not cope with having money, or with the back-slapping companions who helped them spend it and then disappeared as rapidly as had the cash.[96] Sam Adams

TABLE 10. LENGTH OF JOCKEYS' CAREERS

Span in years *	Number of jockeys
1–4	140
5–8	53
9–12	39
13–16	30
17–20	25
21–24	20
25–28	6
29 or more	4
	Total 317

* Based on a study of all jockeys licensed in 1920. The span is not the number of years licensed, but years between obtaining first licence and relinquishing last licence.

Source: calculated from data in *Racing Calendar*

epitomized such prodigal youths. He was just out of his apprenticeship when he won the 1863 Cambridgeshire on *Catch 'em Alive*. Mr Gerald Sturt, who was reported to have won £40,000 on the race, gave Adams £200 and a hunter. Adams's immediate reaction was to marry a local barmaid, lease a neighbouring rectory, hire a groom, and attend the Crichet hounds in immaculate garb. Soon after he annoyed his benefactor by going up and shaking his hand while Sturt was conversing with the Prince of Wales. Less than two years later, Adams was picked up in a state of collapse in the streets of London and taken to Charing Cross hospital where he died; in his hand was a box of matches he had been trying to sell.[97]

Many jockeys whose careers were cut short by lack of

opportunity or surfeit of weight remained associated with racing: it was all they knew. Some progressed to becoming trainers, but not as many as most racing histories imply; of the 317 jockeys licensed in 1920 only 21, less than 7 per cent, subsequently took out a trainer's licence.[98] There is no indication that the experience of being a jockey guaranteed them success as trainers; increasingly education and a business mind were becoming more important than horse sense. Most ex-jockeys who remained in racing were relegated to being stable lads, or eking out their existence by riding the occasional gallop, hanging round stables or race-courses for odd jobs, or even begging from the crowds at race meetings.

Only a few jockeys had made provision for the future. Charley Wood died a rich man, Nat Flatman left £11,000, and Archer much more, but they were in the minority: for too many the end of riding meant poverty.[99] Henry Luke, winner of the Two Thousand Guineas in 1876, died in the workhouse at Sandbach; the even more famous Jem Robinson, victor in six Derbys, two Oaks, nine Two Thousand Guineas, and four One Thousand Guineas, was only saved from a similar fate by the generosity of two former patrons, The Dukes of Bedford and Rutland; Jem Snowden, who at times had earned thousands, died so poor that a few Yorkshire trainers had to pay his funeral expenses; and both Sam and William Chifney, who lived well, died, like their jockey father, in poverty.[100] Jockeys underwent dangerous and, for some, severe toil to earn their living, but they then spent most of their earnings on wine, women and song. They deferred their gratification only for the duration of the racing season; the aforementioned Jem Robinson departed for London with his wife immediately the season ended, there to spend every penny he had earned.[101] It was observable that most jockeys failed to sustain their careers, so why did the attitude of eat, drink, and be merry prevail? Perhaps they rationalized that they would not be the ones to fall by the wayside or possibly the dismal future was simply too horrific to be contemplated.* It

---

* One student of modern American racing has found it very difficult to get jockeys to discuss accidents. 'We never talk about those things,' one rider told him, 'it happens, it happens. There's nothing to talk about.' M. B. Scott, 'The Man on the Horse', in J. W. Loy and G. S. Kenyon, *Sport, Culture and Society*, 1969, p. 429.

may have had nothing to do with being a jockey. A similar pattern of working-class sportsmen rising in their profession, dissipating all they earn, and dying in poverty, can be found among eighteenth-century prizefighters and modern American boxers.[102] This may reflect class background rather than be specific to these occupations, for several studies have suggested that in general the working class put a premium on immediate pleasure and make little provision for the future.[103] Whatever the reason jockeys chose not only to maximize their short-run income but also to spend it. When they ceased to ride the flow of money dried up and with it their style of life.

Social rewards too proved transient. The upper classes who had delighted in his company saw no entertainment value in a stunted, uneducated, ex-jockey; and the adoring crowds found new heroes to worship. The retired jockey sat alone with his memories and his bottle. George Fordham, rider of over two thousand winners, idol of the masses, and fawned over by the rich, was grateful on his death bed for the few 'fair friends, considering all others gave me up and at any moment I may go'.[104] He was only fifty years old and had been third leading jockey in the country when he gave up riding but four years before his death.

10] *Trainers*]

At the beginning of the nineteenth century many trainers were nothing more than training grooms, low-paid servants with few social graces. How would these 'breeches and gaiters' men, living the simple life in 'remote corners of the downs and wolds', have regarded the leading trainers of the late nineteenth century to whom 'it [was] quite the ordinary thing to be tall-hatted, frock-coated, kid-gloved and patent-leather-booted' and who dwelt in 'handsome and comfortable residences . . . with fine gardens, trim lawns for croquet and lawn-tennis, billiard rooms, and cellars containing choice vintages'?[1]

The contrast was a result of the commercialization of racing. As owners reacted to the rise in prize money and increasingly sought the best – in horses, in jockeys, and in trainers – the old-fashioned training groom, looking after fifteen to twenty of his master's horses, gave way to the public trainer who cared for up to a hundred animals from a heterogeneous collection of owners.[2] Private training continued but by the end of the century it was predominantly by doyens of public training easing their way into retirement or by men whose employers were wealthy and ambitious enough to afford to buy their exclusive services.

Recruitment to the profession also changed. The early trainers had generally possessed a degree of literacy (many owners demanded daily training reports) and numeracy (accounts had to be kept), but they were ill-educated in comparison to the trainers of the late nineteenth century, and especially those of the inter-war years when public school accents could increasingly be heard across the Heath.[3] Indeed from the 1890s there was a significant shift into the occupation from the ranks of the gentry, or at least from those to whom the title of gentleman was commonly attributed. Some came as amateurs: here they could compete on equal terms with the professionals without sacrificing the good life. Others turned professional to finance that life.[4]

* Based on data pertaining to fifty-three individuals for whom more than minimal information was available.

Two qualifications were necessary in order to become a trainer, money to set up an establishment and contacts to bring in horses. The money could be one's own as with the gentlemen trainers, successful ex-jockeys, and relatives of some established trainers, or it could be that of one's patrons though this would be unlikely to be offered to a novice, untutored in the arts of training. The need for contacts similarly restricted entry to the trade. Gentlemen taking to training would be well-known in the racing world; a jockey, providing he had attained some success, could expect to be given a chance by a few owners; promoted head lads had had the benefit of understudying their employer and dealing with owners in his absence; and, of course, there were the sons of trainers, brought up in the game and gradually being given more responsibility until they were judged fit to branch out on their own.[5] It is no concidence that several families dominate the history of training in the nineteenth century. What owner would not have taken a gamble with a member of the Day, Scott, Osborne, Darling, Leader, or Dawson dynasties?

The earnings of trainers are less common knowledge than those of jockeys. The standard weekly charge for training a horse rose from £1 15s. 0d. in the 1830s to £2 10s. 0d. in the late nineteenth century and around £5 in the early 1920s.[6] With fifty horses or more in their stables, and the possibility of presents, betting coups, and even salaries,* many trainers could enjoy a high standard of living. Nevertheless earnings could not be guaranteed: only one horse can win a race and without winners it was difficult to retain patrons. Some owners demanded instant success and never gave a trainer a fair chance. The Duchess of Montrose, for one, changed her trainers as often as she changed her mind: 'Ah Mr Peace – the Peace that passeth all understanding' was her imperious dismissal of a not untalented trainer.[7] Even the great John Porter, trainer of 961 winners of races whose prize-money totalled over £600,000, felt the ire of men who lost their patience when they lost races. Late in life he commented to Richard Marsh that the worst

---

* In 1898, for example, Richard Marsh received £2,000 from the five owners who used his stables. This was in addition to the usual training charges. M. Seth-Smith, *Bred for the Purple*, 1969, p. 170.

aspect of training was not bad horses but 'the ingratitude of some of your employers, who made a great fuss of you during your success but quit you like rats from a sinking ship when you are out of luck'.[8] Moreover, even the money that had been earned was not always readily forthcoming. Customarily accounts were settled every three months but, as the famous trainer, William Day, lamented, some owners paid 'yearly, some in a number of years and some not at all'.[9] At one time John Scott, trainer of forty-one classic winners, had over £20,000 owing to him and had not only to beg owners for a remittance but also to request time to settle his own affairs.[10] And Joseph Dawson, one of four brothers who all became top class trainers, eventually had to take Lord Stamford to court in order to get the money due to him.[11]

As with jockeys, this reluctance of owners to pay their debts led many trainers to look to gambling to supplement their incomes.[12] This was as true of trainers at the top of their profession as of the many hard-working men who never hit the big time and whose livelihood depended on two or three successful betting propositions each season. William Day once picked up £22,000 on the 1860 Autumn Double and on one occasion Tom Dawson won £16,000 and very nearly lost it again by leaving it on a train.[13] In the case of jockeys it was frequently assumed that gambling induced dishonesty, but, with the major exception of the American invasion, such allegations were rarely levied publicly against trainers. Certainly few trainers felt the wrath of the Jockey Club, but whether this was because they were doing nothing wrong or merely cleverer than jockeys at getting away with malpractice is a matter for conjecture. An anonymous reviewer did criticize William Day's sanctimonious belief that trainers could do no wrong: 'owners sometimes are, it seems, eccentric; jockeys are not to be trusted; commissioners do dark deeds: the trainer alone walks in the narrow path of uprightness, on which the fierce light of criticism beats in vain'.[14] Nevertheless, despite several strong criticisms of turf morality the reviewer did not (or could not?) cite instances of trainer malfeasance. Moreover, two other contemporary critics of racing practices generally excuse trainers from their strictures. L. H. Curzon opined that 'in all probability, the majority of trainers are most faithful to their employers' and another anonymous critic accepted that in general trainers were men of 'fair integrity and character'.[15] In the absence of hard data no positive statements can be made but a couple of suggestions can be hazarded. First, what little information there is gives the impression that trainers usually bet only on their *own* horses so they were less likely than jockeys to throw a race. Secondly, unlike jockeys, trainers could hardly practice deceit totally unnoticed. If a horse was to be pulled the jockey would have to be taken into confidence, and if it was to run unfit either stable staff or local touts would be aware of the lack of preparation. Doping alone could be done in isolation, but this was very much a product of the American invasion and was cut down severely by drug tests and stringent penalties.*

Trainers were paid for their skill but they 'earned' their money by dint of constant worry. Over the nineteenth century trainers increasingly became managers for their owners as well as trainers, making themselves responsible for selecting the races for the horses, choosing the jockeys, and purchasing yearlings. Thus more decisions were added to the burden of simply getting the horse ready to race. This was difficult enough for there is a fine margin between training and straining. Certainly many old-time trainers ruined horses whose delicate constitutions could not stand up to a regime of drenches, sweats, purges, and in some cases even bleeding.[16] Over time – perhaps as bloodstock became more valuable – it was realized that not every horse could do heavy work wearing equally heavy rugs and blankets: even old John Day grew more merciful in his later years.[17] Eventually, after pioneering work by Tom Dawson at Middleham in the 1850s, sweating was abandoned entirely.[18] Nevertheless there still remained the basic problem of getting the horse ready at the right time, for no horse can be kept continually at top form. Even then the trainer's worries were not over. The horse could be perfectly prepared but all could be lost by the tactics of the jockey: months of training could be brought to nothing by a few minutes ill-judged riding.

There was also the danger of horses being got at. *West Australian*, a star performer trained by John Scott for John

* See above, p. 104.

Bowes, was not unusual in having to be protected prior to a big race. A letter from the trainer's wife tells the story:

> We have had a very narrow escape from the Nobblers; as from what I can hear there is no doubt they intended to get at the horse . . . had they come they would have met with a warm reception as I had two watchmen, one inside and one outside the yard; the inside man had a brace of pistols and would not have hesitated about using them had there been the slightest alarm.[19]

Later there was not merely the risk of losing races but also of losing one's licence to train, since in all cases of doping the trainer was held responsible for the offence.*

This was not the end of a trainer's worries. There was the constant risk of injury and illness. Till the author read the correspondence of John Scott he was unaware of just how many illnesses horses were susceptible to. Even if these were avoided the horse might hit an undetected hole in the training gallops, or the blacksmith might prick the animal when plating it. And what if, heaven forbid, one of the lads failed to extinguish his illegal cigarette: would stables and stock with a value perhaps in six figures go up in smoke? As one trainer rightly commented, 'anxiety is never absent': no wonder the shelter from which the trainer Robinson observed his horses at the gallops was referred to by his lads as 'the governor's unrest'.[20]

* See above, p. 104.

'D for Duke, E for Earl, M for Marquis' – thus Delabere Blaine began his list of abbreviations commonly used in racing in the mid-nineteenth century.[1] This reflected economics as much as class distinction, for, although racing was a sport for all, ownership of thoroughbred bloodstock was predominantly for the rich, and, despite occasional prophecies of impending penury, the British aristocracy was, for the most part, wealthy.[2] Not all could match that great racing patrician, the Duke of Portland, who in 1889 won £73,858 in stakes and gave it all to charity, but many could afford huge racing studs. Others raced on a less impressive, if still expensive, scale.[3] In the 1830s, a third of owners with registered colours were titled and sixty years later, despite an influx of monied men of lesser rank, the proportion of titled owners was about an eighth.[4]

The high proportion of aristocrats among owners led to a belief in some quarters that owning racehorses was an accompaniment not just of wealth but also of social position: certainly patronage of local meetings was an obligation of their place in the social hierarchy and participation at others a self-imposed requirement of society's social diary. It was this belief that tempted new owners, successful men from industry and commerce, to come into racing, particularly in the late nineteenth century.[5] To men such as Fred Gretton, a partner in Bass Brewery, Blundell Maple, a furnishing magnate, and J. B. Joel, who found his fortune in South African mineral fields, owning racehorses symbolized high society. If they too became owners not only would everyone see their names on the racecard alongside those of the nobility, but there was also the chance that introductions in the paddock might lead to invitations elsewhere, an aspiration given support by the behaviour of Edward VII, both when monarch and when Prince of Wales, who readily accepted many of the *nouveau-riche* owners into his social circle.[6]

Although the industrialists and businessmen who took up racing were primarily concerned with the social returns of investment in horseflesh, their spending had important economic consequences for the sport. These men, successful as they were in the economic world, were determined to be equally to the fore on the turf. They wanted success and they wanted it quickly. Unwilling to wait till they bred a good horse of their own, they frequented the sale ring, cheque books in hand, fortunes at their fingertips.[7] A few paid high prices for yearlings simply for the publicity, but most were paying in the hope that the price reflected the quality.[8] Generally it merely reflected the growing demand for bloodstock: competitive bidding pushed up the price of horses thus reinforcing the trend begun by the enclosed course and by increased prize-money. The aristocracy, equally wealthy and equally desirous of owning a great horse, generally had not sought to buy instant success, but had been prepared to wait; to endure patiently years of frustration while trying to breed such an animal. To them, breeding was an essential part of ownership: anyone with money could purchase a horse; it took talent to breed a classic winner. They had always been willing to pay for breeding stock, for proved racing champions; now unproven yearlings and scarcely-raced two-year-olds too were fetching high prices.

Nevertheless, there was still room in racing for the small-scale owner, ranging from the publican who formed a syndicate with two or three friends to buy a broken-down plater which the local vet reckoned he could get on its feet again, to the traders, grocers and other small businessmen imitating their social superiors. Few of these owners ever made the big time: in effect they formed a pool of floating owners, coming into racing when they felt they could afford it and going out again when they realized that their pockets could never match their enthusiasm.

The degree to which owners were in racing for the money is a matter for conjecture, but certainly for one category of owner, the professional gambler or bookmaker, money was all important. Here we are concerned with men such as John Gully and Robert Ridsdale who in the 1830s owned horses specifically to work betting coups; reputedly they won £60,000 on *St Giles*'s Derby and £45,000 on *Margarve*'s St Leger.[9] Another successful confederacy was the astute Druids Lodge syndicate of W. B. Purefoy, E. A. Wigan, A. P. Cunliffe, and Captain F. Forester, who between 1903 and 1910 pulled off four Cambridgeshire coups.[10] For these gamblers, owning horses reduced the number of variables in their betting equations: at the very least they would know if their own horses were trying and, if their horses were in public stables, there was a good chance of learning if others were too.

It is impossible to weight the various categories of ownership because all we have are names not motivations. And even the registered names are a suspect source material because of two major deficiencies. Many owners raced in partnership, either to increase their chance of 'owning' a good horse – the famous *Flying Dutchman* was the property of a ten-man syndicate[11] – or to reduce the costs of ownership. Till 1948, when it was restricted to four, any number of partners could share a horse. There is a tale of eight such partners, each accompanied by a lady, coming to see their horse run at a provincial meeting, where they demanded, and got, free admission and luncheon for all sixteen: all this for an entry costing only two pounds![12] In 1883 the registration of partnerships was made compulsory but the tracing of owners is still difficult because of pseudonyms, for racing under assumed names was common: young bloods anxious that their parents or trustees should not know their degree of involvement in the turf, ladies and others not sure of acceptance by the racing fraternity, and gambling men who felt that anonymity would secure better odds, all raced in disguise.

Owning horses could be an expensive pastime, particularly because it cost just as much to keep a bad horse as a good one. Training bills, entries and forfeits, feeding stuffs, jockeys' fees and presents, travelling costs, stabling at the course, outlays on saddles, cloths and colours, vets' accounts, the Heath Tax on Newmarket-trained animals: for some owners the list must have seemed endless. In the 1840s Richard Tattersall, the famous bloodstock auctioneer, estimated that even without jockeys' fees at least £230 a year was needed to keep a racehorse.[13] Ownership did not get any cheaper. Various estimates in the 1870s and 1880s put the minimum requirement at around £300 and by the inter-war years it averaged somewhere between £400 and £500.[14]

On top of these 'running costs' there was the initial capital cost of the horse. Leasing was possible but rare; generally a lump sum was needed. An owner could pay anything from five guineas (though heaven knows what he might get for this) to five thousand for a horse. Generally a low price implied low quality though there were some notable exceptions. *Crucifix*, bought with her mother by Lord George Bentinck for only fifty-four guineas, ran unbeaten in twelve outings including the Oaks of 1840 and won over £10,000 in stakes; and *Spearmint*, winner of the Derby in 1906 and thereafter able to command a stud fee of 250 guineas, originally cost Major Loder only 300 guineas.[15] Nevertheless, an owner could not buy success. Lord Beaverbrook, the press baron, tried but gave up after spending well over £100,000 with little to show for it. One of his colts was given to Viscount Castlerosse. It proved promising and was fancied to win at Kempton for its new owner but it went lame and did not run: rumour had it that a vengeful Beaverbrook went over at the dead of night and kicked the animal.[16] There was simply no guarantee that owners would get value for their money. Between 1883 and 1892, 277 well-bred yearlings were sold for over 1,000 guineas, for a grand total of 462,640 guineas, but between them they won only 203,337 guineas in stakes;[17] only two in five of such expensive animals ever repaid their purchase price.[18]

Stakes, of course, were not everything. Successful owners could anticipate the value of their bloodstock increasing and, if their champions proved also to be prolific stallions, a substantial income from stud fees. Most owners, however, would not be successful for relatively few horses lived up to aspirations. To the wealthy Earl of Glasgow this was no problem; at the conclusion of each season he used the shotgun to weed out his worst performers.[19] Other owners sought to minimize the capital loss, perhaps by turning to national hunt racing and trying the failure on the flat over hurdles or even fences; the prize-money was less than in flat-racing, but it was better than nothing. And there was always the selling race* where an unexpected turn in form might persuade one owner to make another's troubles his own.

Individual owners could make money, though not constantly –

* See above, p. 44.

the Duke of Portland won thirty-three races worth nearly £74,000 in 1889 but in 1897, with a larger and more valuable stud, he could manage only one race worth £490 – but owners in aggregate could not. Caught in the scissors of rising costs and insufficient prize-money, most owners found racing a losing game. This can be demonstrated by a look at some financial statistics of racing in the first decade of the twentieth century. At the *very least* the total costs of ownership averaged £1,121,670 a year. This is based on Lord Hamilton of Dalzell's ultra-conservative estimate of a minimum of £200 a year to keep a racehorse; plus a 3 per cent opportunity cost on an equally conservative capital cost estimate of £300 a horse;[20] plus entrance fees and forfeits. Undoubtedly the true costs of ownership would be in excess of this since no allowance has been made for either capital loss or capital depreciation and many owners refused to pennypinch on keep and training costs. Nevertheless, even this underestimated minimum cost could not be covered by prize-money which in the same period averaged only £500,166 a year, a shortfall of over £621,000.[21] Moreover, about two-thirds* of the prize-money came from entries and forfeits, i.e. from the owners themselves: basically, owners were racing for each other's money. At least by this time they could count on getting the money. Till 1877 it was up to individual winning owners to collect stakes not already deposited with the official stakeholder; after this date, however, all due monies had to be paid to the stakeholder within fifteen days of the race or the defaulting owner was disbarred from further racing till the debt was discharged.

Clearly the average owner could not expect to cover his costs, let alone make money out of racing. But why should he? Other sportsmen did not. Yachtsmen would spend a small fortune trying to win a fifty-pound trophy; game generally cost the shooting man well in excess of the shop price; and hunting men laid out substantial sums for no material reward at all.[22]

---

* In 1913, the first year for which comprehensive, aggregate data are available, owners supplied 63 per cent of the prize-money (*Bloodstock Breeders Review*, vol. 7, no. 1, April 1918, pp. 18–19). A concerted campaign by owners and breeders lowered this to 53 per cent by 1923 (*ibid.*, vol. 13, 1924, p. 3), but even in 1943 the Ilchester Committee on the *Re-organisation of Racing* (para. 12) was 'definitely of opinion that the owner is called upon to make too great a contribution to stakes'.

Why then should racing men expect not to pay for their sport? Within limits they were prepared to pay, but the very fact that there was prize-money meant that some owners were definitely going to cover costs and encouraged all owners to think it might be them. Certainly most owners were interested in money: even before racing became revolutionized by the railway and gate-money meetings, winning owners generally took the purse rather than the trophy; and clearly the enclosed courses' success in attracting runners showed that owners responded to the cash stimulus.[23] Doubtless there were professional owners, in racing for what they could get out of it, but whether profit was the major motivation of most owners is debatable. Probably most raced principally for pleasure and, within reasonable limits, were prepared to pay for that pleasure, but few would reject the chance of covering or contributing to costs. When that opportunity lessened owners complained about the economics of their sport. Their protest movement began in earnest in the early twentieth century,[24] possibly because of frustrated expectations consequent upon the development of the enclosed course. Gate-money meetings and their offers of increased prize-money had encouraged hopes of covering costs, but the expansion of ownership – partially stimulated by the rise in prize-money – had simultaneously led to a rise in those costs. Then came a growing feeling on the part of owners that they had been exploited by the racing companies; a realization that they were racing predominantly for their own and not the companies' money. This was brought home by an investigation made by Edward Moorhouse for the Thoroughbred Breeders Association which revealed that in France in 1913 owners contributed only 23 per cent of the prize-money and that at no French meeting was the proportion higher than 28 per cent, whereas at Manchester owners contributed 50 per cent, at Hurst Park 62 per cent, at Kempton Park 66 per cent, at Newbury 69 per cent and at Sandown Park an astounding 82 per cent![25]

Could owners find some way of covering their costs? To many, gambling seemed the obvious and simplest solution. It is impossible to be precise about the extent to which owners gambled. There are no hard data on the issue so we have to rely

on contemporary opinion, something never to be trusted absolutely.* Nevertheless, there is an impression that non-gambling
owners were in a minority. Admittedly the Select Committee on
Gaming in 1844 reported that 'it is well known that many of the
most successful owners of racehorses are men who never wager
at all, or only to a trifling extent', and half a century later it was
still being claimed by a leading turf writer that 'a considerable
proportion of the leading owners of horses do not bet at all'.[26]
Yet wealthy leading owners may have seen no reason to gamble;
the same cannot be said of the bulk of losing owners. The very
fact that non-betting owners elucidated comment[27] lends support to the Earl of Suffolk's assertion, in his authoritative
Badminton Library volume on racing, that the great majority of
owners gambled to a greater or lesser degree.[28] Those in
racing purely for pleasure or status reasons had no need to bet,
save to intensify their involvement. Others, however, hoped to
make the bookmaker contribute to the costs of racing. Whether
they succeeded is again a matter of opinion rather than of fact,
though no commentator has been traced who believed that in
aggregate owners could take more from the bookmaker than
they gave to him, whereas opinions to the contrary are easy to
find. William Day, the famous trainer, maintained that in
general gambling increased the costs of ownership and that it
was 'betting rather than racing [which] ruins the majority of
gentlemen on the turf'.[29] Alfred Watson, a leading writer on
turf affairs, agreed: 'if an owner bets, the cost of racing may be
reduced or enhanced; as a general rule he will, at any rate in the
long run, find himself a loser by taking the odds'.[30] As with
ownership, so with gambling: some gambling owners would
make money; most would not.

There was another way for owners to make money. Robert
Black put it clearly: 'horse racing can be practised . . . as a
profitable business only by persons who combine horse breeding

* Cases in point are the tales of the huge gambling winnings of some owners
which have become part of racing folklore. A reading of correspondence of John
Bowes, a heavy better and owner of four Derby winners, suggests that though the
amounts may not be exaggerated, not all the money was for the owner. A proportion, sometimes a good one, of the bets had been for other people, viz. the trainer
and other stable interests, the jockey, and often friends and betting acquaintances
of the owner. (D/St. Box 162, *passim.* Durham County Record Office).

with horse racing and are content with a few successes at the post to enhance the value of what they offer for sale in the paddock'.[31] However, as we shall see in the following chapter, breeding could be just as much of a gamble.

Breeders of horses knew what they were aiming to produce. As early as the fifteenth century the *Boke of St Albans* had laid down what a good horse should be: [1]

> A goode hors sulde have XV propretees and condicions. Yt is to wit III of a man. III of a woman. III of a fox. III of an haare and III of an asse.
> Off a man boolde prowde and hardy
> Off a woman fayre brestid faire of here esy to lip uppon
> Off a fox a faire tayle short eirs with a goode trot
> Off an haare a grete eygh a dry hede and well reunyrig
> Off an asse a bigge chyne a flatte lege and goode bone.

The problem was how to produce such an animal.

Theory had little application, for until the late nineteenth century there was little applicable theory. Not till Mendel's work on heredity became better-known did racehorse breeders begin to act on any explicit theoretical basis. Even then there was a good deal of scepticism; for if breeding could be pursued scientifically why did the brothers and sisters of outstanding horses 'not seldom prove absolutely worthless for racing purposes'? [2] Nineteenth-century breeders did not fully comprehend what they were doing. They appreciated that qualities could be passed on from generation to generation but they did not understand why; nor did they realize that the female line could contribute as much to the development of the breed as could that of the stallion.

The first major attempt to put this right, and at the same time provide a scientific guide to racehorse breeding, was Bruce Lowe's 'figure system' devised in the 1890s. He died, tragically early, before the work was completed but his gospel was enthusiastically espoused by the influential racing writer, William Allison. [3] The basis of the system was that every single mare could be traced back to one of fifty mares in the original *Stud Books* of 1791–1814. Bruce Lowe ranked these fifty families according to the number of St Leger, Derby, and Oaks winners they had produced. Here, he declared, was a guide to breeding success: the higher a mare's family was ranked, the greater was the chance of producing a top-class racehorse. Unfortunately his conclusion was based on a false statistical premiss. The absolute number of classic winners was not a fair guide since there were more brood mares in the top families than in the lower ranked ones: so not only did these families produce most winners, they also produced most failures. If the proportionate number of major winners was taken then the 'figure system' fell by the wayside, for, whereas the top five families produced 6·7 winners per 100 brood mares, the other forty-five families, deemed inferior by Bruce Lowe, produced an average of 7·1.[4] There was no magic formula.[5] Certainly for the decade or so that it was in vogue the 'figure system' did positive harm to the British bloodstock industry by encouraging breeders to cast aside normal principles of breeding such as racecourse performance and immediate family record. On the other hand, and of importance for the future, Bruce Lowe's work drew attention to the vital role of the female line in bloodstock development.

During the inter-war years the work of Professor Robertson on heredity and chromosomes did much to convince breeders, particularly those who read the *Bloodstock Breeders Review*, that a scientific* approach to breeding, considering the potential contribution of both male and female, made sense.[6] However, there is still no guarantee. Racehorse breeding remains a matter of playing the averages: all that can be said is that a judicious union of selected strains of blood is likely to secure more good horses than will random, unscientific coupling. Nevertheless great horses have inflicted, and no doubt will continue to inflict, some wretched offspring on the racing world.

The professed *raison d'être* of racing was the improvement of British bloodstock. In 1844 a Select Committee reported that

---

* Much depended on what the breeder inferred by 'scientific'. Turf historians always point out Lord Wavertree's use of astrology. He was a very successful breeder so his results appear to have justified the means; but one wonders if horses deemed born under an unlucky star were ever given a fair chance. Moreover, he did not rely exclusively on astrology, for he believed that 'there is no royal road to success in breeding, either by the aid of Astrology, Botany, or Physiology: but these all have their uses applied in an intelligent manner'. Quoted in S. G. Galtrey: *Memoirs of a Racing Correspondent*, 1934, p. 138.

'without the stimulus which racing affords, it would be difficult if not impossible, to maintain that purity of blood and standard of excellence which have rendered the breed of English horses superior to that of any other country in the world'.[7]

Over 120 years later this view was echoed in the Duke of Norfolk's Committee on the Pattern of Racing:

> The thoroughbred is a British creation, and is part of our national heritage, which is worth preserving . . . the foreigner looks to the thoroughbred as a typically British creation . . . It is the duty of the Turf authorities to try to preserve the supremacy of the British thoroughbred as far as possible . . . and if they fail in this duty racing is liable to be debased to the level of roulette, and does not deserve to survive.[8]

Certainly the improvement of the thoroughbred led to improvements in the quality of other breeds, particularly light horses, but was racing necessary to attain this?[9] Of course, said the proponents of the turf, for how else could the relative merits of thoroughbreds be assessed adequately. Looks were insufficient for they did not demonstrate the possession of soundness, speed, and stamina: the race-course test alone did this.[10] In a way the argument that racing improved the breed was fallacious for racing performance in itself is not hereditary. Genetic inheritance merely set the limits; how near those limits were approached depended on many factors, not least the abilities of trainer and jockey. Much depended also on how race-course performance was measured. In considering the relative stud merits of stallions, much was made of the total prize-money won by their offspring. Yet in Britain place money was not taken into the reckoning when calculating the winnings (a hangover from the days when the second horse merely got its entry fee back), so the sire of the runner-up in the Derby, even if his offspring was only narrowly beaten, received no credit in the stallions' league table. A more important flaw in the argument was that the type of racehorse produced was dictated not by the needs of the country, or the light horse industry, but by the level of prize-money for different types of racing; and increasingly as the nineteenth century progressed the money was going for two-year-old and sprint racing, not the kind of events to encourage breeding for stamina and strength. How could horses running only five or six furlongs carrying a mere seven stones or so contribute to the improvement, or even the soundness, of hunters, hacks, or, of more importance, cavalry remounts? Lord Coventry, for one, was adamant that 'in England unsound horses are positively encouraged for in these days of light weights and short races, infirmities are but little thought of'.[11]

The first major attack on excessive two-year-old racing was mounted in 1870 by Sir Joseph Hawley, who suggested to his fellow Jockey Club members that there should be no two-year-old racing before 1 September each season; the object was to reduce the risk of breakdown to these immature animals.[12] He received some, but insufficient, support and two-year-old racing was banned only before 1 May and even this decision was rescinded within four years because of pressure exerted on behalf of the spring meetings at Lincoln and Northampton.[13] The development of the enclosed course and the ensuing competition for both spectators and horses further increased the prizemoney available to two-year-olds. By the late 1880s all the principal meetings had valuable events for such horses and at most meetings there was more money for sprints and two-year-old racing than for stamina-testing distance races. The response of owners and breeders was predictable: as can be seen in Table 11, two-year-olds as a proportion of all horses racing increased from about 20 per cent in 1849 to 40 per cent and over in the last decades of the century. Such a concentration on two-year-old racing and sprints was good neither for the turf nor for the bloodstock industry: immature horses were susceptible to breakdown, especially if they raced early in the season, and sprints hid stamina deficiencies. Eventually the Jockey Club took action. In 1899 severe curbs were placed on two-year-old racing: such races were limited to five furlongs till the Epsom Summer meeting and to not more than six furlongs till 1 September; two-year-old horses were not allowed to compete with three-year-olds until June and all handicap races with older horses were forbidden; and until 1 September there were to be no more than two two-year-old races on any racecard, thereafter the maximum was three. The Club also attempted to make other types of racing financially more attractive: at least half the guaranteed stakes were to go to races other than those for two-year-olds and at least half of that had to be for races of over one-and-a-half miles; and there had to be a minimum of two races of more than a mile, aggregating at least two-and-a-half miles, on every daily card.[14]

TABLE 11. PROPORTION OF TWO-YEAR-OLDS

	Number of two-year-olds which raced in that season	Number of horses which raced in that season	Percentage of two-year-olds
1849	265	1,315	20·2
1859	576	1,645	35·0
1869	842	2,534	33·2
1879	844	2,113	39·9
1889	986	2,131	46·3
1899	1,438	3,571	40·3

Source: *Racing Calendar*

For the wealthy members of racing's and society's leisured class, breeding was intimately associated with ownership: the ultimate test of their ability was to breed their own classic winner. Men such as these were breeding for the purposes of their own racing; only the poorer stock would be offered for sale. Most breeders, however, had an eye on the yearling sales: in the early 1870s nine-tenths of horses were bred for sale.[15] Mostly they came from farmers to whom breeding from one or two thoroughbred mares proved a useful income supplement. Others came from the studs of the breeding companies, mainly formed in imitation of Mr Blenkiron's famous and profitable Middle Park Stud which was begun in 1856.[16] Yet few big race winners emerged from the sale ring; privately bred stock continued to dominate racing's major events.[17] Even the Middle Park Stud, the most successful of any, produced only three horses of real class, *Hermit* and *Caractacus*, both Derby winners, and *Seesaw*, a Cambridgeshire victor.[18]

This failure of the companies to breed outstanding horses was probably because they were in breeding for the money and were not prepared to wait for results as were the private breeders to whom time and money were no object. Moreover, whereas the private breeder took pains to select the right stallions for his mares, the companies, in an effort to reduce unit costs, used the same stallion for all mares, whether or not they were psychologically and physiologically suited.[19] Eventually this failure to produce classic winners was reflected in the market and by the mid-1870s 'nearly all the undertakings on a great scale, except the Middle Park Stud, [had] proved eminently unprofitable'.[20] A second wave of stud companies built up in the late nineteenth century as increased prize-money and new owners, wealthy representatives of the industrial and business world, made their influence felt in the bloodstock market. Again they were relatively unsuccessful both in breeding great horses and in making money.[21] Competition for good stallions meant that high prices had to be paid which necessitated the charging of very high stud fees, explicitly to clients or implicitly for the companies' own mares. Neither were justified: generally insufficient clients were forthcoming at the price and insufficient attention had been given to the choice of mares for their yearlings to be guaranteed success in the sale ring.[22]

In seeking to assess whether or not breeders could make money, it is important to distinguish owners of mares from owners of stallions. The bulk of breeders, mostly farmers seeking additional income, fell in the former category.[23] Prior to 1914 it is difficult to make any positive comments because relevant data are too sparse. For the 1920s, however, some rough calculations can be made. If we take the typical stud fee as ranging somewhere between £25 and £50 (see Table 12) and the cost of raising a yearling, including costs attributable to the mare, as between £200 and £300,[24] then the average costs of bringing a horse to the yearling sales lay between £225 and £350. As the average prices fetched by yearlings at the Newmarket and Doncaster sales was £665, or even for the less fashionable horses (those selling for less than 1,000 guineas) £350, it would seem that money was to be made.[25] But we cannot be certain: the breeder still had to play the odds. A third of the mares that were covered failed to become pregnant.[26] The prime reason for this was the artificial breeding season imposed by the Jockey Club rule that all horses take their birthdates as from 1 January. This forced breeders to attempt to produce foals earlier in the year than nature would have dictated. In addition to the lower fertility rates caused by the Jockey Club regulation, there was a 20 per cent death rate among thoroughbred foals and a further wastage rate of 25 per cent before the yearling sales.[27]

What is certain is that few owners of stallions would make money out of breeding because relatively few stallions went to stud. Only stallions with good racing records were given any chance to be sires, whereas with mares even maidens on the race-course were allowed to lose that title at stud. In the 1930s, for example, there were just over 300 stallions being used for thoroughbred breeding but well over 6,000 mares being serviced.[28] However, if a stallion had proved his worth on the track then, providing he was both potent and amenable to stud duties, his owner virtually had a licence to print money. If the horse covered forty mares in a season, the traditionally accepted number, then in the 1840s an owner of even a good rather than an outstanding horse could expect to earn at least £1,000 per annum (on average £5,500 in 1970 purchasing power). No wonder John Bowes was disgruntled that his Derby-winning *Mundig* 'had not met his expectations as a stallion'.[29] As racing became more commercialized the rewards progressively became greater, especially for the best. By the 1890s a good stallion could be bringing in £2,000 (£14,000–£15,000 in 1970 prices) and an outstanding animal like *St Simon*, able to command 600 guineas a service, was earning in excess of £20,000 per annum.[30] Providing that his offspring looked all right and that some of them showed signs of racing ability, then a stud career of ten years or more could be expected.[31] In such a period *St Simon* earned his owner in excess of £200,000.

Clearly the government accepted that racing was important to the bloodstock industry. For most of the nineteenth century it subsidized racing by offering King's and later Queen's Plates of 100 sovereigns to winners of certain long-distance races in which heavy weights were carried. The object was to encourage

TABLE 12. STUD FEES*

	Number of stallions in sample	Percentage of stud fees (guineas)										
		25 or under	26–50	51–75	76–100	101–125	126–150	151–175	176–200	201–225	226–250	More than 250
1839	49	96	4	—	—	—	—	—	—	—	—	—
1850	41	95	5	—	—	—	—	—	—	—	—	—
1860	50	82	12	6	—	—	—	—	—	—	—	—
1869	58	74	22	2	2	—	—	—	—	—	—	—
1879	99	59	32	1	7	1	—	—	—	—	—	—
1889	111	62	23	5	6	1	1	1	—	—	1	—
1899	105	51	30	6	7	2	2	0	1	2	—	—
1909	321	79	12	—	5	—	0	—	0	2	—	1
1920	326	71	15	1	5	0	0	—	1	3	—	3
1929	223	56	18	—	11	—	0	—	4	2	—	11
1939	274	53	22	0	11	—	3	—	5	—	—	7

* Much more detailed information is available for the twentieth than for the nineteenth century. However, most of the higher priced stud fees before 1909 were traced. O signifies that some horses were offered but less than 0·5 per cent of the total.
Source: calculated from data in *Racing Calendar* and *Bloodstock Breeders Review*

the breeding of horses suitable for army remounts. When there was relatively little prize-money about these races may have been successful in attaining their aims, but later they were dismal failures. By the early 1860s walk-overs and fields of only two or three runners were frequent.[32] The issue was raised in Parliament, but it was decided to continue the Plates as it was believed that they had contributed to improving the breed; that they were important to the smaller meetings; and that relatively little money was involved.[33] Indeed the government took more from racing than it gave to the sport: the Plates cost the public purse 3,300 guineas but the tax on racehorses brought in 8,700 guineas.[34] The poor fields continued and in 1876 the number of Plates was reduced in order to increase the prize-money offered for the remainder. Owners and breeders, however, saw greater rewards in two-year-old sprinters than in long-distance stayers. In 1885 a further increase was made in the value of the Plates, again at the expense of the number of races, but eight races attracted only twenty-seven horses.[35] Eventually, following the Royal Commission on Horse Breeding in 1888, the Queen's Plates were abandoned, and the money used to give premiums to thoroughbred stallions suitable for getting 'half-bred' horses of general utility. Perhaps steeplechasing might have proved a good substitute in providing army remounts but no official encouragement was given.

Not till January 1916 did the government again involve the public purse in racing.[36] This was when Col. Hall Walker, M.P., (later Lord Wavertree) offered the nation a gift of his entire stud of valuable thoroughbred stock, providing that the government purchased his breeding establishment at Tully, County Kildare* and his training establishment at Russley Park, Wiltshire. After much hesitation, and under pressure from the Army Council who hoped that the high class thoroughbreds would be the foundation of the Army's light horse stock, the government agreed to pay £65,625 for the properties; the value of the bloodstock acquired gratis was £48,040.

---

* In 1922 the Irish provisional government claimed ownership of the Tully Stud. Eventually it was agreed that the British government would retain the stock and pay £21,300 in lieu of rent. In 1943 Tully was given up and the National Stud was transferred to England.

Much criticism was levied at the creation of a National Stud by the proponents of private enterprise. Some claimed that experience showed that government involvement inevitably led to mismanagement; others objected to what they suspected would be subsidized competition. However, the major organ of private breeders, the *Bloodstock Breeders Review*, gave the stud a cautious welcome:

We feel sure that if the stud is skilfully managed, is developed with a single eye to the purpose it has to serve, is

TABLE 13. FINANCIAL RECORD OF NATIONAL STUD (£)

	Sale of bloodstock	Service of mares	Change in value of stock	Other income *	Net profit (loss)
1919	14,563	2,919	+2,426	32,476	7,653
1920	23,962	3,638	+8,143	48,304	12,392
1921	30,099	2,763	+7,236	50,254	8,347
1922	17,508	4,844	−704	34,576	2,854
1923	13,443	4,998	−1,527	24,893	−3,396
1924	18,615	8,386	−2,013	34,748	3,679
1925	24,000	6,832	+1,744	42,181	9,420
1926	54,910	5,936	+17,592	89,740	39,053
1927	16,115	5,125	−5,320	27,407	−6,816
1928	36,678	10,158	−6,020	52,419	17,656
1929	43,002	7,970	−5,946	60,690	25,728
1930	16,468	5,745	−304	33,801	−701
1931	10,220	565	−11,037	9,047	−21,644
1932	8,060	47	−11,395	7,920	−15,278
1933	6,898	714	−3,927	10,217	−9,954
1934	14,309	84	−1,459	21,335	−1,287
1935	19,866	76	−3,875	23,683	3,414
1936	15,152	—	+3,174	28,695	6,059
1937	20,878	—	+1,473	28,337	10,248
1938	13,526	—	+7,441	23,005	1,942
1939	13,357	183	−2,448	10,217	251

* Includes sale of cattle and pigs from farm associated with the stud and share in stakes won by horses leased for racing purposes.

Source: *Report and Accounts of the National Stud*

not hampered by restrictions of the red tape order to which government departments are so partial, and is generously endowed with funds, it has a great and beneficial future.[37]

In fact the stud was run on strict commercial lines and, as is shown in Table 13, justified itself financially.

However, its economic success was attributable to the demands of racing rather than those of the military. Although the stud was established professedly on strategic considerations the army did not draw its horses directly from the stud; instead the stud concentrated on producing racing stock which it was presumed would somehow exert a beneficial influence on bloodstock in general. In any case by the mid-1920s it was clear, except to those military men with a pathological resistance to technological change, that the days of the cavalry were numbered. This did not deter the supporters of the National Stud. They changed tack by lessening their emphasis on the stud's importance in the improvement of army remounts and concentrating instead on the valuable contribution that the export of thoroughbreds made to the balance of payments, a factor not to be taken lightly in the economic climate of the inter-war years.

Gambling:
The Keystone of Racing]

Betting is the manure to which the enormous
crop of horse racing and racehorse breeding in this
and other countries is to a large extent due.

R. Black, *The Jockey Club and Its Founders* (1891)

To pretend that modern race meetings are held for
the purpose of improving the breed of horses
is mere hypocrisy. They do indirectly improve the
quality of horses, but races are held . . . in
reality to afford the world of betting men an opportunity of winning and losing millions.

S. Sidney, *The Book of the Horse* (1875)

The less custom the bookmaker has, the more
frantically he screams the odds; the
respectable men, with whom our *magnanimi juvenes*
gamble away their patrimony, these are
comparatively silent; so are vultures when their
beaks are in their prey.

'Horse-Racing', *Quarterly Review* (1885)

One for the Rich and
One for the Poor:
*The Law and Gambling**]*

Putting seven pounds extra weight on one's horse may seem a
short cut to losing money but not to Tregonwell Frampton,
keeper of the royal running horses at Newmarket through five
reigns, from Charles II to George I.[1] Frampton was a professional horseman, an astute match-maker who made a good
living from the horses he trained. On one famous occasion,
however, this wily character was outfoxed. He accepted a
challenge from the Yorkshire baronet, Sir William Strickland,
proud owner of *Merlin*, a racehorse acclaimed throughout the
northern counties. The match captured the imagination of the
racing world: the champion of the north versus a favourite of
the greatest southern trainer. *Merlin* was sent to Newmarket
for acclimatization under the care of a jockey-groom named
Hesletine. Acting on his master's instructions, one of Frampton's grooms approached Hesletine who allowed himself to be
'persuaded' to run a secret trial between the two horses in order
that Frampton would know whether or not to hedge his bets.
Although the trial was supposed to be at the weights assigned
for the match, Frampton's horse actually carried seven pounds
excess, so that when *Merlin* won by only a length Frampton felt
certain that the race was his and plunged heavily. So did others;
both those aware of the subterfuge and those merely confident
in Frampton's judgement. However, *Merlin* too had carried half
a stone too much in the trial: the trustworthy Hesletine had not
fallen to his southern tempters and had informed his employer
of the impending trial which Sir William decided to exploit to
his own advantage. The result of the race was a replica of the
trial; with both horses carrying seven pounds less than in their

* This chapter deals almost exclusively with betting on horse racing.

previous encounter, *Merlin* repeated his one-length victory. Many of those who had banked on Frampton and his horse now faced bankruptcy.

Such were the losses incurred and the volume of property that changed hands that it is alleged that Parliament was stimulated to pass an Act in 1710* to inhibit excessive betting. Part of the Act allowed anyone losing over £10 in a bet to take legal action to recover the money.† Presumably it was hoped that the risk of not being able to retain winnings would deter large-scale wagers. In fact the Act remained very much a dead letter, mainly because betting men were generally willing to honour their obligations.[2] If they were not, there was no need for them to invoke the Act as they could simply refuse to pay, there being no legal support for winners claiming their spoils. Only when losers paid out and then changed their minds could the 1710 Act be employed; but losers were reluctant to do this for other legislation passed in the same year had made it illegal to even make a bet of over £10, so to sue for the recovery of losses was to risk prosecution yourself.[3] Generally, however, the authorities turned a blind eye. Perhaps they shared the view of the Victorian commissioner of the City police who believed that it was 'decidedly an evil for a spirit of gambling to prevail among the industrious community' but had 'no desire to interfere with that class of persons who, having ample funds and leisure, choose so to dispose of their property'.[4]

The Act of 1710 had a further important clause which stipulated that anyone informing on transgressors could obtain up to three times the money staked. This legislation too was rarely, if ever, employed. The betting elite would never tell on each other. Some of them may have had a peculiar code of racing morality but honour would preclude informing; they might buy information from the stables but they would never sell evidence to the authorities. Small beer betters would be unattractive to informants for the possible monetary rewards

---

* It is not clear when the race was held. Some authorities suggest 1702 or 1703, others 1708 or 1709. Clearly the latter would lend credence to the imputed motivation for the legislation of 1710.

† In 1745 the limit was raised to £20 in twenty-four hours; this legislation was concerned more with gaming than with bets on horse races. *Select Committee on Betting Duty*, 1923, V, p. v.

were scarcely sufficient to offset the risk of physical assault. In any event the informant could not be involved in the bets himself, or he too could face prosecution: so far as racing was concerned this ruled out much of the potential informing simply because betting books were exceptionally private property.

In 1843, however, Charles Henry Russell, one of the individuals warned off during Lord George Bentinck's determined drive against defaulters,* managed to obtain some evidence and, on the advice of his solicitor brother, elected to take his revenge by raising upwards of thirty actions involving almost half a million pounds. All the actions were against men of substance, not because there was little point in suing the poor, but because Russell wanted more than money; he wanted revenge against the members of the Jockey Club, the institution responsible for his warning off, and generally these men were wealthy. Unfortunately for Russell they possessed influence as well as money. Although Lord Maidstone 'fancied that the action [was] not supportable' and reckoned that if he got into the witness box he would 'kick their arses oratorically', Lord George Bentinck had a better plan.[5] It is clear from his correspondence with John Bowes, the Durham race-horse owner, that Lord George organized a campaign to have the law changed retrospectively.[6] The first action was dismissed on a technicality and, before the second could be commenced, Lord George's friend and racing companion, the Duke of Richmond, chosen because he was a non-gambler and could thus appear to argue disinterestedly, introduced a Bill into Parliament to suspend all these *Qui Tam* actions (so-called because of the opening words of the Act) till a Select Committee had reported on the gaming laws, and Parliament had taken what measures it subsequently thought fit. His Bill was passed, though it faced hostile criticism from a few members who argued that a plea of ignorance of law should not be reason for Parliament to drape its protective mantle around the haughty shoulders of upper-class gamblers, several of whom were magistrates who would not have accepted similar pleas from poachers or beggars arraigned before the bench. The ensuing Select Committee recommended abolition of the law and Parliament agreed. Parliament had not intervened

* See above, p. 89.

in 1842 when the Act was implemented against a gaming house owner named Bond who had been forced to flee the country to avoid paying over £3,500. Perhaps French Hazard was viewed differently from horse racing, but one suspects that it was the social position of the defendants which determined Parliament's line of action. Clearly having friends in high places, or being there yourself, was a useful asset.[7]

Parliament also supported the Select Committee's recommendation of a change in the law respecting gambling debts. The law had been somewhat anomalous on this issue. At common law bets were recoverable unless they offended against public policy, decency, or morals: you could not insist on payment for wagers on whether Britain would declare war against France, on whether an unmarried woman was pregnant, or indeed on whether she was a woman at all. In addition, specific types of bets of over £10 on certain games and pastimes were not recoverable; these included horse racing and various forms of gaming. Thus if £100,000 was risked on a pigeon race or £50,000 wagered on the number of bewigged lawyers crossing Parliament Square it could be collected, but if the bet was on a horse race it could not, unless it was on an issue such as the colours that a jockey might wear.[8] This situation had led to a spate of defaulting on the turf with men making bets that they had no intention of paying should they lose. In 1836 the Hon. Berkeley Craven had shot himself rather than face the disgrace of not being able to settle at Tattersall's; too many other gamblers, however, were not of such mettle. Vincent Dowling, editor of *Bell's Life*, a leading sporting paper, recollected in his evidence to the Select Committee that 'some years back if a man was a defaulter he dare not show his face at Tattersall's or at any place where betting men were in the habit of meeting, but now defaulters obtrude themselves with blushing effrontery'.[9] The Duke of Richmond, chairman of the Select Committee, would have preferred to make all gambling debts enforceable at law. On maturer reflection, however, perhaps aided by Lord George Bentinck's campaign against defaulters and recent court decisions which gave race stewards the right to exclude defaulters from the stands and other enclosed areas, he and the other committee members left it to betters to keep their own house in order.[10] Self-protection lay in refusing to make wagers 'with men of whose honour and solvency they have not sufficient knowledge'.[11] The law thus washed its hands of gambling. Providing that there was no fraud, gambling was left alone; though only for a while.

At the time of the Select Committee the general public probably bet very infrequently on horse racing, perhaps only when actually attending a meeting, and even then their interest lay more with gaming than with betting on horses. The ensuing period, however, witnessed a rapid development of betting lists, aimed specifically at the urban working class. It is frequently alleged that the bookmaker, 'Leviathan' Davis originated these lists. In fact, though Davis popularized them and was the first to make a fortune out of them, they were actually originated by Messrs Drummond and Greville.[12] Whether this was a response to the publicity of the Select Committee or merely a chronological coincidence cannot be ascertained. These lists showed the odds at which a new breed of bookmakers were willing to take ready money bets, and the odds were laid not to the ten pounds that had worried Queen Anne's Parliament but to the sixpences and shillings of the working man and his unemployed brethren. Usually the lists were exhibited in public houses.* Bookmaker and publican made money together: few punters would make bets without buying a drink and too many drinks made for less caution in their wagers. By the early 1850s London had between 100 and 150 of these betting houses and there was a 'considerable number' in most provincial towns.[13]

When Lord Brougham had supported the Duke of Richmond's Gaming Actions Discontinuance Bill in 1844 he had argued that 'gambling had much more fatal consequences, and was far more injurious to morals among the inferior classes than among the superior classes'.[14] Observers from the superior classes felt that the activities of the betting houses bore out his views. Something had to be done, not only to protect the poor from themselves and from bookmakers who tempted them to bet beyond

---

* Possibly the lists stemmed from the sweepstakes which almost every public house organized at the time of the Derby and other major races. *Select Committee on Gaming*, 1844, VI, q.451; Sylvanus, *The Bye-Lanes and Downs of England*, 1850, p. 203.

their means, but also to protect employers and property owners from the nuisance of criminal activities engendered by such excessive betting.[15] Sir Alexander Cockburn, the Attorney General, had no doubts that

the mischief arising from the existence of these betting shops was perfectly notorious. Servants, apprentices, and working men, induced by the temptation of receiving a large sum for a small one, took their few shillings to these places, and the first effect of their losing was to tempt them to go on spending their money, in the hope of retrieving their losses, and for this purpose it not infrequently happened that they were driven into robbing their masters and employers.'[16]

He totally rejected the idea of controlling the betting houses by the use of licences; instead he introduced a Bill to suppress them completely. Both the upper and lower chambers accepted his case without comment and, from 1853, bookmakers operating in betting houses, exhibiting lists, or advertising a willingness to take bets were liable to a hundred pound fine and six months imprisonment.

Sir Alexander acknowledged that one difficulty he had encountered in promoting his legislation was his disinclination to interfere with 'that description of betting which had long existed at Tattersall's* and elsewhere in connexion with the great national sport of horse racing'. However, Tattersall's and its like escaped because there 'individuals bet with each other' whereas at the illegalized betting houses the exhibitor of the list had held himself 'ready to bet with all comers'.[17] This really was a fine distinction because many bookmakers did virtually the same thing at Tattersall's; however, betting there was restricted to members and there was the subtle difference that members also bet with each other and not always with bookmakers offering to bet round. The rich man's betting clubs were thus exempted from the legislation which aimed to close the poor man's betting houses. The working man was effectively

* Having found it impossible to keep gambling transactions out of his sales ring, the horse dealer, Richard Tattersall, had opened a separate subscription room at Hyde Park Corner in 1815. It quickly became the chief betting centre in Britain and Mondays at Knightsbridge had a regular place in the engagements of the sporting nobility and gentry. V. Orchard, *Tattersalls*, 1953, p. 161.

excluded from these clubs by the entrance fee and by the discretionary powers of the proprietors. Tattersall's had a two guinea entry fee in the 1840s, but Richard Tattersall often vetoed the entry of men who could afford this sum. He let people in only on a reference and deliberately put off small tradesmen as 'they are the sort of people who are ruined'. His policy meant that in 1844 his premises had only 350 subscribers. Small betters occasionally made bets at Tattersall's via intermediaries but this was usually at the time of major races not on a day-to-day basis.[18]

But the lower classes did not give up betting. Although betting houses flagrantly open to the street were shut down, others were often tolerated by the local authorities providing that no public nuisance was created. Nevertheless the appointment of a zealous magistrate or police official could always alter the situation. Some bookmakers set up pseudo-betting clubs which took only two minutes to join, but these working man's Tattersalls were a poor imitation of the real thing and when the police elected to take action they were quickly closed down.[19] The general effect of the 1853 Act was to shift the locus of working class betting from the public house into the street. Here the bookmaker felt safer. He could be prosecuted for offering to take bets, but arresting a street bookmaker was no easy task given the public's willingness to assist his escape. Some municipalities obtained special acts to enforce bye-laws relating to obstruction and in these towns loitering for the purposes of making or taking bets could result in a fine of a few pounds. Much depended on the attitude of the police constable and his superior: sometimes it was 'pass along'; at other times arrests were attempted.

Brian Harrison has claimed that the Victorian police failed completely to enforce the laws against betting.[20] Admittedly the authorities were lax in many localities, but the law was enforced sufficiently to produce a relocation of bookmaking activities. If the law was a nullity bookmakers would surely not have bothered to cross the Channel to establish offices on the continent.[21] When the law became prosecuted with increasing severity in the late 1860s no doubt others would have joined them, had it not been discovered that the 1853 Act did not apply to Scotland. Perhaps the legislation had gone through Parliament too quickly for this to be noticed: there had been no debate at all. The result was a migration of bookmakers north of the border, particularly to Glasgow which ironically did not even have a race-course! Within a few years the number of office bookmakers in Glasgow rose from nil to twenty-eight and unlucky Edinburgh possessed thirteen such offices. These betting houses were estimated to make around £20,000 per annum.[22]

Fittingly, it was a Glasgow M.P., Mr Anderson, who in 1874 brought in a Bill to remedy the situation.[23] First, the English law was altered so that all public offers of advice respecting horse races or offers to take bets were made illegal. Then the amended 1853 Act was extended to Scotland. The earlier Act had illegalized betting circulars, but case law had decided that it did not apply to those circulated in England which invited the public to bet in Scotland. Although made illegal by the 1873 Act, circulars continued to be distributed because the privacy of the post was not interfered with. It was hoped that setting the distributor at the mercy of the recipient would inhibit the circulation: it did not.[24] Even before 1873 many newspapers had refused to accept tipsters' advertisements, despite being offered double the scale rate of fees, but this was less true of the provincial press and sporting papers such as the *Sporting Life* or the *Sportsman* whose columns abounded with tipsters' offers. Rather hypocritically the editor of the latter paper warned his readers against tipsters who advertised in his journal. The press continued to flout the law and eventually in 1887 the case of *Cox* v. *Andrews* suggested that tipsters could advertise providing that they did not also act as commission agent or bookmaker.[25] The issue did not really affect working men who did not generally purchase tips as they were too expensive.[26]

Both Mr Anderson and Sir Henry Selwin-Ibbetson, speaking in support of the Bill on behalf of the government, stressed that they were not seeking class legislation. Anderson was adamant that he did not wish to deny the poor man his right to bet; he merely wanted to protect him from abuse and exploitation. Sir Henry wanted betting 'to be carried out on a system of honour, and not on such a system of deposit as now existed'. Neither overtly acknowledged that to bet on credit was an option scarcely open to the less well-off. In one way, however, the 1874 Act did help the lower-class gambler. With ready money postal betting under attack, his easiest outlets were the street book-makers who were generally far more honest men than the postal bookmakers, many of whom had no intention of paying out or when they did insisted on naming their own odds. The street bookmaker did not welsh – perhaps being known by his clients deterred him – and he paid starting price odds which the work-ing man could check in the racing press.

Betting on horses in Britain at the close of the nineteenth century had two distinct structures, both well organized but only one legal.[27] Legal betting took several forms and included both credit and ready money gambling. Betting clubs such as Tattersall's, the Albert, the Beaufort, and the Victoria Sporting Club generally operated on credit, accounts being settled after the races had been run. An initial ten guinea entrance fee plus a further six guineas per annum coupled with an election for membership kept out the less wealthy.[28] Lower-class imitations, such as the Cardiff Cocoa Club, with very small subscriptions were prosecuted out of existence.[29] Bookmakers could operate quite legally in offices providing that all betting was on credit via letter, telegram, or telephone; no-one was to resort there for the purpose of making bets. Again these facilities were the prerogative of the wealthy, or apparently wealthy: most office bookmakers made it plain that 'only gentlemen of standing need apply for an account'. Although the working man was not able to bet on credit, he still had two legal options open: he could send his ready money bets abroad or he could make them on the racecourse. When the Scottish betting houses had been closed the more respectable and honest bookmakers had moved their profitable businesses over the Channel.[30] Within Britain ready money betting could take place at any sporting event where spectators paid an entry fee and where the betting was on the event concerned,* though the bookmaker was not allowed to

---

* This freedom to bet at sports events raised problems of bribery and corruption of the participants. The police could do nothing to eject bookmakers even when requested to do so by the ground proprietors – not that the organizers always objected, as the provision of betting facilities often increased attendances and hence

monopolize any part of the course or stadium by giving it the character of an office by standing on a box or fixing a large umbrella in the ground.* An attempt was made by the Anti-Gambling League to use the 1853 and 1874 legislation against Tattersall's ring at Kempton Park, but on appeal the House of Lords decided that the racecourse company could not be restrained from permitting their enclosure to be used for betting purposes.[31] After this decision the police felt that they could not interfere at race meetings unless bookmakers occupied stands or were on that part of the course licensed for the sale of liquor.[32] Racecourses were left alone on the grounds that there were only a few days racing a year at any one place; that people had to make an effort to get there and were thus presumably interested in the sport; and that racing took place under licence from the Jockey Club who would clamp down on abuse.[33] However, the working man had neither the time nor the money to travel round the country from race meeting to race meeting. Such legal ready money betting by the working class was confined to the occasional local meeting. Credit being unavailable, the only other legal alternative was ready money betting with the continent, but this involved far more effort than passing bets in the street. When all is said and done, it was far more convenient for the working class to involve themselves in illegal street betting.

Such betting probably increased in the late nineteenth century. Although many observers of this phenomenon had axes to grind and were far from unprejudiced in their views, there is a good reason for supposing them to be correct: the same rise in working-class discretionary spending power which stimulated the development of mass, commercial entertainment surely also led to an increase in gambling. It can also be suggested that the addictive nature of gambling would produce a ratchet effect,

the gate money. *Select Committee on Betting*, 1901, V, qq.146, 164. Generally, apart from horse racing, such betting was small scale. *Select Committee on Betting*, 1902, V, q.1403.

* The racecard for the York meeting of 22 May 1901 pointed out that 'no betting in any way contrary to the law will be permitted, nor will any stools, boxes, standings, clogs, joints, umbrellas, colours, placards, or other devices be allowed anywhere upon the Stands or in the Enclosure'. Records of York Race Committee.

with such expenditure being maintained even when real incomes later declined. Many middle-class observers correlated the rise in gambling with increases in criminal activities, destruction of working-class morale, expansions in poverty and debt, and the augmentation of almost any other social evil that could be thought of.[34] At its extreme such views crystallized in a *Contemporary Review* article which declared that 'none can tell all the misery which the Turf has inflicted, because much of it has been born in sad silence. Many a sudden death might, if all were known, be attributed to losses on the Cesarewitch or some other great race – indeed the history of the turf is daily being written in letters of blood in the annals of the nineteenth century.'[35] Such attitudes led the Lord Bishop of Hereford to demand further legislation on the grounds that 'society had the right to protect itself against injurious social acts'.[36] The result was the appointment of a Select Committee to investigate the situation. It confirmed the economic and social evils associated with working-class gambling and elected to solve the problem by the imposition of severer penalties on those involved in such a noxious practice. The existing law had been difficult to enforce providing the street bookmaker had kept on the move and his clients approached him one at a time; one ingenious bookie collected bets while riding a bicycle and escaped the wrath of the law till the day he fell off![37] Moreover, people could not be arrested for obstruction under local bye-laws, merely summoned, which meant they could not be searched for betting slips. In any case the fines levied under these bye-laws were paltry relevant to the betting turnover. The Select Committee thought it ridiculous that one individual with twenty-five convictions in four years had paid only £137 8s. 0d. in fines.[38] Parliament agreed that the answer lay in tougher legislation and under the Street Betting Act of 1906* any person loitering for the purpose of taking or making bets could be fined £10 for the first offence, £20 for the second, and £50 or six months imprisonment on a third conviction. This law applied to any unenclosed ground (except if it was used for horse racing), to which the public had unrestricted access and to any enclosed area

---

* Legislation was first introduced into Parliament in 1903 but its passing was delayed because some of the clauses were deemed impractical.

if the persons in charge of it exhibited notices at the public entrances prohibiting betting.

Lord Durham, an ardent devotee of the turf, opposed the Bill not only because it transformed 'what is only a human instinct into a crime', but also because he saw it as class-biased legislation which 'would seriously interfere with the amusement of the working classes and intensify the monotony of their lives'. The Earl of Faversham agreed that 'it would enact one law for the rich and another for the poor. The rich man may carry on his betting within the enclosure, but the poor man doing the same outside the enclosure, would be liable to arrest by the police.'[39] Many working-class betters did make court appearances, but the general practice of the police was to pursue the bookmaker rather than his client. Even this was made difficult because of public sympathy to the pursued generated by the asymmetrical and class-prejudiced nature of the betting laws.[40] Why should betting be a criminal offence in most public places but a non-criminal act on the racecourse? And why was it legal to telephone or post a credit bet but illegal to pass a ready money stake in the street? Parliament may have decided what was a criminal activity but it failed to convince the public at large. Betting was either right or it was wrong, and if the law refused to recognize this then justice must be given a helping hand. Bookmakers thus could expect the public to warn them of approaching constabulary and even to obstruct the police should arrest seem imminent.

The bookmaker did not rely solely on the public for protection. Corruptible policemen were bribed; others were sympathetic and turned a blind eye; but the best safety device lay in the organization of street betting.[41] Instead of taking bets himself the bookmaker employed regular agents to do the job for him, paying them wages and regarding their fines as inevitable overheads. After a second conviction their services were dispensed with, though frequently the redundant agents were able to move to a new area where they were unknown to police or magistrates. Look-outs were paid to watch out for law officers; unlike the agents who did their best to keep out of court these lookouts attended regularly to familiarize themselves with the faces of the police and detectives.

Not all agents collected bets in the streets. Small shop-keepers and traders, especially in industrial areas, were paid commission for allowing their premises to function as illicit betting houses; often their earnings from betting exceeded those from their legitimate business. Some slips were passed in public houses but generally not with the permission of the land-lord who was genuinely frightened of losing his licence. Workers collected bets from their mates; if over a score of men worked together one of them was almost certain to be a book-maker's agent. Women who worked were encouraged to bet by such agents; those who remained at home were canvassed by other agents between nine and eleven before they went to meet their street clientele. Clearly the working man was not going to be prevented from betting by any legislation. A Select Com-mittee of 1923, set up to inquire into the feasibility of a betting duty, was frankly 'amazed at the extent to which betting existed' in Britain.[42] Moreover, although practically every class in Britain was involved in betting, the Committee noted that it was especially prevalent among clerks and artisans. The bulk of their gambling was with moderate stakes, but many small bets added up to some substantial sums and responding to the demand for betting facilities could prove a short cut to riches.[43] The organization of illegal betting was designed both to protect this income and enlarge it: as the 1923 Committee commented, 'the business is so lucrative . . . of such dimensions and so steadily increasing in volume that this organisation has been perfected to a marvellous degree'.[44]

Although this Committee acknowledged the futility of trying to suppress street betting, it was not prepared to legalize it. It felt that betting was 'a foolish occupation or habit. It [was] a pure luxury and a fitting subject matter for taxation unless there [were] strong reasons for allowing this luxury to escape.'[45] In the opinion of the Committee such reasons did exist. If taxed, street betting could have yielded a substantial sum, but it could only be taxed if it was made legal and this would sanction an activity which most of the Committee found morally offensive. Street betting, it was argued, had a de-moralizing effect on one's character; it was a serious moral danger to the rising generation, and it established disrespect for the law.[46] (The latter could, of course, have been avoided by legalizing the activity!) A minority report went further: betting was worse than foolish; it was a waste of economic resources; it destroyed the spirit essential to regular industry; it led to debt and the ruin of the home; and it encouraged crime and dishonesty.[47] So, although street betting could not be put down, it was nevertheless not to be tolerated. The betting tax was to apply only to racecourse and credit bookmakers; those who operated in the streets were to pay fines not taxes.

Another parliamentary investigation in the early 1930s adopted the same attitude.[48] Not till the Betting and Gaming Act of 1960 was the working man free to place ready money bets within Britain off the racecourse: and all this time those capable of obtaining credit could bet almost without restriction.* One law for the rich another for the poor is undoubtedly the theme of Britain's gambling legislation throughout most of the nineteenth and twentieth centuries.

* In the 1930s football pools became a major attraction for the working man's bets – over ten million people were involved each week – and these were operated on credit. It has been argued above that the working class could not obtain credit from bookmakers so why could he get it from the pools companies? The answer lies in the market situation: the pools companies operated oligopolistically; if the money was not sent the following week then all the pools firms agreed to blacklist the offender. This was a much easier task for the relatively few pools companies to organize than it would have been for the multitude of legal and illegal bookmakers. J. Hilton, *Rich Man Poor Man*, 1945, pp. 125–6.

14]   *Bookmakers and their*
Betters]

No-one knows the true extent of gambling in Britain. The official figure of £1,526 millions bet on dog and horse racing in 1972 is no doubt understated simply because such official betting is taxable.[1] Estimates relating to earlier periods are even more likely to fall short of actuality because of the illegal nature of so much gambling. All nineteenth-century estimates, and many twentieth-century ones, are totally unscientific, the products of fertile but prejudiced minds. The economist, A. R. Prest, a less biased calculator, has made estimates for the first two decades of the twentieth century, but he is the first to admit that they 'are little more than guesses', based as they are on extrapolation of inter-war data.[2] This data has been utilized more relevantly to its time period by Stone and Rowe in their study of consumption patterns between the wars. They estimate that betting on horses rose from £58·2 millions in 1920 to £119·2 millions in 1938. However, their basic data is sporadic – information on bookmakers' taxed incomes between 1919 and 1923 and on the revenue raised by the betting duty between 1926 and 1929 – and their calculations rest on some dubious assumptions regarding the extent of tax evasion and illegal betting.[3]

Notwithstanding the difficulties of quantification, few would gainsay that gambling is deep-rooted in British life, a passion pursued at all levels of society from the bingo hall to the bridge parlour but, of course, particularly associated with horse racing. Nevertheless, despite, or perhaps because of, its widespread nature, gambling has its critics. It is frequently attacked as an unnecessary evil, as an immoral and unproductive* activity seducing its protagonists into excessive involvement and

---

* The 'waste' of financial resources is generally exaggerated by a confusion between betting turnover and betting expenditure. The former is often financed out of winnings and involves much double counting because of hedging and laying-off. Technically there is no waste, for bookmakers provide a service and hence their output is recorded in the Gross National Product.

tempting them into crime and corruption. Admittedly the relatively tax-free* rewards of gambling have attracted a criminal element, and unquestionably addiction to the level of Dostoevsky's 'hero', masochistically losing his money, his outlays a prelude to orgasm, is a clear manifestation of sickness. Most gamblers, however, are far from being social deviants.

The overt rationale behind betting on horses is to make money, but, apart from those owners, trainers, and jockeys in the know, and a select group (though one hesitates to use the collectivity with such highly individualistic men) of professional gamblers, most backers cannot hope even for a regular income and certainly not for a fortune. Most of them do not have the means to finance the huge outlays which big winnings require.† Moreover, to be successful in the long run the backer needs to know form, genealogy, and probability theory; the bookmaker merely has to wait for the punters' mistakes. Over time most gamblers lose; they know they lose; yet they continue to bet. What they are seeking is the occasional windfall, the finance for a spree be it in the saloon or shopping centre. In effect, for them gambling is an inefficient but exciting alternative to saving. Indeed, excitement is perhaps the real motivation for most gamblers. Win or lose, gamblers obtain 'a considerable amount of excitement . . . [and] a diversion from the cares and worries of daily life'.[4] Gambling has an important temporal aspect, the delay between making a bet and knowing the result. The consequence is that on the racecourse 'some of the most exciting moments in a man's life . . . are those which pass between the time when the horses have flashed by the post and when the winner's number is hoisted', and off the course the tension can be prolonged till the press rush out the early editions.[5] For many, gambling is an opportunity to brighten their lives: taking a chance destroys routine be it the daily grind of the factory operative, the endless unrewarded tasks of the

* Betting duty (in force between 1926 and 1929 and since 1966), is generally passed on by bookmakers to winning clients, but gambling winnings have never been subject to the more onerous income tax. Bookmakers do pay income tax but there is a good deal of scope for tax avoidance and evasion.

† The recently introduced tote jackpots and their betting shop equivalents do pay long odds, but as yet no one has approached anywhere near the returns of a major football pools win.

housewife, or the boredom of the leisured classes, trapped by the obligations of the social calendar. Perhaps for the rich gambling is a form of conspicuous consumption, a way of putting their wealth in evidence. For the poor gambling is, in the words of George Orwell, 'the cheapest of luxuries': [6] an outlay of ten new pence or even less gives them a chance to beat the system; for a moment they are able to try and control their fate. And make no bones about it, betting on horses has more to do with skill than luck. Although they utilize imperfect data, most backers make a genuine mental effort, selecting their choices by a deliberate application of rational criteria. Finally, gambling also performs a social function in providing an open sesame to certain sub-cultures: 'What won the 3.30?' is a safe conversational gambit in any working-class bar. In such cultures the ability to pick winners brings social recognition, and the willingness to share knowledge, particularly the hot tip straight from the stable via dubious friends of friends, serves to cement relationships. Clearly gambling has its positive side and is not merely the irresponsible, anti-social activity, caricatured and condemned by the anti-gambling brigade.

At the fulcrum of betting lie the bookmakers. Although decried by critics and moralists as 'illiterate crooks' and 'parasitical excrescences', they have been very important to racing. [7] Admittedly many of them, particularly the street bookmakers, made no contribution to the welfare of the sport, but certainly the development of turf accountancy enabled owners, without whom there would be no racing, to bet more freely. No longer did they have to limit their wagers to fellow owners who, of course, might not be willing to accept the proffered bet. Bookmakers were willing to offer odds on all horses, and also long ante-post odds on yearlings and other unraced young horses, something no-one dare risk unless they were betting round. When bookmakers first made their appearance is unclear, though Admiral Rous dates it with naval precision at 1804. [8] Certainly there are reasons for supposing that it was around the end of the eighteenth century with owners becoming more money-minded and possibly being pressed by wartime inflation. There was an obvious attraction for a man to bet round. If sufficient bets were forthcoming, and if the odds were manipulated correctly, then he stood to win no matter which horse was first at the post. Some were extraordinarily successful. 'Leviathan' Davis, once a carpenter working for Messrs Cubitt – one of his jobs was on the subscription room at Newmarket – retired with a huge fortune; the inappropriately named Fred Swindell, the man who took rooms next to Admiral Rous so as to observe which owners visited the aristocratic handicapper, began his working life as an engine-cleaner in a Derby firearms factory, but left £146,000; and who would have imagined that Joe Pickersgill, a butcher's boy, would eventually parcel up nearly three-quarters of a million pounds out of horseflesh?[9] Such success stories can be culled from any racing history, but they were the exception rather than the rule. The profession was too easy to enter for there to be monopoly profits: the betting duty returns of the 1920s show that there were some 14,625 bookmakers in existence. Safe but unspectacular profits, however, were there for the taking: in the 1920s audited accounts of Ladbroke and Co. showed a gross profit (before expenses and bad debts) of 4·89 per cent on turnover.[10] But, despite their larger-than-life image, bookmakers are only human and many, perhaps too many, were tempted to seek higher rewards by not rounding their books and risking a disproportionate share of money on one or two horses. This was gambling rather than turf accounting. Those who were knowledgeable or lucky made money; the others did not.

In a speech at the opening of his new betting rooms in 1865, Richard Tattersall commented on the

> occupation of the bookmaker [which] was a few years since a
> very small business. It was confined to but few persons. Like
> the electric telegraph and the railways, it has sprung into
> importance only of late years, and has now passed from noblemen and gentlemen of high standing and means to persons of
> lower rank, who, years since, would as soon have thought of
> keeping a tame elephant as a book.[11]

Possibly he exaggerated the exclusive nature of early bookmaking, but there is no doubting that by the later nineteenth century men from humble backgrounds dominated all forms of bookmaking: certainly by this time gentlemen were rare enough in the profession to elicit specific comment when they did appear.[12] One nineteenth-century historian reckoned that 'every successful professional layer of odds began as a backer'.[13] In this he was probably correct: how else could a working man have amassed sufficient capital to enter the trade? Some budding bookmakers no doubt took advantages of money and knowledge acquired when working as commission agents. These were middle men who acted for owners not wishing to reveal possible stable *coups*, for outwardly respectable persons wishing to preserve their anonymity, and for anyone wishing to bet large sums without disturbing the market, as when John Bowes requested his commissioner to put the money on his Derby horse 'very quietly and by degrees'.[14]

Whatever their backgrounds, it did not matter if they were prompt in payment:

> the most shady antecedents, the vilest habits, a language compounded of the slang of thieves and the oaths of Lancashire miners, are compatible with a high position as a bookmaker, if prepared to bet on the largest scale against everything, and pay on the fixed settling day without quibbling evasions.[15]

Bookmaking morality may have stooped to stopping a horse, but it generally drew the line at refusing to pay a client.[16] Indeed, such was the reputation of men like Davis that his betting tickets were negotiable financial instruments.[17] Of course there were some welshers, but most bookmakers played straight: not to do so was to risk almost certain long run income for short term gain and the chance of a broken bone or two. A bookmaker's reputation, and hence his turnover, was based on his honesty and fair play: there was no profit without honour.

Their clients were less reliable. The old school of betters, typified by Squire Osbaldeston, was adamant that 'we must pay at Tattersall's, or our character and credit will be gone'.[18] In practice, however, the stigma of not settling died with Berkeley Craven who shot himself rather than default. By the mid-nineteenth century young bloods thought no more of bilking their bookmaker than their tailor and other traders. But it was not only young men about town who refused to pay: bad debts became an occupational hazard. In the early 1920s Ladbroke and Co., the largest firm of bookmakers in the country, estimated that 12½ per cent of the money owed them at that time would not be recoverable.[19] Gambling debts were not enforceable by law so there was little that the bookmakers could do. They were reluctant to post defaulters because any deterrent effect could well be outweighed by the loss of potential punters, who feared similar treatment should they ever not be able to settle in the short run, even if they had every intention of settling when they could.[20] The best solution lay in never opening dubious accounts, but, if the credit-worthiness of prospective betters was to be assessed adequately, bookmakers had to organize themselves so that inquiries were not wastefully duplicated and so that some bookmakers did not remain ignorant of information known to others. Yet bookmaking was a highly competitive trade in which great emphasis was placed on individual rather than collective action. It was the opponents of gambling who eventually brought the bookmakers together. In 1902, in anticipation of Parliamentary promotion of strong anti-gambling legislation, the *Sporting Life* helped found the National Sporting League to defend betting interests. The League soon became an association of off-course bookmakers and while retaining its initial lobbying function, added the further objectives of preventing fraud and malpractice and checking the credit rating of punters.[21] The Bookmakers' Protection Association developed in the inter-war years to serve the same function for on-course bookmakers.[22] Street bookmakers had no such organization: they protected themselves by refusing credit to anyone.

Clients who won too frequently were no problem: their accounts were simply closed. Far more worrying was the danger of being caught with too much to pay out. This was more a risk facing the street or office bookmaker, for on the course bets could be laid off relatively easily further up the rails. The off-course bookmaker, however, confronted two major difficulties. First, much of his betting was at starting price odds and these were determined by on-course betting, so a local favourite, if not also course favourite, could prove expensive should it come home. Secondly, telegrammed bets could arrive at his office after the race had been run, possibly leaving him with un-anticipated payments to make. George Drake, a bookmaker himself, once exploited the system to the full in the early twentieth century. When his horse *George Crag* ran at Sandown Park he put £300 on and his commissioners £50 each; all of them making a big show in doing so. The horse came nowhere. When it next ran, at Manchester, Drake was present but did not bet on it. The odds drifted out to 8–1. Meanwhile a small army of men on bicycles were busy sending off perhaps a hundred telegrams, all at the last minute so that the book-makers receiving them would not have time to lay them off and thus lower the starting price. Drake collected some £60,000.[23] This particular *coup* led to a bookmakers' ruling which limited the amount that could be staked via late-arriving telegrams. At least if bets arrived before the race there was the possibility of laying them off. In the nineteenth century leading office book-makers kept hansom cabs at the door so as to rush excessive last-minute money to other offices. Later the telephone simpli-fied the operation. Even better was the development of the London and Provincial Sporting News Agency, more com-monly known as the 'blower', which provided direct and instant communication with the racecourse. The agency was begun in 1921 by F. Trueman, with interests in course bookmaking, and A. L. Forster, a racing journalist. It became organized as a limited company in 1929, by which time it offered bookmakers not only laying-off facilities but also a complete racing informa-tion service.[24] Certainly bookmakers would no longer be fooled, as they were at the turn of the century, by the deceiver who sent three racing papers, a programme and later the results, of an imaginary meeting at Todmore. *Bell's Life* and the *Sporting Life* were gullible enough to fall for the ploy.[25] No-one knows how much this cost unsuspecting bookmakers.

In betting the odds favour the professional, be he bookmaker or backer. The betting market was, and still is, an imperfect one with knowledge not available equally to both sides; those who can afford to pay for information are at an advantage. Clearly the working man in the nineteenth century could not compete effectively in the pursuit of racing information. He could not employ a tout, most of whom could expect to earn more than the average industrial worker; nor could he regularly purchase tipsters' circulars, many of which cost upwards of ten shillings.[26] But help was at hand: for only a few pence the racing press threw wide the stable door.

The working man's racing paper was a development of the later nineteenth century. There were sporting journals before this but they catered for a clientele from a different social strata, horse racing being covered along with other pastimes of the leisured classes. In 1840 there were four such monthlies, the *Old Sporting Magazine*, the *New Sporting Magazine*, the *Sporting Review* and the *Sportsman*. As the latter cost 1s. 6d. and the others 2s. 6d. they were all beyond the pocket of the working man.[27] Two weekly sporting magazines, *Bell's Life* and the *Sunday Times* were cheaper, but they were clearly aimed above the heads of even the literate lower-class punter. Provincial newspapers would break out into a rash of turf articles at the time of their local meeting, but racing columns were not a regular feature. Really there was no racing press as such. However, coincident with the substantial rise in working class spending power came a rapid development of the popular racing press. By the late 1870s there were one daily, one bi-weekly, and six weekly papers wholly devoted to sporting, particularly racing matters; by the early 1890s three dailies and a dozen weeklies were exclusively devoted to horse-racing; and at the turn of the century twenty-five sporting papers were published in London alone.[28] In addition there were innumerable tipsters' circulars masquerading as newspapers, and racing sheets emerging at intervals on racing days from 10 a.m. onwards.[29] Clearly there was now more to read on racing and most of it was written for working men, an increasingly literate, numerate, and wealthy audience. Events in the inter-war years further increased the information available to the racing public. The great national dailies engaged in a struggle for readers and, as part of their campaign, the press barons turned to the sport of kings. A run of successful tipping was found to have a marked influence on circulation figures and the racing correspondent became a valued journalist, the best ones, often university graduates, earning up to £2,000 a year.³⁰ By the 1930s, the stay-at-home punter received an infinitely more informative and comprehensive racing service than he had sixty years before.

Initially the racing press faced strong opposition to its attempts to obtain information. Owners and trainers would have nothing to do with reporters so touts had to be utilized. This merely increased the hostility between owners and the press, for, though many owners were not averse to employing touts themselves, the information gleaned was for their ears alone, whereas that supplied to the papers was read by thousands and was thus bound to affect the odds.³¹ In an attempt to fool the touts, horses were sometimes disguised at their training, but it rarely worked; they knew the animals too well. Occasionally violence was resorted to by angry trainers but this frequently led to appearances before the bench: one such assault cost Tom Jennings a £200 fine.³² In the late 1870s, as the racing press got into its stride, a number of owners and trainers petitioned the Jockey Club stewards on the issue:

We desire to call their attention to a system of recent creation, but avowedly recognized now by certain cheap sporting papers, and which system, if persisted in, will become intolerable. Some few years ago were published what are called 'Training Reports' professing to give detailed information respecting the horses at the various training quarters in England, information, that is to say, as to their work, their health, their condition, their capabilities, and their private trials for public racing. This information is largely obtained from Servants, Boys, and even Apprentices, who attempted to violate their masters' secrets by an organized staff of paid Horse-watchers and Touts, who are, as we believe, maintained at the Chief Training establishments in the country, at the expense of those Papers.

The result of their efforts is to corrupt and demoralize, and in many cases to cause the discharge and ruin of servants and boys in training stables, and a further result is the entire destruction of confidence between the employer and the employed. It is against this system, so dishonourable in practice, so injurious to owners and trainers, and so entirely subversive to the morality and best interests of the Turf, that we earnestly protest, and we trust that the Jockey Club will take such immediate steps as may be desirable to arrest its future progress.[33]

The Club took its customary line and did nothing. But what could it have done? It was beyond its power to control the press or its contents. In any event, certainly by the turn of the century, touting was accepted by the stables as 'a necessary evil, so anxious are the public to know how the horses in the trainers' hands are progressing'.[34] After the First World War both racing journalism and racing journalists changed. Public school and university men were recruited into the profession; and increasingly leading owners and trainers found themselves dealing with men of their own rank.[35] Confidences were exchanged, and respected; because trust was not abused, other publishable information was freely given.[36] Indeed many trainers became part-time journalists, actually supplying training reports to the racing papers.[37]

The increased facilities offered to the press by the expansion of the railway and telegraph system played a vital role in updating the information available to the punters. In the early nineteenth century those awaiting results had to rely on homing pigeons, dogs trained to follow a trail, and the garrulous guards of the mail coaches. By the latter years of the century the Post Office had created a specialist corps of turf telegraphists; at the St Leger meeting of 1901, for example, eighty-two operators despatched 184,000 words of racing news direct from the Doncaster course.[38] No longer was it possible for bookmakers to exploit their clients, as some from Edinburgh used to do following the Derby and other important races. These astute fellows employed a rider to meet the English mail coach at Haddington where he would collect details of the winners, and then race to Auld Reekie with the news, exclusive, of course, to his employers. They would then widen the odds on losing horses to tempt unsuspecting backers to wager on them. It is satisfying to note that on one occasion two officers flying pigeons from Haddington hoisted the bookmakers with their own petard.[39]

Altruism was not the prime motive of the press: racing was

publicized because it sold papers. Nevertheless, in helping themselves the newspaper proprietors helped others, particularly the
working-class better. His chances of being defrauded by local
bookmakers was lessened by the widespread printing of starting
prices. Prior to this, bookmakers either offered their own odds
or alleged starting prices, neither of whose validity, working
men in their ignorance, could assess. Independent estimates of
starting prices began to be published in the 1850s and gradually
over the rest of the century they began to be given as general
practice by most papers, whether specialist racing journals or
not. Indeed, even anti-gambling newspaper proprietors were
forced to publish them – or risk falling circulation figures.[40] By
the end of the century the prices were determined, by universal
consent, by representatives of two leading racing papers, the
Sportsman and the *Sporting Life*. Most bookmakers saw the
wisdom of adopting these press-determined prices; it cut down
the chances of dispute and discontent, publicity about which
could prove detrimental in what was generally a highly competitive business. Leading bookmakers went so far as to allow
the press representatives to consult their books in order to
determine genuine starting prices – technically the odds available at starting to substantial money. In general the press made
the betting market less imperfect, less one-sided. With information on form and suggestions as to fancies, the working man's
betting became less akin to buying tickets in a lottery; at one
extreme, no more would ignorant punters put their money on
horses long deceased, dead certs only for the bookmakers.

15]   *The Totalizator*[1]]

The French took much from British racing: most of the rules, official colours for jockeys, and several semantic transfers, including *'le turf'*, *'le sweepstake'* and even *'le betting room'* at the headquarters of the French Jockey Club.[2] The insular British took little in return save the *pari-mutuel* (anglicized to the totalizator and popularized as the tote) and even this was a long time in coming; the French had one in operation in 1872 but it did not make its official appearance in Britain till 1929. A lower-class entrepreneur, named Andrew Anderson, had pedalled an elementary apparatus of his own around the racing circuit in the late nineteenth century, but he was soon stopped by a sentence of three months hard labour for breaking the law relating to gaming machines, the same law which, firmly applied, put paid to the roulette tables and gaming booths on many racecourses.[3]* So-called 'parry-pitches' did develop. Here the names of the backers were listed below their selections and the pool of bets, less entrepreneurial deductions, divided amongst the winners. However, their popularity waned as it became apparent that many bookmakers exploited their clients by writing in false names so as to reduce the pay-out.[4]

It was not that there was no interest in the idea of a tote. For many years prior to its adoption, influential racing men had considered that the coming of the tote could give racing a much-needed shot in the arm by diverting money from the book-makers' satchels into the coffers of racing itself. Since the tote would deduct a percentage from the total pool of bets before distributing rewards to the winning backers, it seemed certain to make money, providing it was run reasonably efficiently. This money could then be used for the benefit of racing and race-goers. The problem lay in convincing Parliament that the betting law should be changed to allow the tote to function. Before the First World War there was little chance of this happening; Parliamentary opinion, as reflected in both committee reports and actual legislation, was concerned more with restrict-

* See above, pp. 140–1.

ing betting facilities than extending them. * In 1916 a petition†
signed by many leading owners, trainers, and breeders in favour
of the tote was presented to the Jockey Club stewards who
received it sympathetically, but decided that, as it was wartime
when the very existence of racing hung in the balance, it was
both inappropriate and inopportune to approach the government
on the issue.[5] Interest in the tote increased in the 1920s when
many participants, particularly owners and breeders, became
seriously concerned about the financial rewards of racing.
Gambling thrived on horse racing but gave nothing to the sport;
increasingly owners and others began to argue that bookmakers
should make a financial contribution to racing, or that the tote
should be set up, or, preferably, both.

The imposition of the betting duty in 1926 was the green
light to the advocates of the tote; if the government now saw fit
to dip its bucket into the ever-flowing stream of gambling, why
should not racing, the very basis of the gambling, do the same?
Representatives of both the Jockey Club and the National Hunt
Committee approached Winston Churchill, who, as Chancellor
of the Exchequer, had been responsible for introducing the duty.
He made it clear that while the government was not prepared to
take the initiative, it would be prepared to allocate parliamentary time should any private member's bill aiming to
legalize tote betting reach the stage of a second reading. Perhaps
the government did not expect matters to go this far, for the
odds against drawing a favourable place in the ballot for such
bills were those of the outsider. However, several M.P.s
expressed their willingness to sponsor a bill (to be prepared by
the Jockey Club's legal advisers), should they be lucky. One of
them, Major Ralph Glyn, Conservative member for Abingdon
and skilled parliamentarian, drew fifth place, so the battle was
on. And what a struggle it was. Those with moral objections to
betting united with the supporters of the bookmakers to oppose
the Bill; a second reading was gained only by a short head; and
in committee every line was contested. Nonetheless, the Bill

* See Chapter 13.

† Actually it was a substitute petition compiled from the collective memory of
the organizers. The original mysteriously disappeared when Mr Kennedy, the
breeder of *Tetrach*, took it to a Curragh meeting. S. Galtrey, *Memoirs of a Racing
Journalist*, 1934, pp. 24–5.

went through, though not in its original form for less than two lines of the first draft remained intact. Flesh and blood had been added to the skeletal outline to create a new body: the opponents of the tote had refused to allow the Jockey Club to take responsibility for its operations and had insisted on a statutory authority, the Racecourse Betting Control Board (R.B.C.B.), being established with five of its twelve members appointed by the government.* The R.B.C.B. was given power to authorize tote operations under licence but it elected to secure economies of scale, administration, and experience by organizing most operations itself.

Much was expected of the tote. Perhaps too much, for many saw it as the panacea to each and every racing ill. The views of breeders and owners were epitomized in a speech by Lord Derby, a non-betting owner:

> The race horse breeding industry is entirely dependent on racing. Do away with racing and bloodstock is for ever destroyed in England. Racing is my greatest amusement, and one that is not getting any cheaper. In England every racehorse has to earn £650 before it pays its expenses. In France you have to earn only £180. In my opinion the difference is always entirely attributable to the presence of the Totalizator.[6]

Others looked forward to 'the undoubted improvement that would be effected on our racecourses';[7] racegoers stood to gain from both better facilities and cheaper admissions; certainly punters would not be welshed by the tote; and ladies might be encouraged to bet if they could deal with anonymous totalizator clerks rather than with raucous, flamboyant bookmakers.

Everything, of course, depended upon the tote making money. The R.B.C.B. was convinced that this was almost inevitable; indeed they anticipated a 'substantial surplus' available for distribution after a full year's operations. Alas, they

---

* The make-up of the Board was a chairman and another member appointed by the Home Secretary, three members appointed by the Jockey Club, two by the National Hunt Committee, and one each by the Secretary of State for Scotland, the Minister of Agriculture and Fisheries, the Chancellor of the Exchequer, the Racecourse Association, and the Committee of Tattersall's.

were wrong: as is shown in Table 14, there was no surplus till 1933 and this was less than £10,000. The tote had been caught in the pincers of excessive expenditure and over-estimated revenue. The decentralized nature of British racing led to high unit fixed costs, for whereas Longchamps had thirty days racing each year, the typical British course had only between six and ten days. It was hoped that a way round this would be to have regional pools of transportable equipment, but in practice this proved impractical and uneconomic. Verdicts on the tote's early operations ran the gamut from 'fiasco' to 'encouraging'. Untried

TABLE 14. FINANCIAL RECORD OF THE TOTE

	Racing days in operation	Turnover £	Retained by R.B.C.B. £	Grants and donations £
1929	76	534,281	40,861	—
1930	456	3,259,502	261,324	—
1931	583	3,886,650	371,898	—
1932	595	4,017,578	362,142	—
1933	572	4,411,668	375,573	9,841
1934	586	5,135,972	463,717	27,872
1935	592	6,149,253	564,216	107,565
1936	552	7,367,925	668,897	120,354
1937	558	7,903,721	722,517	151,500
1938	569	9,093,482	758,515	177,550

Source: calculated from *Reports and Accounts of R.B.C.B.*

machines were in use, or rather, were in use where delivery dates had not proved unduly optimistic. British rights to the proven equipment, the Julius apparatus, had been purchased by a speculative enterprise, Totalisators Limited, in anticipation of the tote becoming legal; but the R.B.C.B. had refused to agree to its demands for a high fee plus royalties and had turned to other, less demanding but also less reliable, suppliers. Nevertheless, despite the setbacks, the tote proved popular with the racing public; it accepted two shilling stakes and place betting, something that most bookmakers, save those in the cheapest enclosure, were unwilling to do. Unfortunately the early years of the tote coincided with a severe financial crisis which was 'felt with some severity amongst those classes who are habitual racegoers and amongst a larger class, who, in more prosperous times, would probably have attended race meetings in the area where they live'.[8] When the economy picked up, so did the tote.

In Britain, unlike elsewhere, the tote did not have a monopoly of on-course betting; nor was it always competing on equal terms with the bookmakers. Admittedly, the Act establishing the tote gave course executives the right to charge bookmakers five times the normal admission fee, but the bookies were still able to set up in front of the stands, whereas most totes were located less advantageously to the rear because of the need for buildings.* And, no matter where located, the tote clearly found it difficult to attract the big gambler. The analysis of tote ticket sales shown in Table 15 demonstrates that big money was not forthcoming. The large-scale backer had no desire to carry huge sums of money with him – the post-war race-course ruffianism was not that long ago – but, whereas the bookmakers would extend him credit, the tote allowed only cash betting. One attempt to ease this obstacle to big money bets was the institution of the chit system whereby books of vouchers (from £1 to £100) could be purchased at most major banks; if they were stolen the thief could not benefit as they were non-negotiable and any winnings would be credited to the bank account of the original owner. But perhaps the greatest deterrent to big money was the lack of opportunity to negotiate the odds; all tote bets were as at starting, whereas on-course bookmakers offered odds at the time the bet was struck. Because of this, even owners, men who hoped to benefit from the tote surplus, preferred to use the bookmaker for their larger bets. Indeed Lord Hamilton of Dalzell, a prime mover in getting the tote established, declared that he had no wish of a tote monopoly for 'without them [bookmakers] owners of horses would be deprived of the chance they have of backing their horses at a good price, one of the few advantages they get in return for the money they put into the game. Their disappearance would be a misfortune.'[9] Aggravating the situation was the fact that the tote declared its dividend

* This is discussed in detail in the *Second Report and Accounts of the R.B.C.B.*, 1930–31, XVII.

to a two shilling unit which inevitably increased administrative costs and affected the competitive position *vis-à-vis* the book-makers where favourites were concerned. Undoubtedly the tote was better for outsiders as here bookmakers tended to offer nominal but limited odds, whereas the tote backer faced no such limit. Big money, however followed favourites, not outsiders.

TABLE 15. TOTE SALES (PERCENTAGES)

	2s.	10s.	£1	£5	£10	Doubles, trebles and special pools*	On-course (chits and T.I.L.)	Off-course
1930	25·2	23·0	31·9*	—	1·5	3·3	2·2	12·9
1931	24·1	21·9	22·0	0·2	0·6	5·7	12·1	13·2
1932	23·9	20·1	17·7	—	0·4	4·6	14·6	18·9
1933	20·9	16·9	15·0	—	0·3	5·3	17·1	24·6
1934	19·7	15·6	14·3	—	0·3	8·6	15·5	25·1
1935	18·6	14·4	13·0	—	0·3	10·0	15·9	27·8
1936	18·7	14·4	13·2	—	2·1†	7·6	15·2	28·7
1937	18·9	14·5	13·5	2·2	0·4	6·1	15·6	28·8
1938	19·4	12·5	13·4	2·6	0·4	5·5	14·9	31·5
1939	20·1	12·5	12·7	2·4	0·4	4·9	13·2	33·9

* Usually to a 10s. stake.
† Includes £5 units.
Source: calculated from *Reports and Accounts of R.B.C.B.*

The tote was relatively slow to tap off-course betting. It could not open offices because it operated on a cash not a credit basis and off-course cash betting was illegal. From the beginning, however, an arrangement was made with the London and Provincial News Agency Limited to pay them a commission for all bets they laid off to the tote via the chit system. Then, during 1931, a deal was concluded with the Guardian Pari-Mutuel Limited (later Tote Investors Limited (T.I.L.)), a private enterprise venture organized principally by Lord Milford, a well-known owner and breeder, for credit bets concluded in T.I.L. offices to be transferred via chits to the tote, again in return for a commission. After protests from the National Sporting League, the off-course bookmakers association, the courts decided in March 1934 (appeal dismissed October 1934), that it was legal for such commission to be paid. By the late 1930s, as is shown in Table 16, T.I.L. was responsible for over 40 per cent of tote turnover and about two-thirds of this came from off the course. Nevertheless, off-course betting on the tote totalled only two and a half million pounds in 1938, whereas even *legal* off-course betting with bookmakers has been estimated at eighty-five millions.[10]

TABLE 16. MONEY TRANSMITTED BY T.I.L.
TO R.B.C.B. POOLS

	Off-course £	On-course £	Total £	Percentage of total tote turnover
1930	100,994	—	100,994	3·1
1931	352,431	324,764	677,195	17·4
1932	646,225	422,696	1,068,921	26·0
1933	959,997	590,807	1,550,804	35·1
1934	1,131,809	739,763	1,871,572	36·4
1935	1,408,152	956,392	2,364,544	38·5
1936	1,820,923	1,112,543	2,933,466	39·8
1937	1,968,290	1,221,047	3,189,337	40·4
1938	2,529,072	1,318,918	3,847,990	42·3

There were many claims for the funds that did become available for distribution. The money was disbursed under three basic heads: direct aid to racing, assistance to horse breeding (including veterinary science and education), and grants to charities associated with racing. In 1935 aid to horse breeding was classed as charity when a charitable trust was formed for tax avoidance purposes. Grants to assist horse breeding had almost suffered a legal setback when it had been suggested that direct aid to veterinary science was not within the powers of the R.B.C.B. as laid down in the original Act, but a sanctioning clause was tagged on to the Betting and Lotteries Act of 1934.

At least one authority maintains that these grants saved light horse breeding in Britain.[11] There was no debate over offering assistance to owners by increasing prize-money and subsidizing transport costs, or to the policy of underwriting losses of racecourses who reduced admission charges. Where controversy did rage was on the question of financing the improvement of racetracks or racecourse amenities, for basically this was subsidizing shareholders in the racing companies by improving their capital assets. In France the *pari-mutuel* was not allowed to assist racecourses which were run for private profit; but in France such courses were the exception whereas in Britain they were the rule. Eventually the R.B.C.B. decided that the benefits that the improvements offered to owners and the race-going public were the prime consideration. By 1938 over £158,000 was being distributed for the benefit of racing. At the time it may have seemed too little too late, but it set a precedent for further state intervention into both the gambling and racing industries, an intervention which has enabled racing to survive.*

* See Chapter 16.

Epilogue]

It is nonsense to argue, as some do, that business
and sport cannot mix. In another age racing
may have been purely a sport. But for a long time it
has been an industry, and as an industry it has
declined because the administrators of racing have
had neither the business experience to run it
effectively, or apparently the will or even the desire
to bring in that experience for the benefit of
racing. You now see before you the spectacle of a
once proud sport reduced to utter dependence
on public money.

Mr David Robinson, Gimcrack Dinner Speech, 1969

16] *A Declining Industry?*
The Benson Report and
Beyond]

For some owners, perhaps for most, and certainly for the
majority of spectators, racing still performs a social function,
but it is not the social institution that it was in the eighteenth
and early nineteenth centuries. It is an entertainment industry in
competition with many others and as such it is economic considerations that are to the fore: unless it can provide a level of
rewards sufficient both to maintain the interest of existing
participants and to attract new entrants, then it cannot hope to
survive. In the 1960s many observers felt that British racing
was on such an inclined plane to oblivion. Their suspicions were
reinforced in 1968 by the publication of the Benson Report, an
internal Jockey Club enquiry, which declared that a number of
trends 'in a greater or lesser degree indicate a decline in the
racing industry in this country in recent years'.[1]

Finance, especially prize money, was at the root of the problem. The level of prizes was insufficient to enable or encourage
British owners and breeders to compete with foreign buyers for
the best bloodstock. Thus the general standard of British racing
stock declined and with it the quality of British racing. In turn
this lessened the public appeal of the sport. It was a vicious
circle; for it was the paying spectator who supplied the basis of
the prize fund. Average daily attendances fell from 11,194 in
1953 to 7,530 in 1967 and thus, despite increased admission
charges, and partly because of them, the racing fund failed to
keep pace with racing's needs. Marginal racegoers had been
seduced away by the temptations of the betting shop and live
television coverage. Betting shops were legalized in 1960;
by 1967 there were 15,535 in operation attracting their clientele
by their convenience, cheapness (at least as regards admission)

and commentaries. Live television coverage had begun much earlier, in 1946, but had really developed with the coming of commercial television: in 1955 races at 28 meetings were televised; by 1967 179 meetings were being covered. Armchair racing men missed the atmosphere of the racecourse, but also its entry charges, inadequate facilities, and travelling costs while obtaining a better view of the horses and free, expert, up-to-the-minute, advice. Some attempts were made to arrest the decline in course attendances by offering more evening races, but, although relatively more profitable than weekday afternoon racing, about two-thirds of the meetings still ran at a loss. Sunday racing might have helped, but not without a change in the law which prohibited Sunday betting; and there was little chance of that occurring.

If the public was less willing to pay at the gate then alternative sources of funds were necessary. The obvious candidate was the betting sector. In 1943 the Ilchester Committee had argued that it was to the totalizator that racing must look 'for an important source of augmentation of the financial assistance in the future'.[2] But in fact only 2 per cent of the tote turnover was returned to racing compared to between 3 and $7\frac{1}{2}$ per cent in other countries; and in total this was even less significant than abroad where the tote often had a monopoly of legal betting. In Britain the tote handled only a small proportion of betting due to a combination of a too high minimum stake and insufficient off-course facilities. Once betting shops were legalized the disparity was even greater. Clearly there was a case for asking bookmakers to contribute financially to racing.

When the betting shops were made legal the government decided to compensate racecourses for the expected fall in attendances by the creation of the Horserace Betting Levy Board. This body was assigned the task of assessing and collecting a levy on bookmakers and the tote, and utilizing the funds to promote technical services, modernize racecourses, improve veterinary science, and contribute to prize money. Nevertheless, up to the time of the Benson Report the levy had seemed to fall disproportionately upon the tote – 32 per cent on what was less than 5 per cent of total betting turnover.

Despite receiving this assistance, and also contributions

from commercial sponsors (in 1967 equal to 8 per cent of the prize money offered), taken as a whole British racecourses did not earn a reasonable rate of return on the assets employed in their enterprise. Information supplied by thirty courses suggested that in 1967 the rate of return on their capital was around 1·4 per cent, a ridiculously low level. Such returns did not attract new capital, so the Levy Board had an important role to play if courses were to be modernized: indeed the bulk of the three million pounds spent on modernization schemes between 1963 and 1966 came from that source.

It is, however, arguable that some of the fault for the low rates of return lay in the inefficiency of the racing industry itself. The Ilchester Committee had considered that economies could have been achieved by concentrating racing on a reduced number of racecourses and also by improving the quality of racecourse management.[3] Twenty-five years later, when the Benson Committee reported, little progress had been made. Racecourse management at some courses still left much to be desired, though this was partly attributable to the financial problems of an industry which could not offer sufficient remuneration to attract talented men. A few racecourses had become defunct, but because of economic pressures not Jockey Club edict, for the Club was extremely reluctant to incur local resentment by withdrawing fixtures from any course. Instead of concentrating racing on fewer courses, many executives endeavoured to cover their fixed costs by increasing their volume of racing, thus putting severe strain on the limited financial and manpower resources of both themselves and the racing industry. The Ilchester Committee had also argued that it would be beneficial to racing if more courses were run on a non-dividend basis so that all surplus revenue could be ploughed back into racing.[4] Here, more had been achieved: when Ilchester reported there were five such racecourses; by the time of Benson there were nineteen.

In 1967 24 per cent of prize-money came from the owners themselves; without that contribution racecourses would have been in even greater financial difficulties. But asking owners to race for their own money did not solve the problems of the industry as a whole. The real value of prize-money in 1967 was only 52 per cent of that of 1937 and on average owners could only hope to recoup around 40 per cent of the costs of keeping, training and racing their horses. Thus, even without considering the initial capital outlay, it cost most owners almost £4,000 a year to keep a horse. Although most people interested in owning racehorses were willing, as they always had been, to pay for their enjoyment, the pressures of inflation and taxation were limiting the amount of money available for such spending.

In turn the financial problems of owners reacted on the breeders, for British owners could not offer the breeder a price sufficient to cover the costs of raising yearlings; in 1967 the average shortfall was 270 guineas. Foreign owners, however, could offer reasonable prices mainly because their prize-money was higher than that in Britain: in 1966 the average British prize was £824 compared with £2,170 in France, with a smaller proportion coming from the owners than it did in Britain.* Without the foreign demand, the British bloodstock industry could not have remained viable, but increasingly the exports were of the better class horses and this was sowing the seeds of possible disaster.† As the Benson Committee saw it, 'the horses bred in Britain will in future tend to be of indifferent quality; the standard of racing will deteriorate; Britain's position in the racing world will steadily decline and public interest will diminish'.[5]

Fortunately British racing is still with us. Enterprising race-course managers, more of them full-time appointees than before, have stemmed the rate of decline in attendances by offering improved amenities, by catering for the family, by encouraging parties of racegoers, and by greater showmanship as exhibited in the development and expansion of ladies' races. Nevertheless this was hardly sufficient to solve racing's financial problems. So how can we explain the remarkable rise in prize money from £3,801,000 in 1967 to £6,112,000 by 1972?‡ Owners marginally increased their percentage from 28 to 29, but this

---

* These figures include national hunt racing.

† It could be argued that the rot had set in some years earlier when the Aga Khan exported *Blenheim*, *Mahmoud* and *Bahram* to the United States.

‡ For both flat and national hunt racing.

was probably a response to the increased rewards offered.
Commercial sponsors contributed 13 per cent of the total prize
money: indeed the Jockey Club, via the Racing Information
Bureau, has made a real effort to attract sponsors by publicizing
the value of sponsorship as an advertising medium. In contrast
the proportion of the prize money coming from the racecourses
dropped from 45 per cent to 26 per cent, primarily because of
the great increase in the prize money contributed by the Levy
Board, some 32 per cent of the total.

Unquestionably it is the Levy Board that has saved racing.
In 1972–3 the levy raised over £6·2 million as compared to the
first levy in 1962–63 which obtained £1·8 million; and some
97 per cent of it came from the bookmaker, a much fairer reflection of the betting scene than the earlier disproportionate
exactions made on the tote. Since the inception of the levy to
1973 some £34 million has been spent in bringing 'nearly all
racecourses back to solvency':[6] of this, £15·3 million has gone
in assistance to racehorse owners and £9·5 million in direct
assistance to racecourses. Via its wholly-owned subsidiary, the
Metropolitan and Country Racecourse Management and Hold-
ings Ltd, the Levy Board has actually acquired control of the
Epsom Grand Stand Association, and also of Sandown and
Kempton Park racecourses, ironically the pioneers of the
enclosed, gate-money meeting.

The growing financial involvement of the Levy Board has
weakened the dominance of the Jockey Club. In the case of the
Racecourse Betting Control Board, racecourses used to submit
claims to the Jockey Club, which then forwarded those it agreed
with to the Control Board which, provided the claims were
within the general purposes of the legislation, normally
accepted them. However, the chairmen of the Levy Board
refused to accept this as precedent and fought for the right to
allocate funds as they saw fit. They have used their financial
patronage to influence decisions about the reorganization of the
fixture list, allocation of prize money, and improvement of
safety measures; though the Jockey Club retains its traditional
sole responsibility on matters affecting the conduct of racing
such as rules, licences and discipline.

Racing has been rescued by the acknowledgement that

Britain is more a nation of punters than of racegoers. Whereas the Ilchester Committee refused 'to encourage the stay-at-home backer – a person who contributes nothing to the business of racing nor to its finance',[7] The Levy Board has insisted on the continuation of mid-week meetings, many of them not directly viable, simply because they provided a daily betting market, so vital if funds were to be raised by a levy on betting turnover. The reason has not been merely to provide a gambling mechanism: the ultimate objective was the preservation and improvement of the racing industry.

Certainly the racing scene has changed since the eighteenth century when paternalistic race committees provided races for the free enjoyment of the local community. Now the gambling activity of the betting population, racegoers or not, helps provide employment for professional racecourse executives. Private philanthropy has given way to public money.

Notes]

INTRODUCTION

1. *Badminton Magazine*, vol. 3, October 1896, p. 428.
2. L. H. Curzon, 'The Horse as an Instrument of Gambling', *Contemporary Review*, vol. 30, August 1877, p. 391.

PROMOTION: THE DEVELOPMENT OF RACING

1. RACING BEFORE 1840

1. H. Reeve (ed.), *The Greville Memoirs*, vol. 2, 1874 (5 June 1831).
2. Quoted in J. C. Whyte, *History of the British Turf*, 1840, p. xviii.
3. J. Ford, *Prizefighting*, 1971, pp. 89–90.
4. See e.g. A. J. Kettle, 'Lichfield Races', *Transactions of the Lichfield and South Staffordshire Archaeological and History Society*, vol. 6, 1964–1965. The surveys of racing in the *Victoria County Histories* also bring out this point.
5. E. P. Thompson, 'Time, Work-Discipline, and Industrial Capitalism', *Past and Present*, vol. 38, December 1967, p. 73. See also K. Thomas, 'Work and Leisure in Pre-Industrial Society', *Past and Present*, vol. 29, December 1964.
6. H. Perkin, *The Age of the Railway*, 1971, p. 210.
7. M. W. Flinn, 'Trends in Real Wages, 1750–1850', *Economic History Review*, vol. 27, no. 3, August 1974, pp. 395–411.
8. *Select Committee on Gaming*, 1844, VI, q. 1031.
9. J. C. Whyte, *History of the British Turf*, 1840, p. 322.
10. *Select Committee on Gaming*, 1844, VI, q. 1209.
11. J. Ford, *Cricket*, 1972, p. 41; J. Ford, *Prizefighting*, 1971, p. 96. See also the *Victoria County Histories*.
12. See e.g. *Select Committee on Gaming*, 1844, VI, qq. 1267–70.
13. *ibid.*, qq. 1167, 1181, 1257–61, 1281.
14. *ibid.*, q. 1331.
15. *ibid.*, qq. 1388, 1392.
16. *ibid.*, q. 1381.
17. H. Perkin, *The Origins of Modern English Society, 1780–1880*, 1972, p. 280.
18. C. J. Apperley, 'The Turf', *Quarterly Review*, vol. 49, July 1833, p. 382.
19. H. Perkin, *The Origins of Modern English Society, 1780–1880*,

1972, p. 277. On this see also R. W. Malcolmson, *Popular Recreation in English Society, 1700–1850*, 1973, chapters 6 and 7.

20. E. P. Thompson, 'Time, Work-Discipline and Industrial Capitalism', *Past and Present*, vol. 38, December 1967, p. 84; K. Thomas, 'Work and Leisure in Pre-Industrial Society', *Past and Present*, vol. 29, December 1964, p. 61.

21. B. Harrison, 'Religion and Recreation in Nineteenth Century England', *Past and Present*, vol. 38, December 1967, pp. 98–100.

22. C. J. Apperley, 'The Turf', *Quarterly Review*, vol. 49, July 1833, p. 388.

23. G. J. Cawthorne and R. S. Herod, *Royal Ascot*, 1900, p. 58; R. Onslow, *The Heath and the Turf*, 1972, p. 41, citing the *New Sporting Magazine* of 1833.

24. Entry for 1842 in Minute Book of York Race Committee, quoted in *Notes for York Race Committee*, p. 5.

25. J. C. Whyte, *History of the British Turf*, 1840, p. 199.

26. C. J. Apperley, 'The Turf', *Quarterly Review*, vol. 49, July 1833, p. 434.

27. A full survey of British racing in 1839 can be found in J. C. Whyte, *History of the British Turf*, 1840. See also the comprehensive surveys in the *Victoria County Histories*, though beware those written by historians who know little about racing and those by racing men ignorant of history.

28. J. C. Whyte, *History of the British Turf*, 1840, p. 209.

29. *ibid.*, p. 208; *Racing Calendar*, 1830–40.

30. Rous, *op. cit.*, p. x; J. C. Whyte, *History of the British Turf*, 1840, pp. xiv, 189.

31. *Sunday Times*, 4 and 25 June 1837; R. Longrigg, *The History of Horse Racing*, 1972, pp. 142–4; J. Rice, *The History of the British Turf*, 1879, pp. 202–5; J. C. Whyte, *History of the British Turf*, 1840, pp. 274–7; D. P. Blaine, *Encyclopaedia of Rural Sports*, 1870, p. 375.

32. Earl of Suffolk, *Racing and Steeplechasing*, 1886, p. 211.

33. *ibid.*, p. 43.

2. THE RAILWAY REVOLUTION: RACING 1840–70

1. H. P. White, *A Regional History of the Railways of Great Britain*, vol. 2, *Southern England*, 1961, p. 113; C. H. Ellis, *British Railway History 1830–1876*, 1954, p. 81.

2. J. C. Whyte, *History of the British Turf*, 1840, p. 344.

3. Quoted in M. Robbins, *The Railway Age*, 1965, p. 43.

4. The Druid, *Post and Paddock*, 1895 ed., p. 4.

5. Earl of Suffolk, *Racing and Steeplechasing*, 1886, p. 75.

6. Sylvanus, *The Bye-Lanes and Downs of England*, 1850, p. 117.

7. Memory of S. Clayton cited in *Bloodstock Breeders Review*, vol. 8, December 1919, p. 4; E. Moorhouse, 'Then and Now – Racing', *Badminton Magazine*, vol. 36, May 1913, p. 480.

8. D. I. Gordon, *A Regional History of the Railways of Great Britain*, vol. 5, *The Eastern Counties*, 1968, pp. 139–41; K. Brown, 'A Derelict Railway', *Proceedings of the Cambridge Antiquarian Society*, 1931, pp. 1–16.

9. Earl of Suffolk, *Racing and Steeplechasing*, 1886, p. 43.

10. R. Onslow, *The Heath and the Turf*, 1971, pp. 41–7.

11. J. Kent, *The Racing Life of Lord George Cavendish Bentinck*, 1892, pp. 60–70.

12. The Druid, *Scott and Sebright*, 1895 ed., p. 67; R. Mortimer, *The Jockey Club*, 1958, p. 59.

13. Earl of Suffolk, *Racing and Steeplechasing*, p. 212; R. Rodrigo, *The Racing Game*, 1960, p. 25.

14. Quoted in J. Fairfax-Blakeborough, *The Racecourses of Scotland*, 1954, p. 25.

15. James Radford to John Bowes, 4 July 1840, Bowes Papers, D/St. Box 162, Durham County Record Office.

16. C. Richardson, *The English Turf*, 1901, p. 156.

17. The Druid, *Scott and Sebright*, 1895 ed., pp. 171–2.

18. R. Ord, 'Horse Racing in the North of England', *Badminton Magazine*, vol. 15, August 1902, pp. 168–74; C. Richardson, *The English Turf*, 1901, p. 122.

19. H. Rous, *On the Laws and Practice of Horse Racing*, 1866, p. 6.

20. *ibid.*, p. 2. See also 'Turf Ethics in 1868', *Broadway*, vol. 1, 1868, pp. 379–80.

21. M. W. Flinn, 'Trends in Real Wages 1750–1850', *Economic History Review*, vol. 27, no. 3, August 1974, p. 396.

22. E. J. Hobsbawm, *Industry and Empire*, 1968, p. 74.

23. Calculations based on B. R. Mitchell and P. Deane, *Abstract of British Historical Statistics*, 1962, p. 343.

24. E. P. Thompson, 'Work, Time-Discipline and Industrial Capitalism', *Past and Present*, vol. 38, December 1967, pp. 90–91.

25. M. B. Smith, 'The Growth and Development of Popular Entertainment and Pastimes in the Lancashire Cotton Towns 1830–1870', M. Litt. thesis, University of Lancaster, 1970, pp. 136, 146.

26. H. Rous, *On the Laws and Practice of Horse Racing*, 1866, p. 5; H. Rous to R. Johnson, 1 March, 20 August 1865, York Racing Museum.

27. H. Rous to R. Johnson, 23 February 1865, York Racing Museum.

28. H. Rous to R. Johnson, 1 March 1865, York Racing Museum.

29. J. C. Whyte, *History of the British Turf*, 1840, pp. 199–201; G. J. Cawthorne and R. S. Herod, *Royal Ascot*, 1900, p. 95.

30. H. Rous, *On the Laws and Practice of Horse Racing*, 1866, p. 4.

31. 'Modern Horse Racing', *Edinburgh Review*, vol. 151, April 1880, p. 412.

32. *ibid.*; 'Turf Ethics in 1868', *Broadway*, vol. 1, 1868, pp. 379–80. See also *Hansard*, vol. 237, 29 January 1878; vol. 240, 13 June 1878; vol. 243, 14 February 1879.

33. E. Spencer, *The Great Game*, 1900, pp. 223–6; R. Mortimer, *The Jockey Club*, 1958, p. 115.

34. 'Modern Horse Racing', *Edinburgh Review*, vol. 151, April 1880, p. 412.

35. 'Turf Ethics in 1868', *Broadway*, vol. 1, 1868, pp. 379–80.

3. THE ENCLOSED COURSE

1. F. Gale, *Modern English Sports*, 1885, pp. 80–81.

2. J. Myerscough, 'The Transformation of Popular Recreation', Unpublished seminar paper, University of Sussex, 1972, pp. 10–11, citing G. Stedman Jones, *Outcast London*, 1971, pp. 19–32.

3. J. Porter and E. Moorhouse, *John Porter of Kingsclere*, 1919, pp. 444–7.

4. C. Richardson, *The English Turf*, 1901, p. 212; 'Pages From a Country Diary', *Badminton Magazine*, vol. 11, July 1900, p. 29.

5. C. Richardson, *The English Turf*, 1901, p. 212; C. Ramsden, *Farewell Manchester*, 1966, pp. 20, 31.

6. J. D. Astley, *Fifty Years of My Life*, 1895, pp. 351–2.

7. J. Fairfax-Blakeborough, *The Racecourses of Scotland*, 1954, p. 53.

8. C. Richardson, *The English Turf*, 1901, p. 176.

9. *ibid.*

10. C. Richardson, *Racing at Home and Abroad*, vol. 1, 1923, p. 262.

11. A. E. Dingle, 'Drink and Working-Class Living Standards in Britain, 1870–1914', *Economic History Review*, vol. 25, November 1972, pp. 615–16.

12. *ibid.*, p. 618; E. J. Hobsbawm, *Industry and Empire*, 1968, p. 138.

13. H. Perkin, *The Age of the Railway*, 1971, chapter 8; J. Myerscough, 'The Transformation of Popular Recreation', unpublished seminar paper, University of Sussex, 1972, p. 10. A. Hern, *The*

Seaside Holiday, 1967, chapter 5; P. Young, *A History of British Football*, 1969, chapters 9 and 10.

14. C. Richardson, *The English Turf*, 1901, p. 175.

15. *ibid.*, pp. 185–212; R. K. Mainwaring, 'The Prospects of the Racing Season', *Badminton Magazine*, vol. 4, April 1897, p. 445.

16. C. Richardson, *The English Turf*, 1901, p. 205.

17. *ibid.*, pp. 176–7; A. E. T. Watson, 'Racing', in Earl of Suffolk, H. Peck and F. G. Aflalo (eds.), *The Encyclopaedia of Sport*, 1900, pp. 198–9; 'Racing, Past and Future', *Badminton Magazine*, vol. 26, March 1908, pp. 268–9.

18. C. Richardson, *The English Turf*, 1901, p. 197; J. Rickman, *Homes of Sport: Horse Racing*, 1952, p. 30.

19. Lord Hamilton of Dalzell, 'The Financial Aspects of Racing', *Badminton Magazine*, vol. 23, September 1906, p. 252.

20. H. Custance, *Riding Recollections and Turf Stories*, 1894, pp. 194–6.

21. The surveys of racing in the *Victoria County Histories* commonly attribute the decline of meetings in the late 1870s to the 300-sovereign rule.

22. R. Mortimer, *The Jockey Club*, 1958, p. 117.

23. C. Richardson, *Racing at Home and Abroad*, vol. 1, 1923, p. 39.

24. C. Richardson, *The English Turf*, 1901, pp. 149–55.

25. L. H. Curzon, *The Blue Riband of the Turf*, 1890, p. 19; C. Richardson, *The English Turf*, 1901, p. 178.

26. G. J. Cawthorne and R. S. Herod, *Royal Ascot*, 1900, pp. 123, 191–3.

27. Richardson, *The English Turf*, 1901, p. 74.

28. Earl of Suffolk, *Racing and Steeplechasing*, 1886, pp. 74–5.

29. *ibid.*, p. 95.

30. Number of horses taken from the *Racing Calendar*. Bloodstock estimates from L. H. Curzon, 'The Horse as an Instrument of Gambling', *Contemporary Review*, vol. 30, August 1877, p. 378; L. H. Curzon, *The Mirror of the Turf*, 1892, p. 61, and *Bloodstock Breeders Review*, vol. 5, July 1917, p. 189.

31. E. Moorhouse, 'Then and Now – Racing', *Badminton Magazine*, vol. 36, May 1913, p. 490; 'Horse-Racing', *Quarterly Review*, vol. 161, October 1885, p. 455.

32. Earl of Suffolk, *Racing and Steeplechasing*, 1886, pp. 74–5.

4. THE AMERICAN INVASION

1. G. Lambton, *Men and Horses I Have Known*, 1924, p. 260.

2. J. Rice, *The History of the British Turf*, vol. 2, 1879, p. 69.

3. T. H. Bird, *Admiral Rous and the English Turf*, 1939, pp. 199–200; 'The American Jockey Invasion', *Badminton Magazine*, vol. 24, April 1907, pp. 422–4; The Sportsman, *British Sports and Sportsmen – Racing*, 1920, p. 146.

4. C. Richardson, *The English Turf*, 1901, pp. 231–4; A. E. T. Watson, 'American Training Methods', *Badminton Magazine*, vol. 13, July 1901, pp. 35–40.

5. *ibid.*, p. 41.

6. G. Lambton, *Men and Horses I Have Known*, 1924, pp. 253–4; A. E. T. Watson, 'American Training Methods', *Badminton Magazine*, vol. 13, July 1901, p. 37.

7. T. Sloan, *Tod Sloan*, 1915, p. 213.

8. H. Custance, *Riding Recollections and Turf Stories*, 1894, p. 26.

9. T. Sloan, *Tod Sloan*, 1915, p. 69.

10. A. E. T. Watson, 'Racing – Past and Future', *Badminton Magazine*, vol. 8, July 1899; C. Richardson, *The English Turf*, 1901, p. 264; 'Notes', *Badminton Magazine*, vol. 7, November 1898, p. 588; *Badminton Magazine*, vol. 10, February 1900, p. 179.

11. 'The American Jockey Invasion', *Badminton Magazine*, vol. 24, April 1907, p. 429.

12. T. Sloan, *Tod Sloan*, 1915, p. 97.

13. G. Lambton, *Men and Horses I Have Known*, 1924, p. 241; C. Richardson, *The English Turf*, 1901, p. 265; 'Notes', *Badminton Magazine*, vol. 11, November 1900, p. 585.

14. 'The American Jockey Invasion', *Badminton Magazine*, vol. 24, April 1907, pp. 424–5.

15. *ibid.*, pp. 425–8; C. Richardson, *The English Turf*, 1901, p. 262; T. Sloan, *Tod Sloan*, 1915, pp. 47–8; 'Notes', *Badminton Magazine*, vol. 8, November 1898, p. 588.

16. H. E. Rowlands, 'American Jockeyship', *Badminton Magazine*, vol. 10, February 1900, pp. 180–2.

17. 'Notes', *Badminton Magazine*, vol. 9, November 1899, p. 586.

18. C. Richardson, *The English Turf*, 1901, pp. 255–6; H. E. Rowlands, 'American Jockeyship', *Badminton Magazine*, vol. 10, February 1900, pp. 183–6; T. Sloan, *Tod Sloan*, 1915, pp. 284–5.

19. D. Maher, 'On Race Riding', *Badminton Magazine*, vol. 20, May 1905, p. 557.

20. A. B. Portman, 'Prospects of the Racing Season', *Badminton Magazine*, vol. 6, March 1898, p. 331; A. E. T. Watson, 'Racing – Past and Future, *Badminton Magazine*, vol. 8, July 1898, p. 26; E.

Saville, 'Training and Staying', *Badminton Magazine*, vol. 41, June 1913, p. 700.

21. T. Sloan, *Tod Sloan*, 1915, p. 48.

22. A. E. T. Watson, 'Racing – Past and Future', *Badminton Magazine*, vol. 8, January 1899, p. 27.

23. C. Richardson, *The English Turf*, 1901, p. 264.

24. 'Notes', *Badminton Magazine*, vol. 11, September 1900, p. 351; *Badminton Magazine*, vol. 4, June 1902, p. 696.

25. *Badminton Magazine*, vol. 12, February 1901, pp. 252–3; 'The State of the Turf', *Badminton Magazine*, vol. 19, December 1904, p. 664; R. F. Meysey-Thompson, 'A Trial of the Monkey Seat', *Badminton Magazine*, vol. 28, March 1914, p. 370.

26. *ibid.*, pp. 362–3.

27. G. Lambton, *Men and Horses I Have Known*, 1924, p. 271.

28. T. A. Cook, *A History of the English Turf*, 1905, vol. 3, p. 525.

29. *Bloodstock Breeders Review*, vol. 5, December 1916, p. 329.

30. *Bloodstock Breeders Review*, vol. 3, December 1914, p. 337; 'Notes', *Badminton Magazine*, vol. 13, November 1901, pp. 589–90.

31. T. Sloan, *Tod Sloan*, 1915, pp. 101, 187.

32. *ibid.*, pp. 89, 155; R. Rodrigo, *The Racing Game*, 1960, p. 201.

33. An unnamed British newspaper quoted in T. Sloan, *Tod Sloan*, 1915, p. 191.

34. G. Lambton, *Men and Horses I Have Known*, 1924, p. 246.

35. 'Sportsmen of Mark – Andrew Jackson Joyner', *Badminton Magazine*, vol. 28, June 1909, pp. 590–91; G. Lambton, *Men and Horses I Have Known*, 1924, p. 250.

36. The following is based on R. Mortimer, *The Jockey Club*, 1958, pp. 138–43, and T. H. Browne, *A History of the English Turf 1904–1930*, vol. 1, 1931, pp. 91–2.

37. *Bloodstock Breeders Review*, vol. 2, July 1913, p. 129.

5. THE FIRST WORLD WAR AND AFTER

1. The narrative of this chapter is based on contemporary evidence in *Hansard*, and the *Bloodstock Breeders Review*; hence only quotations are specifically acknowledged.

2. *The Times*, 4 May 1915.

3. Quoted in *Bloodstock Breeders Review*, vol. 3, October 1914, pp. 196–7.

4. Rosallian, 'Summer Sport in 1915?', *Badminton Magazine*, vol. 41, March 1915, pp. 326–32; F. A. M. Webster, 'War and the Sports of the Nations', *Badminton Magazine*, vol. 42, May 1915, pp. 62–71.

5. E. E. Dorling, *Epsom and the Dorlings,* 1939, p. 109.

6. Quoted in *Bloodstock Breeders Review,* vol. 6, July 1917, p. 111.

7. E. Moorhouse, 'The Racing Year', *Bloodstock Breeders Review,* vol. 8, 1919, p. 48.

8. R. H. Tawney, 'The Abolition of Economic Controls, 1918–21', *Economic History Review,* 1943.

9. For examples of the revisionist literature, see D. H. Aldcroft, 'Economic Growth in Britain in the Inter-War Years: A Reassessment', *Economic History Review,* vol. 20, 1967; H. W. Richardson, 'The Basis of Economic Recovery in the 1930s: A Review and a New Interpretation', *Economic History Review,* vol. 15, 1962.

10. K. Roberts, *Leisure,* 1970, pp. 12–15.

11. Pilgrim Trust, *Men Without Work,* 1938, *passim*; H. G. Brown, 'Some Effects of Shift Work on Social and Domestic Life', *Yorkshire Bulletin of Economic and Social Research,* Occasional Paper 2, 1959; K. Roberts, *Leisure,* 1970, p. 48.

12. Calculations based on D. H. Aldcroft, *The Inter-War Economy,* 1970, p. 364.

13. What follows is based on the *Royal Commission on Lotteries and Betting,* 1932–3, XV, pp. 7–10.

14. R. Graves and A. Hodge, *The Long Weekend,* 1941, p. 384.

15. J. Hilton, *Rich Man, Poor Man,* 1945, pp. 125–6.

16. J. Hilton, *Why I Go In For The Pools,* 1936, *passim.*

17. Quoted in *Bloodstock Breeders Review,* vol. 17, 1928, p. 19.

18. Calculated from *Reports of the Racecourse Betting Control Board.*

19. *Seventh Report of R.B.C.B.,* 1935–6, vol. 14.

20. See the *Report of the Racing Re-organisation Committee (The Ilchester Committee),* 1943, paras 32–58.

21. *ibid.,* para. 3.

CONTROL: THE MORALITY OF RACING

6. THE JOCKEY CLUB

1. Statement of the Club's senior steward to the *Select Committee on Betting Duty,* 1923, V, q. 1443.

2. J. C. Whyte, *History of the British Turf,* vol. 1, 1840, p. 149; D. P. Blaine, *Encyclopaedia of Rural Sports,* 1870, p. 375.

3. H. Custance, *Riding Recollections and Turf Stories,* 1894, p. 191.

4. R. Black, *The Jockey Club and Its Founders,* 1891, p. 361.

5. R. Mortimer, *The Jockey Club,* 1958, p. 172.

6. J. Ford, *Prizefighting,* 1971, chapter 5.

7. R. Mortimer, *The Jockey Club,* 1958, p. 11.

8. *ibid.*, p. *36*.

9. This account is based on R. Mortimer, *The Jockey Club*, 1958, pp. *36–44*; R. Rodrigo, *The Racing Game*, 1960, pp. 138–40; Thormanby, *Famous Racing Men*, 1882, p. *52*; M. Seth-Smith, *Bred for the Purple*, 1969, pp. 33–64; and *The Times*, 26 October 1792.

10. J. Ford, *Prizefighting*, 1971, p. 84.

11. J. S. Fletcher, *The History of the St Leger Stakes*, 1902, p. *35*; Thormanby, *Famous Racing Men*, 1882, p. *33*; E. Moorhouse, *The Romance of the Derby*, 1908, p. 8.

12. J. S. Fletcher, *The History of the St Leger Stakes*, 1902, pp. 148–150.

13. R. C. Lyle, *Royal Newmarket*, 1945, p. *52*.

14. R. Mortimer, *The Jockey Club*, 1958, p. 48.

15. R. Black, *The Jockey Club and Its Founders*, 1891, p. *257*; G. Hawkins, *The Jockey Club*, 1827.

16. R. Mortimer, *The Jockey Club*, 1958, p. *59*.

17. B. Darwin, *The Life and Times of John Gully*, 1935, *passim*.

18. H. Reeve (ed.), *The Greville Memoirs*, vol. 2, 1874; 17 December 1832.

19. A. E. Watson, *The Turf*, 1898, p. 171.

20. M. Ayres and G. Newbon, *Over the Sticks*, 1971, p. 20.

21. C. J. Apperly, 'The Turf', *Quarterly Review*, vol. 49, July 1833, p. 383.

22. Details based on E. Moorhouse, *The Romance of the Derby*, 1908 pp. 258–70; R. Mortimer, *The Jockey Club*, 1958, pp. 72–6; J. Kent, *The Racing Life of Lord George Cavendish Bentinck*, 1892, pp. 152–61.

23. J. Ford, *Prizefighting*, 1971, pp. 184–9.

24. G. Stone, 'Wrestling: The Great American Passion Play', in E. Dunning, *The Sociology of Sport*, 1971, p. 306.

25. Quoted in J. Ford, *Prizefighting*, 1971, p. 188.

26. *ibid.*, p. 99.

27. *ibid.*, pp. 97–8.

28. K. Chesney, *The Victorian Underworld*, 1970, pp. 276–7.

29. J. Ford, *Cricket*, 1972, p. 102.

30. J. Kent, *The Racing Life of Lord George Cavendish Bentinck*, 1892, p. 151.

31. H. Reeve (ed.), *The Greville Memoirs*, vol. 2, 1885; 28 September 1848.

32. J. Kent, *The Racing Life of Lord George Cavendish Bentinck*, 1892, *passim*; R. Rodrigo, *The Racing Game*, 1960, pp. 24–5; H. Reeve (ed.), *The Greville Memoirs*, vol. 2, 1885; 28 September 1848.

33. J. Kent, *The Racing Life of Lord George Cavendish Bentinck*,

1892, pp. 296–7; T. H. Bird, *Admiral Rous and the English Turf*, 1939, pp. 178–9.

34. R. Mortimer, *The Jockey Club*, 1958, p. 76; E. Spencer, *The Great Game*, 1900, p. 18.

35. The following is based on J. Kent, *The Racing Life of Lord George Cavendish Bentinck*, 1892, pp. 152–9; R. Mortimer, *The Jockey Club*, 1958, pp. 72–6; R. Rodrigo, *The Racing Game*, 1960, p. 141; K. Chesney, *The Victorian Underworld*, 1970, pp. 279–80; The Sportsman, *British Sports and Sportsmen – Racing*, 1920, pp. 131–2; E. Moorhouse, *The Romance of the Derby*, 1908, pp. 258–70; H. Reeve (ed.), *The Greville Memoirs*, vol. 2, 1885; 28 September 1848.

36. *Annual Register*, 1844, p. 352.

37. J. Kent, *The Racing Life of Lord George Cavendish Bentinck*, 1892, p. 152.

38. The Sportsman, *British Sports and Sportsmen – Racing*, 1920, pp. 298–9; R. Mortimer, *The Jockey Club*, 1958, pp. 106–7.

39. Quoted in C. E. Hardy, *John Bowes and the Bowes Museum*, 1970, p. 69.

40. H. Reeve (ed.), *The Greville Memoirs*, vol. 2, 1885; 28 September 1848.

41. The Sportsman, *British Sports and Sportsmen – Racing*, 1920, p. 216; R. Mortimer, *The Jockey Club*, 1958, p. 108.

42. J. Kent, *The Racing Life of Lord George Cavendish Bentinck*, 1892, p. 253; B. Disraeli, *The Political Life of Lord George Bentinck*, 1852, p. 539.

43. *Hansard*, 3rd series, vol. 73, 21 February 1844.

44. T. H. Bird, *Admiral Rous and the English Turf*, 1939, pp. 4–8.

45. *ibid.*, pp. 52–4; W. Day, *Turf Celebrities I Have Known*, 1891, p. 207.

46. T. H. Bird, *Admiral Rous and the English Turf*, 1939, p. 171; R. Black, *The Jockey Club and Its Founders*, 1891, p. 326.

47. R. Black, *The Jockey Club and Its Founders*, 1891, p. 326.

48. Quoted in R. Rodrigo, *The Racing Game*, 1960, p. 29.

49. T. H. Bird, *Admiral Rous and the English Turf*, 1891, p. 4.

50. H. Rous, *On the Laws and Practice of Horse Racing*, 1866, p. xiii; T. H. Bird, *Admiral Rous and the English Turf*, 1939, pp. 162–3.

51. 'Modern Racing', *Edinburgh Review*, vol. 151, April 1880, p. 432.

52. 'Horse-Racing', *Quarterly Review*, vol. 161, October 1885, p. 465.

53. W. L. Burn, *The Age of Equipose*, 1964, p. 236.

54. S. G. Galtrey, *Memoirs of a Racing Journalist*, 1934, p. 162.

55. A. E. Watson, *The Turf*, 1898, p. 131.

56. *ibid.*, p. 132; *Select Committee on Betting*, 1902, V, qq. 2453–4.

57. *Hansard*, 3rd series, vol. 156, 16 February 1860; vol. 159, 12 June 1860.

58. *ibid.*, vol. 237, 29 January 1878; vol. 240, 13 June 1878; vol. 243, 14 February 1879.

59. R. Mortimer, *The Jockey Club*, 1958, p. 103.

60. J. Rice, *The History of the British Turf*, 1879, vol. 2, p. 352.

61. The following is based on R. Mortimer, *The Jockey Club*, 1958, pp. 86–90; T. H. Bird, *Admiral Rous and the English Turf*, 1939, pp. 126–32; E. Spencer, *The Great Game*, 1900, p. 9; Thormanby, *Famous Racing Men*, pp. 96–112.

62. R. Mortimer, *The Jockey Club*, 1958, p. 86.

63. *ibid.*, p. 87.

64. *ibid.*, p. 88.

65. The Sportsman, *British Sports and Sportsmen – Racing*, 1920, pp. 297–8; R. Mortimer, *The Jockey Club*, 1958, p. 105.

66. E. D. Cuming, *Squire Osbaldeston: His Autobiography*, 1926, p. 2.

67. R. Mortimer, *The Jockey Club*, 1958, p. 95.

68. *The Times*, 19 July 1857.

69. R. Rodrigo, *The Racing Game*, 1960, p. 140.

70. G. Lambton, *Men and Horses I Have Known*, 1924, pp. 253–4.

71. *ibid.*, p. 255; Earl of Ellesmere, 'Concerning Stewards', *Badminton Magazine*, vol. 12, 1901, p. 393.

72. G. Lambton, *Men and Horses I Have Known*, 1924, p. 256.

73. J. M. Hogge, *Betting and Gambling*, 1904, p. 16, quoting the *Sportsman*.

74. 'Doping', *Badminton Magazine*, vol. 41, January 1913, p. 88.

75. For evidence that doping could take place without the knowledge of the stable see T. Weston, *My Racing Life*, 1952, pp. 78–83.

76. R. Mortimer, *The Jockey Club*, 1958, p. 49.

77. *ibid.*, p. 83.

78. A full transcript of the trial can be found in the appendix to volume two of G. Chetwynd, *Racing Reminiscences*, 1891. It makes interesting reading.

79. *Saturday Review*, 3 March 1888, p. 270.

80. R. Black, *The Jockey Club and Its Founders*, 1891, p. 319.

81. Earl of Ellesmere, 'Concerning Stewards', *Badminton Magazine*, vol. 12, 1901, p. 394.

82. Lord Beaufort to Mr Greenfield, 9 February 1893, York Racing Museum.

83. Lord Durham to C. Wood, 27 January 1897, York Racing Museum.

84. Rapier, 'Notes', *Badminton Magazine*, vol. 2, March 1896, p. 425.

85. L. H. Curzon, *Mirror of the Turf*, 1892, pp. 270, 276.

86. A. F. T. Watson, 'Racing in 1896', *Badminton Magazine*, vol. 3, December 1896, p. 686.

87. S. G. Galtrey, *Memoirs of a Racing Journalist*, 1934, p. 20.

88. *ibid.*

89. 'Racing', *Badminton Magazine*, vol. 25, July 1907, p. 18; E. Rickman, *Come Racing With Me*, 1951, pp. 97–100; M. Good, *The Lure of the Turf*, 1957, p. 185.

90. See, for example, the speech of the Association's chairman, Lord D'Abernon, in the *Bloodstock Breeders Review*, vol. 8, 1919, p. 195.

91. S. G. Galtrey, *Memoirs of a Racing Journalist*, 1934, pp. 26–7.

92. *ibid.*, p. 26.

93. J. D. Astley, *Fifty Years of My Life*, 1895, pp. 269–71; J. Fairfax-Blakeborough, *The Analysis of the Turf*, 1927, p. 69.

94. J. Fairfax-Blakeborough, *The Analysis of the Turf*, 1927, p. 69.

95. A. W. Coaten, 'The Evolution of Racing', in Earl of Harewood (ed.), *Flat Racing*, 1940, p. 127.

7. RACING OFFICIALS

1. L. H. Curzon, *A Mirror of the Turf*, 1892, pp. 94–5; The Sportsman, *British Sports and Sportsmen – Racing*, 1920, p. 206.

2. The account of the 1827 St Leger is based on Thormanby, *Famous Racing Men*, 1882, p. 76; R. Rodrigo, *The Racing Game*, 1960, pp. 84, 111; J. S. Fletcher, *The History of the St Leger Stakes*, 1902, p. 217; The Druid, *Post and Paddock*, 1895, p. 127.

3. H. A. Bryden and E. D. Cuming, 'Racing', *Victoria County History (Derbyshire)*, vol. 2, 1907, p. 290.

4. E. D. Cuming, *Squire Osbaldeston: His Autobiography*, 1926, pp. 142–3.

5. F. Bonnet, 'Racing', *Victoria County History (Nottingham)*, vol. 2, 1910, pp. 388–92; E. E. Dorling, *Epsom and the Dorlings*, 1939, *passim*.

6. J. Fairfax-Blakeborough, *The Analysis of the Turf*, 1927, p. 193; G. J. Cawthorne and R. S. Herod, *Royal Ascot*, 1900, p. 173.

7. Earl of Suffolk, *Racing and Steeplechasing*, 1886, p. 62.

8. J. Fairfax-Blakeborough, *The Analysis of the Turf*, 1927, p. 254.

9. *ibid.*, p. 258.

10. Earl of Suffolk, *Racing and Steeplechasing*, 1886, p. 63.

11. J. C. Whyte, *History of the British Turf*, vol. 1, 1840, p. 495.

12. J. S. Fletcher, *The History of the St Leger Stakes*, 1902, pp. 148–150, 158.

13. The Druid, *Post and Paddock*, 1895, p. 127.

14. Thormanby, *Famous Racing Men*, 1882, p. 66; The Sportsman, *British Sports and Sportsmen – Racing*, 1920, p. 127.

15. The Sportsman, *British Sports and Sportsmen – Racing*, 1920, p. 123; J. Kent, *The Racing Life of Lord George Cavendish Bentinck*, 1892, p. 305.

16. J. Kent, *The Racing Life of Lord George Cavendish Bentinck*, 1892, pp. 303–4.

17. The Sportsman, *British Sports and Sportsmen – Racing*, 1920, p. 216.

18. H. Rous, *On the Laws and Practice of Horse Racing*, 1866, p. 25.

19. T. H. Bird, *Admiral Rous and the English Turf*, 1939, p. 190.

20. *ibid.*

21. H. Rous, *On the Laws and Practice of Horse Racing*, 1866, p. 25.

22. Earl of Suffolk, *Racing and Steeplechasing*, 1886, p. 64.

23. E. Moorhouse, *The Romance of the Derby*, 1902, p. 376.

24. 'Starters and Starting', *Badminton Magazine*, vol. 18, January 1904, p. 31.

25. P. E. Ricketts, 'The Handicapper, the Starter, the Judge', in Earl of Harewood (ed.), *Flat Racing*, 1940, p. 191.

26. *ibid.*, p. 190.

27. 'Notes', *Badminton Magazine*, vol. 5, July 1897, p. 124.

28. 'Starters and Starting', *Badminton Magazine*, vol. 18, January 1904, pp. 28–9.

29. J. Fairfax-Blakeborough, *The Analysis of the Turf*, 1927, p. 204.

30. F. J. Ridgway, 'Racehorses and Others in 1897', *Badminton Magazine*, vol. 5, December 1897, p. 740.

31. A. E. T. Watson, 'Sportsmen of Mark – Mr Hugh Owen', *Badminton Magazine*, vol. 23, July 1906, p. 11.

32. T. H. Bird, *Admiral Rous and the English Turf*, 1939, p. 197.

33. H. Rous, *On the Laws and Practice of Horse Racing*, 1850 ed., p. 124.

34. J. Fairfax-Blakeborough, *The Analysis of the Turf*, 1927, p. 174.

35. A. E. T. Watson, 'Racing', in Earl of Suffolk, H. Peek & F. G. Aflalo (eds.), *The Encyclopaedia of Sport*, 1900, p. 192.

36. 'Handicapping', *Saturday Review*, vol. 72, 19 September 1891, p. 325; G. J. Cawthorne and R. S. Herod, *Royal Ascot*, 1900, pp. 176–

177; 'Handicappers and Handicapping', *Badminton Magazine*, vol. 16, May 1903, *passim*.

37. G. Chetwynd, *Racing Reminiscences*, vol. 2, 1891, p. 77.

38. 'Handicapping', *Saturday Review*, vol. 72, 19 September 1891, p. 325.

39. G. Chetwynd, *Racing Reminiscences*, vol. 2, 1891, p. 77.

40. A. E. T. Watson, 'Sportsmen of Mark – Mr W. F. Lees', *Badminton Magazine*, vol. 22, May 1906, p. 480; 'Racing', *Badminton Magazine*, vol. 25, July 1907, p. 21.

41. H. Rous, *On the Laws and Practice of Horse Racing*, 1850 ed., pp. xi, xii. See also evidence of the trainer, John Day, to the *Select Committee on Gaming*, 1844, VI, qq. 1466–7.

42. What follows is based on Thormanby, *Famous Racing Men*, 1882, pp. 107–12; T. H. Bird, *Admiral Rous and the English Turf*, 1939, *passim*; R. Mortimer, *The Jockey Club*, 1958, p. 82; H. Rous to R. Johnson, 3 January 1868, York Racing Museum; H. Rous to J. Bowes, 22 November 1863, D/St. Box 162, Durham County Record Office.

43. 'Handicappers and Handicapping', *Badminton Magazine*, vol. 16, May 1903, p. 503.

44. H. Rous to J. Bowes, 30 November 1863, D/St. Box 162, Durham County Record Office.

45. A. E. T. Watson, 'Racing – Past and Future', *Badminton Magazine*, vol. 10, January 1900, p. 39; 'Notes', *Badminton Magazine*, vol. 10, January 1900, p. 120.

46. Quoted in R. Onslow, *The Heath and the Turf*, 1971, p. 140.

47. 'Judges and Judging', *Badminton Magazine*, vol. 17, November 1903, p. 562; J. D. Astley, *Fifty Years of My Life*, 1895, p. 243; The Druid, *Post and Paddock*, 1895, p. 129.

48. E. Moorhouse, 'Then and Now – Racing', *Badminton Magazine*, vol. 36, May 1913, p. 480.

49. 'Modern Horse-Racing', *Edinburgh Review*, vol. 151, April 1880, p. 425.

50. M. Cobbett, *Racing Life and Racing Characters*, 1903, p. 47.

51. Quoted in J. Fairfax-Blakeborough, *The Analysis of the Turf*, 1927, p. 151.

52. Earl of Suffolk, *Racing and Steeplechasing*, 1886, p. 73; 'The State of the Turf', *Badminton Magazine*, vol. 14, March 1902, p. 332.

53. R. Rodrigo, *The Racing Game*, 1960, p. 31.

54. See e.g. two articles entitled 'The State of the Turf', *Badminton Magazine*, vol. 19, November 1904, p. 551; vol. 20, February 1905, p. 187.

55. J. Fairfax-Blakeborough, *The Analysis of the Turf*, 1927, p. 149.
56. A. E. T. Watson, 'Sportsmen of Mark – Lord Hamilton of Dalzell', *Badminton Magazine*, vol. 27, September 1905, pp. 246–247.
57. S. G. Galtrey, *Memoirs of a Racing Journalist*, 1934, p. 30.

8. THE CROWD

1. H. Rous, *On the Laws and Practice of Horse Racing*, 1850, p. v.
2. *Select Committee on the Laws Respecting Gaming*, 1844, VI, p. v.
3. See J. Ford, *Prizefighting*, 1971, p. 149; D. C. Itzkowitz, 'Peculiar Privilege: A Social History of English Foxhunting', Ph.D. thesis, Columbia University, 1973, pp. 65–72.
4. J. Rice, *The History of the British Turf*, vol. 2, 1879, p. 31.
5. For details of such junketing at Doncaster, see J. S. Fletcher, *The History of the St Leger Stakes*, 1902, pp. 75–6.
6. E. T. Sachs, 'Autumn Racing', in F. G. Aflalo (ed.), *The Sports of the World*, vol. 1, 1903, p. 44; L. H. Curzon, *A Mirror of the Turf*, 1892, p. 39.
7. H. Reeve (ed.), *The Greville Memoirs*, vol. 1, 1874; 20 August 1831.
8. *ibid.*; 27 May 1833.
9. P. B. Power, *Some Observations upon the Question 'Will Horse Racing Benefit Worthing?'*, 1859.
10. H. Reeve (ed.), *The Greville Memoirs*, vol. 1, 1874; 14 June 1843; Rosebery Papers, Box 109, Memoranda 22 June 1895, National Library of Scotland.
11. *ibid.*
12. Wm Chayton to John Bowes, 10 December 1846, D/St. Box 162, Durham County Record Office.
13. W. Day, *The Racehorse in Training*, 1880, p. 285.
14. H. Reeve (ed.), *The Greville Memoirs*, vol. 1, 1874; 27 May 1833.
15. *ibid.*; 23 October 1839.
16. *Manchester Guardian*, 29 May 1847.
17. *Select Committee on Gaming*, 1844, VI, q. 1773; *Select Committee on Laws Respecting Gaming*, 1844, VI, q. 404.
18. Earl of Suffolk, *Racing and Steeplechasing*, 1886, pp. 91–2.
19. See e.g. E. T. Sachs, 'Autumn Racing', in F. G. Aflalo (ed.), *The Sports of the World*, vol. 1, 1903, p. 42; C. Richardson, *Racing at Home and Abroad*, vol. 1, 1923, p. 215; J. Rice, *The History of the British Turf*, vol. 2, 1879, p. 40.

20. A. E. T. Watson, 'Some Recent St Legers', *Badminton Magazine*, vol. 5, September 1897, p. 265.

21. The Druid, *Post and Paddock*, 1895, p. 20.

22. C. Richardson, *The English Turf*, 1901, p. 89.

23. *ibid.*, p. 213.

24. *ibid.*, pp. 30–31; L. H. Curzon, *A Mirror of the Turf*, 1892, p. 115.

25. Quoted in J. Rice, *The History of the British Turf*, vol. 2, 1879, p. 19.

26. *Carlisle Patriot*, quoted in J. Fairfax-Blakeborough, *The Analysis of the Turf*, 1927, p. 296.

27. 'Turf Ethics in 1868', *Broadway*, vol. 1, 1868–9, p. 380.

28. M. Fane, *Racecourse Swindles*, 1936, p. 11; K. Chesney, *The Victorian Underworld*, 1970, pp. 151–7.

29. L. H. Curzon, *A Mirror of the Turf*, 1892, p. 328; K. Chesney, *The Victorian Underworld*, 1970, p. 138; E. Spencer, *The Great Game*, 1900, pp. 171–2.

30. M. Fane, *Racecourse Swindles*, 1936, p. 11.

31. K. Chesney, *The Victorian Underworld*, 1970, p. 249.

32. W. Tait, *Magdalenism*, 1840, p. 3.

33. View of Major O'Gorman, *Hansard*, 3rd series, vol. 244, 6 March 1879.

34. S. Sidney, *The Book of the Horse*, 1875, p. 199.

35. K. Chesney, *The Victorian Underworld*, 1970, pp. 268–78; also information supplied by J. Hutchinson, postgraduate student at the University of Edinburgh working on the commercialization of football.

36. K. Chesney, *The Victorian Underworld*, 1970, pp. 301–6.

37. G. Sanger, *Seventy Years a Showman*, 1926, p. 62.

38. J. Fairfax-Blakeborough, *The Analysis of the Turf*, 1927, p. 271.

39. L. H. Curzon, *A Mirror of the Turf*, 1892, p. 328.

40. K. Chesney, *The Victorian Underworld*, 1970, p. 287; W. Russell, *The Reminiscences of Jock Thirlestane, Yokel and Detective at Musselburgh Races in Days Gone Bye*, n.d., p. 100.

41. The Sportsman, *British Sports and Sportsmen – Racing*, 1920, p. 74.

42. T. A. Cook, *A History of the English Turf*, vol. 3, 1905, p. 485.

43. The Sportsman, *British Sports and Sportsmen – Racing*, 1920, pp. 108–9; R. Black, *Horse-Racing in England*, 1893, p. 185.

44. C. J. Apperley, 'The Turf', *Quarterly Review*, vol. 49, July 1833, pp. 432–3; C. W. Searle, *The Origin and Development of Sunninghill*

and Ascot, 1937, p. 82; J. Fairfax-Blakeborough, *The Analysis of the Turf*, 1927, p. 159.

45. M. Cobbett, *Racing Life and Characters*, 1903, p. 168.

46. J. S. Fletcher, *The History of the St Leger Stakes*, 1902, pp. 96–7; *Select Committee on Gaming*, 1844, VI, qq. 1019–29.

47. J. H. Peart to J. Bowes, 7 June 1870, D/St. Box 162, Durham County Record Office.

48. S. Sidney, *The Book of the Horse*, 1875, p. 199.

49. E. Moorhouse, 'Then and Now – Racing', *Badminton Magazine*, vol. 36, May 1913, p. 498; E. Spencer, *The Great Game*, 1900, pp. 168–9; C. Richardson, *Racing at Home and Abroad*, vol. 1, 1923, pp. 168–9; G. E. Wilkinson, 'The Arrangement and Running of Racecourses', in Earl of Harewood (ed.) *Flat Racing*, 1940, p. 397; J. Fairfax-Blakeborough, *The Analysis of the Turf*, 1927, pp. 247–53.

50. R. Ord, 'Horse-Racing in the North of England', *Badminton Magazine*, vol. 14, August 1902, p. 174.

51. E. Rickman, *On and Off the Racecourse*, 1937, pp. 255–60.

52. *Select Committee on the Betting Duty*, 1923, V, qq. 4529, 8234.

53. Quoted in E. Rickman, *On and Off the Racecourse*, 1937, p. 266.

54. *ibid.*, p. 270.

55. W. Russell, *The Reminiscences of Jock Thirlestane, Yokel and Detective at Musselburgh Races in Days Gone Bye*, n.d., p. 101.

PARTICIPATION: THE MEN OF RACING

9. JOCKEYS

1. H. B. Bromhead, 'Derby Anecdotes', *English Illustrated Magazine*, vol. 10, 1892–3, p. 669; J. Welcome, *Fred Archer: His Life and Times*, 1967, p. 88.

2. T. A. Cook, *A History of the English Turf*, 1905, p. 521.

3. C. H. Curzon, *A Mirror of the Turf*, 1892, p. 346.

4. J. Burnett, *A History of the Cost of Living*, 1969, p. 253. See also 'Returns of Wages Published Between 1830 and 1886', *Parliamentary Papers*, 1887, LXXXIX, and various articles by A. L. Bowley published in the *Journal of the Royal Statistical Society*, 1895–1906.

5. C. H. Curzon, *A Mirror of the Turf*, 1892, p. 344.

6. *ibid.*

7. *Pierce Egan's Book of Sports*, vol. 1, pp. viii, 117; Thormanby, *Famous Racing Men*, 1882, pp. 31–2.

8. The Druid, *Post and Paddock*, 1895, p. 38; R. Rodrigo, *The Racing Game*, 1960, p. 68.

9. Earl of Suffolk, *Racing and Steeplechasing*, 1886, p. 243.

10. *ibid.*

11. 'The Turf: Its Frauds and Chicaneries', *Contemporary Review*, vol. 22, June 1873, p. 32.

12. 'Modern Horse-Racing', *Edinburgh Review*, vol. 151, April 1880, p. 419.

13. T. A. Cook, *A History of the English Turf*, 1905, p. 544.

14. *ibid.*; J. Welcome, *Fred Archer: His Life and Times*, 1967, p. 88; C. Richardson, *The English Turf*, 1901, p. 276.

15. 'The Turf: Its Frauds and Chicaneries', *Contemporary Review*, vol. 22, June 1873, p. 32; The Druid, *Scott and Sebright*, 1895, p. 61.

16. S. G. Galtrey, *Memoirs of a Racing Journalist*, 1934, pp. 184, 217.

17. J. Runciman, 'The Ethics of the Turf', *Contemporary Review*, vol. 55, April 1889, p. 163.

18. W. Day, *The Racehorse in Training*, 1880, p. 163.

19. Earl of Suffolk, *Racing and Steeplechasing*, 1886, p. 245.

20. E. M. Humphris, *The Life of Fred Archer*, 1923, p. 76; J. Welcome, *Fred Archer: His Life and Times*, 1967, p. 120.

21. T. A. Cook, *A History of the English Turf*, 1905, p. 393; R. W. Jeffrey (ed.), *Dyott's Diary 1781–1845*, p. 106, quoted in A. J. Kettle, 'Lichfield Races', *Transactions of Lichfield and Staffordshire Archaeological and Historical Society* 1964–5, vol. 6, p. 43.

22. T. H. Bird, *Admiral Rous and the English Turf*, 1939, p. 173.

23. 'The Turf: Its Frauds and Chicaneries', *Contemporary Review*, vol. 22, June 1873, p. 32.

24. J. Welcome, *Fred Archer: His Life and Times*, 1967, pp. 161–2; The Sportsman, *British Sports and Sportsmen – Past Sportsmen*, vol. 2, 1920, p. 290.

25. See letters to John Bowes from W. Read (26 November 1863) and from Captain White (March 1863), D/St. Box 162, Durham County Record Office.

26. T. A. Cook, *A History of the English Turf*, 1905, p. 522.

27. C. Richardson, *The English Turf*, 1901, p. 226.

28. *ibid.*

29. J. Welcome, *Fred Archer: His Life and Times*, 1967, p. 150.

30. J. Fairfax-Blakeborough, *The Analysis of the Turf*, 1927, p. 102.

31. J. Rice, *The History of the British Turf* vol. 1, 1879, pp. 269, 300; J. Runciman, 'The Ethics of the Turf', *Contemporary Review*, vol. 55, April 1889, p. 615; *Bloodstock Breeders Review*, vol. 2, no. 4, December 1913, p. 346.

32. S. G. Galtrey, *Memoirs of a Racing Journalist*, 1934, p. 217; E. Spencer, *The Great Game*, 1900, p. 117.

33. R. Onslow, *The Heath and the Turf*, 1971, p. 51; Q. Gilbey, *Champions All*, 1971, p. 156.

34. J. Kent, *The Racing Life of Lord George Cavendish Bentinck*, 1892, p. 122.

35. J. D. Astley, *Fifty Years of My Life*, 1895, p. 176.

36. *Hansard*, 3rd series, vol. 156, 11 February 1860; vol. 159, 12 June 1860.

37. Earl of Suffolk, *Racing and Steeplechasing*, 1886, p. 53.

38. T. A. Cook, *A History of the English Turf*, 1905, pp. 543–4.

39. The Druid, *Scott and Sebright*, 1895, p. 42.

40. *ibid.*, p. 32.

41. T. Weston, *My Racing Life*, 1952, p. 13; C. H. Curzon, *A Mirror of the Turf*, 1892, p. 340.

42. J. D. Astley, *Fifty Years of My Life*, 1895, pp. 358–60.

43. C. Richardson, *The English Turf*, 1901, p. 223.

44. The following is based on W. Day, *The Racehorse in Training*, 1880, pp. 15–21, and J. Porter, *Kingsclere*, 1896, pp. 217–8.

45. E. Spencer, *The Great Game*, 1900, p. 111; J. C. Whyte, *History of the British Turf*, 1840, p. 493.

46. C. J. Apperley, 'The Turf', *Quarterly Review*, vol. 49, July 1833, p. 403.

47. D. P. Blaine, *Encyclopaedia of Rural Sports*, 1870, p. 375.

48. Q. Gilbey, *Champions All*, 1971, p. 61.

49. E. M. Humphris, *The Life of Fred Archer*, 1923, pp. 48–9.

50. R. Scott to Mr D. Swannell, March 1965, York Racing Museum.

51. J. Porter, *Kingsclere*, 1896, p. 223.

52. M. Cobbett, *Racing Life and Racing Characters*, 1903, p. 232; Q. Gilbey, *Champions All*, 1971, pp. 139–41.

53. 'Jockeys and Jockeyship', *Badminton Magazine*, vol. 18, February 1904, p. 148.

54. T. A. Cook, *A History of the English Turf*, 1905, p. 537.

55. 'Otto Madden on Race Riding', *Badminton Magazine*, vol. 20, April 1905, p. 417.

56. *Bloodstock Breeders Review*, vol. 26, 1937, p. 277.

57. J. Porter, *Kingsclere*, 1896, p. 219.

58. C. Richardson, *The English Turf*, 1901, p. 221.

59. W. Day, *The Racehorse in Training*, 1880, pp. 163, 273; J. Porter, *Kingsclere*, 1896, pp. 72–3.

60. For an example of complaint about the apprentice allowance see 'The Racing Season', *Badminton Magazine*, vol. 22, April 1906, p. 427.

61. R. K. Mainwaring, 'The Prospects of the Racing Season', *Badminton Magazine*, vol. 4, April 1897, p. 454.

62. 'Jockeys, Betting and Bookmakers', *Badminton Magazine*, vol. 14, May 1902, pp. 488–91.

63. Earl of Suffolk, *Racing and Steeplechasing*, 1886, p. 53.

64. P. J. Sloane, 'The Labour Market in Professional Football', *British Journal of Industrial Relations*, vol. 7, 1969, p. 186.

65. J. Welcome, *Fred Archer: His Life and Times*, 1967, p. 86; A. E. T. Watson, 'Racing', in Earl of Suffolk, H. Peek and F. G. Aflalo (eds.), *The Encyclopaedia of Sport*, 1900, p. 194.

66. Earl of Suffolk, 'Gentlemen Riders', *Badminton Magazine*, vol. 11, April 1896, p. 478.

67. Quoted in M. Seth-Smith, *Bred for the Purple*, 1969, pp. 95–6.

68. J. C. Whyte, *History of the British Turf*, 1840, p. 608.

69. Quoted in J. Fairfax-Blakeborough, *The Analysis of the Turf*, 1927, p. 143.

70. J. C. Whyte, *History of the British Turf*, 1840, pp. 596–7.

71. See e.g. the pleading letter of Frank Butler to John Bowes, 12 January 1855, D/St. Box 162, Durham County Record Office.

72. M. B. Scott, 'The Man on the Horse', in J. W. Loy and G. S. Kenyon, *Sport, Culture and Society*, 1969, p. 427.

73. The Druid, *Post and Paddock*, 1895, p. 36; J. Welcome, *Fred Archer: His Life and Times*, 1967, p. 57.

74. E. Spencer, *The Great Game*, 1900, p. 128.

75. *ibid.*

76. T. Weston, *My Racing Life*, 1952, p. 169.

77. D. Batchelor, *The Turf of Old*, 1951, p. 181; J. Fairfax-Blakeborough, *The Analysis of the Turf*, 1927, p. 123; E. Moorhouse, *The Romance of the Derby*, vol. 2, 1908, p. 65.

78. T. H. Bird, *Admiral Rous and the English Turf*, 1939, p. 85.

79. R. Rodrigo, *The Racing Game*, 1960, p. 62.

80. J. Fairfax-Blakeborough, *The Analysis of the Turf*, 1927, p. 133; T. Weston, *My Racing Life*, 1952, p. 171.

81. The Druid, *Post and Paddock*, 1895, p. 91; The Druid, *Scott and Sebright*, 1895, p. 60; Earl of Suffolk, *Racing and Steeplechasing*, 1886, p. 239.

82. D. J. Hanes, *The First British Workmen's Compensation Act 1897*, 1968, p. 103; A. Wilson and H. Levy, *Workmen's Compensation*, 1939, pp. 101–2.

83. Q. Gilbey, *Champions All*, 1971, pp. 19–24.

84. *Select Committee on Gaming*, 1844, VI, q. 3105.

85. J. Welcome, *Fred Archer: His Life and Times*, 1967, p. 88. Letters from Frank Butler to John Bowes showed that he bet heavily, £50 being a not uncommon stake, e.g. 23 September 1851, 5 November 1852, D/St. Box 162, Durham County Record Office.

86. Earl of Suffolk, *Racing and Steeplechasing*, 1886, p. 105.

87. T. Sloan, *Tod Sloan*, 1915, p. 101.

88. T. Weston, *My Racing Life*, 1952, pp. 26–8 is quite explicit on this.

89. Sylvanus, *The Bye-Lanes and Downs of England*, 1850, p. 28.

90. Earl of Suffolk, *Racing and Steeplechasing*, 1886, p. 233.

91. W. Read to J. Bowes, 17 November 1863, D/St. Box 162, Durham County Record Office.

92. H. Rous to J. Bowes, 30 November 1863, D/St. Box 162, Durham County Record Office.

93. D. Batchelor, *The Turf of Old*, 1951, p. 174.

94. J. Rice, *The History of the British Turf*, vol. 1, 1879, p. 273; C. H. Curzon, *A Mirror of the Turf*, 1892, p. 359.

95. C. Richardson, *The English Turf*, 1901, pp. 225–6.

96. J. Porter and E. Moorhouse, *John Porter of Kingsclere*, 1919, p. 63; L. H. Curzon, *The Blue Riband of the Turf*, 1890, p. 91.

97. W. and A. J. Day, *The Racehorse in Training*, 1925, p. 75.

98. Calculated from data in *Racing Calendar*.

99. M. Good, *The Lure of the Turf*, 1957, p. 54; T. H. Bird, *Admiral Rous and the English Turf*, 1939, p. 182.

100. *Bloodstock Breeders Review*, vol. 6, October 1917, p. 393; T. A. Cook, *A History of the English Turf*, 1905, pp. 384–6; Earl of Suffolk, *Racing and Steeplechasing*, 1886, p. 231; J. Fairfax-Blakeborough, *The Analysis of the Turf*, 1927, p. 124.

101. Earl of Suffolk, *Racing and Steeplechasing*, 1886, p. 231.

102. J. Ford, *Prizefighting*, 1971, chapter 3; S. K. Weinberg and H. Arond, "The Occupational Culture of the Boxer', *American Journal of Sociology*, vol. 57, March 1952, 460–69.

103. J. Klein, *Samples from English Culture*, 1965, pp. 196–7.

104. G. Fordham to C. Wood, 1 October 1887, York Racing Museum.

10. TRAINERS

1. Earl of Suffolk, *Racing and Steeplechasing*, 1886, pp. 98–100; C. Richardson, *The English Turf*, 1901, p. 218.

2. Earl of Suffolk, *Racing and Steeplechasing*, 1886, pp. 98–100.

3. *ibid.*; L. H. Curzon, *A Mirror of the Turf*, 1892, p. 88; 'Modern

Horse-Racing', *Edinburgh Review*, vol. 151, April 1880, p. 417; C. Richardson, *Racing at Home and Abroad*, vol. 1, 1923, p. 334; W. and A. J. Day, *The Racehorse in Training*, 1925, p. 30.

4. 'Sportsmen of Mark, *Badminton Magazine*, vol. 23, February 1907; C. Richardson, *The English Turf*, 1901, p. 234; L. H. Curzon, *The Blue Riband of the Turf*, 1890, p. 100.

5. W. Day, *The Racehorse in Training*, 1880, p. 224; W. Day, *Reminiscences of the Turf*, 1886, p. 355.

6. Earl of Suffolk, *Racing and Steeplechasing*, 1886, p. 98; C. Richardson, *The English Turf*, 1901, p. 221; *Bloodstock Breeders Review*, vol. 10, December 1921, p. 182.

7. Quoted in J. Welcome, *Fred Archer: His Life and Times*, 1967, p. 231.

8. Quoted in M. Seth-Smith, *Bred for the Purple*, 1969, p. 211.

9. W. Day, *The Racehorse in Training*, 1880, pp. 216–18.

10. J. H. Peart to J. Bowes, 2 November 1848, D/St. Box 162, Durham County Record Office.

11. R. Onslow, *The Heath and the Turf*, 1971, p. 55.

12. J. Fairfax-Blakeborough, *The Analysis of the Turf*, 1927, p. 73; 'Racing', *Badminton Magazine*, vol. 25, July 1907, p. 19.

13. W. and A. J. Day, *The Racehorse in Training*, 1925, p. 157; The Sportsman, *British Sports and Sportsmen – Racing*, 1920, p. 144.

14. 'Horse-Racing', *Quarterly Review*, vol. 161, October 1885, p. 444.

15. L. H. Curzon, *The Blue Riband of the Turf*, 1890, p. 105; 'Modern Horse-Racing', *Edinburgh Review*, vol. 151, April 1880, p. 416.

16. W. Day, *The Racehorse in Training*, 1880, p. 75; The Druid, *Post and Paddock*, 1895, p. 136; Earl of Suffolk, *Racing and Steeplechasing*, 1886, p. 100.

17. The Druid, *Post and Paddock*, 1895, p. 24; W. Day, *The Racehorse in Training*, 1880, p. 75.

18. Earl of Suffolk, *Racing and Steeplechasing*, 1886, p. 209; J. Rice, *The History of the British Turf*, vol. 2, 1879, p. 207; H. Custance, *Riding Recollections and Turf Stories*, 1894, p. 196.

19. Quoted in C. E. Hardy, *John Bowes and the Bowes Museum*, 1970, p. 117.

20. A. E. T. Watson, *The Racing World and Its Inhabitants*, 1904, p. 29.

11. OWNERS

1. D. P. Blaine, *Encyclopaedia of Rural Sports*, 1870, p. 371.

2. See e.g. the discussion in P. Wilsher, *The Pound in Your Pocket 1870–1970*, 1970, pp. 36–7 on the wealth of the aristocracy in the 1870s.

3. V. Orchard, *Tattersalls*, 1953, p. 253.

4. Calculated from data in the *Racing Calendar*.

5. 'Notes', *Badminton Magazine*, vol. 5, December 1897, p. 745.

6. R. Cecil, *Life in Edwardian England*, 1972, p. 9.

7. C. Richardson, *The English Turf*, 1901, p. 274.

8. 'Owners and Owning', *Badminton Magazine*, vol. 17, September 1903, p. 313.

9. Thormanby, *Famous Racing Men*, 1882, p. 77.

10. E. Rickman, *Come Racing with Me*, 1951, pp. 95–6.

11. V. Orchard, *Tattersalls*, 1953, p. 192.

12. E. Rickman, *Come Racing with Me*, 1951, p. 92.

13. *Select Committee on Laws Respecting Gaming*, 1844, VI, q. 419.

14. 'The Turf: Its Frauds and Chicaneries', *Contemporary Review*, vol. 22, June 1873, p. 36; L. H. Curzon, 'The Horse as an Instrument of Gambling', *Contemporary Review*, vol. 30, August 1877, p. 378; 'Modern Horse-Racing', *Edinburgh Review*, vol. 151, April 1880, p. 432; *Bloodstock Breeders Review*, vol. 18, 1929, p. 264; E. Rickman, *On and Off the Course*, 1937, pp. 6, 21.

15. The Sportsman, *British Sports and Sportsmen – Racing*, 1920, pp. 102–4; A. E. T. Watson, 'Major Eustace Loder', *Badminton Magazine*, vol. 31, August 1910, p. 119.

16. S. G. Galtrey, *Memoirs of a Racing Journalist*, 1934, p. 157.

17. Calculated from data in C. Richardson, *The English Turf*, 1901, p. 273.

18. *ibid.*, p. 276.

19. H. Custance, *Riding Recollections and Turf Stories*, 1894, p. 187.

20. Lord Hamilton, 'The Financial Aspects of Racing', *Badminton Magazine*, vol. 23, September 1906, p. 253; bloodstock valuation based on Doncaster and Newmarket sales data cited in *Bloodstock Breeders Review, passim*.

21. Calculated from data in the *Racing Calendar*.

22. G. H. Verrall, 'The Financial Aspect of Racing from Another Point of View', *Badminton Magazine*, vol. 23, November 1906, p. 504.

23. H. Rous, *On The Laws and Practice of Horse Racing*, 1850, p. 51.

24. An impression gained from a reading of racing and sporting magazines.

25. *Bloodstock Breeders Review*, vol. 7, no. 1, April 1918, pp. 18–19.

26. *Select Committee on Gaming*, 1844, VI, p. vi; A. E. T. Watson, 'Racing in 1896', *Badminton Magazine*, vol. 3, December 1896, p. 687.

27. See e.g. L. H. Curzon, 'The Horse as an Instrument of Gambling', *Contemporary Review*, vol. 30, August 1877, p. 383; J. Runciman, 'The Ethics of the Turf', *Contemporary Review*, vol. 55, April 1889, p. 605.

28. Earl of Suffolk, *Racing and Steeplechasing*, 1886 and 1907, p. 157.

29. W. Day, *The Racehorse in Training*, 1880, p. 243.

30. A. E. T. Watson, *The Turf*, 1898, p. 153.

31. R. Black, *Horse-Racing in England*, 1893, p. 269.

12. BREEDERS

1. Quoted in R. Longrigg, *The History of Horse Racing*, 1972, p. 28.

2. A. E. T. Watson, 'Racing' in Earl of Suffolk, H. Peck & F. G. Aflalo (eds.), *The Encyclopaedia of Sport*, 1900, p. 179.

3. See B. Lowe, *Breeding Race Horses by the Figure System*, 1895, and W. Allison, *The British Thoroughbred Horse*, 1901.

4. *Bloodstock Breeders Review*, vol. 1, no. 1, April 1912, pp. 37–40.

5. For a detailed criticism see J. B. Robertson, 'The Figure System', *Badminton Magazine*, vol. 36, March 1913.

6. See e.g. J. B. Robertson, 'The Principles of Heredity Applied to the Racehorse', in Earl of Harewood (ed.), *Flat Racing*, 1940, pp. 93–116.

7. *Select Committee on the Laws Respecting Gaming*, 1844, VI, p. v.

8. *Report of the Duke of Norfolk's Committee on the Pattern of Racing*, 1965, para. 4.

9. See e.g. W. S. Dixon, *The Influence of Racing and the Thoroughbred Horse on Light Horse Breeding*, 1924.

10. See e.g. A. E. T. Watson, 'The Turf', *Badminton Magazine*, vol. 4, June 1897, p. 732; *Report of the Duke of Norfolk's Committee on the Pattern of Racing*, 1965, para 4.

11. Lord Coventry to Lord Rosebery, 18 February 1873, Rosebery Papers, Acc. 4070, Box 109, National Library of Scotland.

12. For a full discussion of Hawley's proposals see R. Mortimer, *The Jockey Club*, 1958, pp. 86–7.

13. Earl of Suffolk, *Racing and Steeplechasing*, 1886, pp. 127–8; J. Porter and E. Moorhouse, *John Porter of Kingsclere*, 1919, p. 101.

14. The Sportsman, *British Sports and Sportsmen – Racing*, 1920, pp. 174, 182–3.

15. *Select Committee on Horses*, 1873, XIV, q. 3846.

16. J. Rice, *The History of the British Turf*, vol. 2, 1879, p. 339.

17. *Select Committee on Horses*, 1873, XIV, q. 3846; C. Richardson, *Racing at Home and Abroad*, vol. 1, 1923, p. 169.

18. The Sportsman, *British Sports and Sportsmen – Breeding and Agriculture*, 1926, p. 120.

19. *Select Committee on Horses*, 1873, XIV, q. 3846.

20. S. Sidney, *The Book of the Horse*, 1875, p. 554; see e.g. a study of the Cobham Stud in *Bloodstock Breeders Review*, vol. 5, no. 3, October 1913, pp. 209–21.

21. C. Richardson, *The English Turf*, 1901, p. 5.

22. *ibid.*

23. *Select Committee on Betting Duty*, 1923, V, q. 7677; *Bloodstock Breeders Review*, vol. 14, 1930, p. 147.

24. Information supplied by J. V. Baillie, breeder, in a letter of 15 November 1972; data from the *Reports and Accounts of the National Stud*.

25. Calculated from data in *Bloodstock Breeders Review*.

26. C. Leicester, *Bloodstock Breeding*, 1959, p. 27; J. B. Robertson; 'The Principles of Heredity Applied to the Racehorse', in Earl of Harewood (ed.), *Flat Racing*, 1940, p. 105.

27. *Bloodstock Breeders Review*, vol. 6, no. 2, July 1917, pp. 109–110.

28. Calculated from data in *Bloodstock Breeders Review*.

29. George Bryatt to W. J. Scott, 24 July 1843, Bowes Papers D/St. Box 162, Durham County Record Office.

30. T. A. Cook, *A History of the English Turf*, 1905, pp. xxi–xxii.

31. *Bloodstock Breeders Review*, vol. 4, no. 2, July 1915, p. 132.

32. 'Our Breeds and Races', *Saturday Review*, vol. 11, May 1864, p. 323.

33. J. Rice, *The History of the British Turf*, vol. 2, 1879, p. 334.

34. *Select Committee on Horses*, 1873, XIV, q. 3383.

35. J. Rice, *The History of the British Turf*, vol. 2, 1879, p. 334; 'Horse-Racing', *Quarterly Review*, vol. 161, October 1885.

36. What follows is based on T. H. Brown, *A History of the English Turf 1904–1930*, 1931, contemporary issues of the *Bloodstock Breeders Review*, and the *Reports and Accounts of the National Stud*.

37. *Bloodstock Breeders Review*, vol. 4, no. 4, January 1916, p. 223.

GAMBLING: THE KEYSTONE OF RACING

13. ONE FOR THE RICH AND ONE FOR THE POOR:
THE LAW AND GAMBLING

1. What follows is based on Thormanby, *Famous Racing Men*,

1882, pp. 10–12; R. Rodrigo, *The Racing Game*, 1960, pp. 9–10; *Select Committee on Betting Duty*, 1923, V.

2. *Select Committee on Gaming*, 1844, VI, p. iv.

3. *Select Committee on Betting Duty*, 1923, V, p. vi.

4. *Select Committee on Gaming*, 1844, VI, q. 801.

5. Lord Maidstone to J. Bowes, 19 December 1844, D/St. Box 162, Durham County Record Office.

6. C. E. Hardy, *John Bowes and the Bowes Museum*, 1970, pp. 67–70. Copies of these letters are retained at the Bowes Museum, Barnard Castle, County Durham.

7. *Hansard*, 3rd series, vol. 72, 5, 8, 14, 21 February 1844.

8. *ibid.*

9. *Select Committee on Laws Respecting Gaming*, 1844, VI, qq. 238–9.

10. *ibid.*, V.

11. *ibid.*

12. L. H. Curzon, *A Mirror of the Turf*, 1892, p. 230.

13. *Hansard*, 3rd series, vol. 129, 11 July 1853.

14. *ibid.*, vol. 72, 8 February 1844.

15. J. Rice, *The History of the British Turf*, vol. 1, 1879, p. 255.

16. *Hansard*, 3rd series, vol. 129, 11 July 1853.

17. *ibid*; J. Rice, *The History of the British Turf*, vol. 2, 1879, p. 275.

18. *Select Committee on Gaming*, 1844, VI, qq. 1072–9; *Select Committee on Laws Respecting Gaming*, 1844, VI, qq. 410, 446–61.

19. J. Rice, *The History of the British Turf*, vol. 2, 1879, pp. 274–5.

20. B. Harrison, *Drink and the Victorians*, 1971, pp. 376–7.

21. J. Rice, *The History of the British Turf*, vol. 2, 1879, p. 276.

22. *Hansard*, 3rd series, vol. 218, 15 April 1874.

23. *ibid.*

24. *Select Committee on Betting*, 1902, V, q. 3079.

25. *ibid.*; 'Horse-Racing', *Quarterly Review*, vol. 161, October 1885, p. 454.

26. *Select Committee on Betting*, 1902, V, q. 3074.

27. A full survey of the law relating to betting at this time can be found in W. Coldridge and C. V. Hawksford, *The Law of Gambling*, 1895.

28. *Select Committee on Betting*, 1902, V, qq. 2817, 2820; *Select Committee on Betting*, 1901, V, q. 183.

29. *Select Committee on Betting*, 1901, V, q. 183.

30. 'Horse-Racing', *Quarterly Review*, vol. 161, October 1885, p. 453; *Select Committee on Betting*, 1902, V, q. 862; *Bloodstock Breeders Review*, vol. 3, December 1914, p. 328.

31. J. M. Hogge, *Betting and Gambling*, 1904, p. 33.

32. *Select Committee on Betting*, 1902, V, q. 425.
33. *Royal Commission on Lotteries and Betting*, 1932–3, XIV, p. 73.
34. *Select Committee on Betting*, 1902, V, *passim*.
35. 'The Turf: Its Frauds and Chicaneries', *Contemporary Review*, vol. 22, June 1873, p. 36.
36. *Hansard*, 4th series, vol. 94, 20 May 1901.
37. J. M. Hogge, *Betting and Gambling*, 1904, p. 33.
38. *Select Committee on Betting*, 1902, V, p. viii.
39. *Hansard*, 4th series, vol. 122, 18 May 1903.
40. *Select Committee on Betting Duty*, 1923, V, qq. 1361–3.
41. The following description is based on *ibid.*, p. xiv.
42. *ibid.*, p. xl.
43. *ibid.*, qq. 375, 1371, 1674.
44. *ibid.*, p. xiii.
45. *ibid.*, p. xl.
46. *ibid.*, p. xv.
47. *ibid.*, p. liii.
48. *Royal Commission on Lotteries and Betting*, 1932–3, XIV.

14. BOOKMAKERS AND THEIR BETTERS

1. R. Holloway, 'More Gambling, Less Tax?', *Lloyds Bank Review*, October 1973, no. 110, p. 32.
2. A. R. Prest, *Consumers' Expenditure in the United Kingdom 1900–1919*, 1954, p. 158.
3. R. Stone and D. Rowe, *The Measurement of Consumer Expenditure and Behaviour in the U.K. 1920–1938*, vol. 2, 1966, pp. 84–92.
4. 'Reviews', *Badminton Magazine*, vol. 21, September 1905, p. 339.
5. Rapier, 'Short Heads', *Badminton Magazine*, vol. 19, October 1904, p. 368.
6. G. Orwell, *The Road to Wigan Pier*, 1937, p. 89.
7. 'The Turf: Its Frauds and Chicaneries', *Contemporary Review*, vol. 22, June 1873, p. 34; R. Black, *Horse-Racing in England*, 1893, p. 192.
8. According to R. Longrigg, *The History of Horse Racing*, 1972, p. 117.
9. E. Spencer, *The Great Game*, 1900, p. 227; J. Fairfax-Blakeborough, *The Analysis of the Turf*, 1927, pp. 263–5; L. H. Curzon, *A Mirror of the Turf*, 1892, p. 233; T. H. Bird, *Admiral Rous and the English Turf*, 1939, p. 151.
10. Cited in E. Rickman, *Come Racing with Me*, 1951, pp. 166–7.
11. J. Rice, *The History of the British Turf*, vol. 2, 1879, p. 305.

12. E. Spencer, *The Great Game*, 1900, p. 170; L. H. Curzon, 'The Horse as an Instrument of Gambling', *Contemporary Review*, vol. 30, August 1877, p. 339.

13. J. Rice, *The History of the British Turf*, vol. 2, 1879, p. 271.

14. G. Payne to J. Bowes, 11 July 1843, D/St. Box 162, Durham County Record Office; *Select Committee on Gaming*, 1844, VI, qq. 1680, 1683; Earl of Suffolk, *Racing and Steeplechasing*, 1886, p. 260; The Druid, *Post and Paddock*, 1895, p. 51.

15. S. Sidney, *The Book of the Horse*, 1875(?), p. 195.

16. J. Runciman, 'The Ethics of the Turf', *Contemporary Review*, vol. 55, April 1889, p. 606.

17. J. Rice, *The History of the British Turf*, vol. 2, 1879, p. 273.

18. E. D. Cuming, *Squire Osbaldeston: His Autobiography*, 1926, p. 220.

19. *Select Committee on Betting Duty*, 1923, V, qq. 3663, 3758, 3987.

20. Earl of Suffolk, *Racing and Steeplechasing*, 1886, pp. 258, 265–7.

21. H. P. Eriksson, *A History of the National Sporting League*, 1970, p. 1.

22. E. Rickman, *On and Off the Course*, 1937, p. 268.

23. T. Weston, *My Racing Life*, 1952, pp. 17–18.

24. E. Rickman, *On and Off the Course*, 1937, pp. 218–19.

25. *ibid.*, p. 227; M. Cobbett, *Racing Life and Racing Characters*, 1903, pp. 88–9.

26. 'Touts and Touting', *Badminton Magazine*, vol. 17, December 1903, 622–30; The Druid, *Post and Paddock*, 1895, p. 169; 'The Turf: Its Frauds and Chicaneries', *Contemporary Review*, vol. 22, June 1873, p. 31.

27. J. C. Whyte, *History of the British Turf*, 1840, p. xiii.

28. J. Rice, *The History of the British Turf*, vol. 2, 1879, pp. xi–xii; L. H. Curzon, *A Mirror of the Turf*, 1892, p. v; *Select Committee on Betting*, 1902, V, q. 3842.

29. *Select Committee on Betting*, 1902, V, q. 1600.

30. E. Rickman, *On and Off the Course*, 1937, p. 185; E. Rickman, *Come Racing with Me*, 1951, p. 9; S. G. Galtrey, *Memoirs of a Racing Journalist*, 1934, pp. 284–5.

31. 'Tipsters and Tipping', *Badminton Magazine*, vol. 18, August 1904, p. 399; The Druid, *Post and Paddock*, 1895, p. 170.

32. J. Porter, *Kingsclere*, 1896, pp. 248–9.

33. Quoted in R. Mortimer, *The Jockey Club*, 1958, p. 112.

34. J. Porter, *Kingsclere*, 1896, p. 249.

35. E. Rickman, *Come Racing with Me*, 1951, p. 4.

36. E. Rickman, *On and Off the Course*, 1937, p. 180.

37. *ibid.*, p. 38.
38. *Select Committee on Betting*, 1902, V, qq. 2971–3003.
39. L. H. Curzon, *The Blue Riband of the Turf*, 1890, pp. 218–22.
40. *Select Committee on Betting*, 1902, V. q. 1624.

15. THE TOTALIZATOR

1. The basic material for this chapter has been taken from *Bloodstock Breeders Review*, 1909–31; *Reports and Accounts of the Racecourse Betting Control Board*; and Lord Hamilton of Dalzell, 'The Tote', in Earl of Harewood (ed.), *Flat Racing*, 1940, pp. 378–94.
2. J. Richardson, 'Hunting, Fishing and Cricket: Anglomania under the Second French Empire', *History Today*, vol. 21, no. 4, April 1971, pp. 243–4; N. Elias, 'The Genesis of Sports as a Sociological Problem', in E. Dunning, *The Sociology of Sport*, 1971, p. 189.
3. E. Spencer, *The Great Game*, 1900, pp. 161–3.
4. *ibid.*, p. 163.
5. For details of the debate as to whether the government should be approached, see A. W. Coaten, 'Is the Pari-Mutuel wanted in England?', *Badminton Magazine*, vol. 45, May 1916.
6. Quoted in T. Weston, *My Racing Life*, 1952, p. 123.
7. *Bloodstock Breeders Review*, vol. 16, 1927, p. 7.
8. *Report and Accounts of the R.B.C.B.*, 1930–31, XVII, p. 6.
9. Quoted in R. Mortimer, *The Jockey Club*, 1958, p. 154.
10. R. Stone and D. Rowe, *The Measurement of Consumer Expenditure and Behaviour in the U.K. 1920–1938*, vol. 2, 1966, p. 91.
11. S. G. Galtrey, *Memoirs of a Racing Journalist*, 1934, p. 22.

EPILOGUE

16. A DECLINING INDUSTRY? THE BENSON REPORT AND BEYOND

1. *The Racing Industry*, 1968, para. 33. Since most of what follows is based on Benson no further references are given except for direct quotations.
2. *Report of the Racing Reorganisation Committee*, 1943, para. 93.
3. *ibid.*, paras. 70, 92.
4. *ibid.*, para. 92.
5. *The Racing Industry*, para. 49.
6. *Twelfth Report of Horserace Betting Levy Board*, 1973, para. 5.
7. *Report of the Racing Reorganisation Committee*, para. 53.

Select Bibliography]

MANUSCRIPT SOURCES

Bowes Papers: Racing and Personal Letters of John Bowes, D/St. Box 162, Durham County Record Office.
Rosebery Papers: Acc. 4070, Boxes 108, 109, National Library of Scotland.
The Western Meeting, Ayr, Minute Books.
York Racing Committee Records.
York Racing Museum.

PARLIAMENTARY PAPERS

Hansard's Parliamentary Debates.
National Stud: *Annual Reports of Ministry of Agriculture and Fisheries.*
Racecourse Betting Control Board: *Annual Reports.*
Report of the Commissioners of Inland Revenue on the Duties under their Management, 1870, XX.
Royal Commission on Betting, Lotteries and Gaming, 1950–51, VIII.
Royal Commission on Horse Breeding, 1888, XLVIII.
Royal Commission on Horse Breeding, 1890, XXVII.
Royal Commission on Lotteries and Betting, 1932–3, XIV.
Select Committee on Betting, 1901, V.
Select Committee on Betting, 1902, V.
Select Committee on Betting Duty, 1923, V.
Select Committee on Gaming, 1844, VI.
Select Committee on Horses, 1873, XIV.
Select Committee on Laws Respecting Gaming, 1844, VI.

OTHER REPORTS

Report of Dalzell Committee of Inquiry into Racing, 1919.
Horserace Betting Levy Board: *Annual Reports.*
Report of Duke of Norfolk's Committee on the Pattern of Racing, 1965.
Racecourse Association Ltd: *Annual Reports.*
Report of the Working Party on Racecourse Management (Cohen Report), 1969.
The Racing Industry (Benson Report), 1968.
Report of the Racing Reorganisation Committee (Ilchester Report) 1943.

Report of the Committee on the Scheme for the Suppression of Doping (Paton Committee), 1971.

NEWSPAPERS AND PERIODICALS

Badminton Magazine
Bloodstock Breeders Review
General Stud Book
Racing Calendar
Ruffs Guide to the Turf
Sporting Life

ARTICLES (excluding those in above periodicals)

'Bookmaking', *All the Year Round*, vol. 20, 1868.
'The Derby', *The Broadway*, vol. 2, 1869.
'Doncaster: Yorkshire Racecourses', *All the Year Round*, vol. 17, September 1876.
'Handicapping', *Saturday Review*, vol. 72, September 1891.
'Horse-Racing', *Quarterly Review*, vol. 161, October 1885.
'The Intellectual Side of Horse-Racing', *New Statesman*, vol. 15, June 1920.
'A Mirror of the Turf, *Saturday Review*, vol. 73, May 1892.
'Modern Horse-Racing', *Edinburgh Review*, vol. 151, April 1880.
'Our Breeds and Races', *Saturday Review*, vol. 11, May 1864.
'Sir E. Sullivan on the Turf', *Saturday Review*, vol. 65, March 1888.
'Turf Ethics in 1868', *The Broadway*, vol. 1, 1868-9.
'The Turf: Its Frauds and Chicaneries', *Contemporary Review*, vol. 22, June 1873.
'Whitewall', *All the Year Round*, vol. 4, October 1870.
'Work and Leisure in Industrial Society', *Past and Present*, vol. 30, April 1965.

C. J. APPERLEY, 'The Turf', *Quarterly Review*, vol. 49, July 1833.
H. A. BLOCH, 'The Sociology of Gambling', *American Journal of Sociology*, vol. 57, November 1951.
H. B. BROMHEAD, 'Derby Anecdotes', *English Illustrated Magazine*, vol. 10, 1892-3.
L. H. CURZON, 'The Horse as an Instrument of Gambling', *Contemporary Review*, vol. 30, August 1877.
A. E. DINGLE, 'Drink and Working-Class Living Standards in Britain, 1870-1914', *Economic History Review*, vol. 25, November 1972.

M. W. FLINN, 'Trends in Real Wages 1750–1850', *Economic History Review*, vol. 27, August 1974.

A. P. L. GORDON, 'Statistics of Totalisator Betting', *Journal of Royal Statistical Society*, vol. 94, 1931.

B. HARRISON, 'Religion and Recreation in Nineteenth Century England', *Past and Present*, vol. 38, December 1967.

R. HOLLOWAY, 'More Gambling, Less Tax?', *Lloyds Bank Review*, vol. 110, October 1973.

A. J. KETTLE, 'Lichfield Races', *Transactions of Lichfield and South Staffordshire Archaeological and History Society*, vol. 6, 1964–5.

J. MYERSCOUGH, 'History and Philosophies of the Use of Leisure Time', Unpublished seminar paper, University of Sussex, 1972.

J. MYERSCOUGH, 'The Transformation of Popular Recreation', Unpublished seminar paper, University of Sussex, 1972.

J. RICHARDSON, 'Hunting, Fishing and Cricket: Anglomania under the Second French Empire', *History Today*, vol. 21, April 1971.

J. RUNCIMAN, 'The Ethics of the Turf', *Contemporary Review*, vol. 55, April 1889.

P. J. SLOANE, 'The Labour Market in Professional Football', *British Journal of Industrial Relations*, vol. 7, 1969.

K. THOMAS, 'Work and Leisure in Pre-Industrial Society', *Past and Present*, vol. 29, December 1964.

E. P. THOMPSON, 'Time, Work-Discipline, and Industrial Capitalism', *Past and Present*, vol. 38, December 1967.

S. K. WEINBERG and H. AROND, 'The Occupational Culture of the Boxer', *American Journal of Sociology*, vol. 57, March 1952.

BOOKS

F. G. AFLALO (ed.), *The Sports of the World* (2 vols), London, 1903.

S. ALEXANDER, *St Gile's Fair 1830–1914*, Oxford, 1970.

J. D. ASTLEY, *Fifty Years of My Life*, London, 1895.

M. AYRES and G. NEWBON, *Over the Sticks*, Newton Abbot, 1971.

D. BATCHELOR, *The Turf of Old*, London, 1951.

G. BEST, *Mid-Victorian Britain 1851–75*, London, 1971.

T. H. BIRD, *Admiral Rous and the English Turf*, London, 1939.

R. BLACK, *Horse-Racing in England*, London, 1893.

R. BLACK, *The Jockey Club and Its Founders*, London, 1891.

D. P. BLAINE, *Encyclopaedia of Rural Sports*, London, 1870.

E. BLAND (ed.), *Flat Racing Since 1900*, London, 1950.

H. BLYTH, *The Pocket Venus*, London, 1966.

T. H. BROWNE, *A History of the English Turf 1904–1930* (2 vols), London, 1931.

W. L. BURN, *The Age of Equipose*, London, 1964.

C. J. CAWTHORNE and R. S. HEROD, *Royal Ascot*, London, 1900.

R. CECIL, *Life in Edwardian England*, Newton Abbot, 1972.

P. R. CHALMERS, *Racing England*, London, 1939.

R. H. CHARLES, *Gambling and Betting*, Edinburgh, 1928.

S. G. CHECKLAND, *The Rise of Industrial Society in England 1815–85*, London, 1964.

K. CHESNEY, *The Victorian Underworld*, London, 1970.

G. CHETWYND, *Racing Reminiscences* (2 vols), London, 1891.

M. COBBETT, *Racing Life and Racing Characters*, London, 1903.

W. COLDRIDGE and C. V. HAWKSFORD, *The Law of Gambling*, London, 1895.

T. A. COOK, *A History of the English Turf* (3 vols), London, 1905.

D. CRAIG, *Horse-Racing*, London, 1963.

E. D. CUMING, *Squire Osbaldeston: His Autobiography*, London, 1926.

B. W. R. CURLING, *British Racecourses*, London, 1951.

L. H. CURZON, *The Blue Riband of the Turf*, London, 1890.

L. H. CURZON, *A Mirror of the Turf*, London, 1892.

H. CUSTANCE, *Riding Recollections and Turf Stories*, London, 1894.

B. DARWIN, *John Gully and His Times*, London, 1935.

W. DAY, *The Racehorse in Training*, London, 1880.

W. DAY, *Reminiscences of the Turf*, London, 1886.

W. DAY, *The Horse: How to Breed and Rear Him*, London, 1888.

W. DAY, *Turf Celebrities I Have Known*, London, 1891.

W. and A. J. DAY, *The Racehorse in Training*, London, 1925.

A. DELGADO, *Victorian Entertainment*, Newton Abbot, 1972.

W. S. DIXON, *The Influence of Racing and the Thoroughbred Horse on Light Horse Breeding*, London, 1924.

E. E. DORLING, *Epsom and the Dorlings*, London, 1939.

THE DRUID, *Saddle and Sirloin*, London, 1870.

THE DRUID, *Post and Paddock*, London, 1895.

THE DRUID, *Scott and Sebright*, London, 1895.

E. DUNNING, *The Sociology of Sport*, London, 1971.

H. EDWARDS, *Sociology of Sport*, Homewood (Illinois), 1973.

P. EGAN, *Pierce Egan's Book of Sports*, London, 1832.

H. P. ERIKSSON, *A History of the National Sporting League*, Unpublished manuscript, 1970.

J. FAIRFAX-BLAKEBOROUGH, *The Analysis of the Turf*, London, 1927.

J. FAIRFAX-BLAKEBOROUGH, *Racecourses of Yorkshire*, London, 1954.

J. FAIRFAX-BLAKEBOROUGH, *The Racecourses of Scotland*, London, 1954.

M. FANE, *Racecourse Swindles*, London, 1936.

W. FAWCETT, *Racing in the Olden Days*, 1933(?).

J. S. FLETCHER, *The History of the St Leger Stakes*, London, 1902.

J. FORD, *Prizefighting*, Newton Abbot, 1971.

J. FORD, *Cricket*, Newton Abbot, 1972.

S. G. GALTREY, *Memoirs of a Racing Journalist*, London, 1934.

Q. GILBEY, *Champions All*, London, 1971.

E. GOFFMAN, *Interaction Ritual*, London, 1972.

M. GOOD, *The Lure of the Turf*, London, 1957.

C. E. HARDY, *John Bowes and the Bowes Museum*, Newcastle, 1970.

LORD HAREWOOD (ed.), *Flat Racing*, London, 1940.

B. HARRISON, *Drink and the Victorians*, London, 1971.

J. F. C. HARRISON, *The Early Victorians*, London, 1971.

G. HAWKINS, *The Jockey Club*, London, 1827.

R. D. HERMAN, *Gambling*, New York, 1967.

J. HILTON, *Why I Go In for the Pools*, London, 1936.

J. HILTON, *Rich Man Poor Man*, London, 1945.

E. J. HOBSBAWM, *Industry and Empire*, London, 1968.

J. M. HOGGE, *Betting and Gambling*, Edinburgh, 1904.

E. M. HUMPHRIS, *The Life of Fred Archer*, London, 1923.

E. M. HUMPHRIS, *The Life of Matthew Dawson*, London, 1928.

J. KENT, *Racing Life of Lord George Cavendish Bentinck M.P.*, London, 1892.

J. KENT, *Records and Reminiscences of Goodwood and the Dukes of Richmond*, London, 1896.

VISCOUNT KNEBWORTH, *Boxing*, London, 1931.

G. LAMBTON, *Men and Horses I Have Known*, London, 1924.

C. LEICESTER, *Bloodstock Breeding*, London, 1959.

R. LONGRIGG, *The History of Horse Racing*, London, 1972.

J. W. LOY and G. S. KENYON, *Sport, Culture and Society*, London, 1969.

R. C. LYLE, *Royal Newmarket*, London, 1945.

R. W. MALCOLMSON, *Popular Recreations in English Society 1700–1850*, Cambridge, 1973.

S. MARGETSON, *Leisure and Pleasure in the Nineteenth Century*, Newton Abbot, 1971.

P. C. McINTOSH, *Sport in Society*, London, 1968.

E. MOORHOUSE, *The Romance of the Derby* (2 vols), London, 1908.

R. MORTIMER, *The Jockey Club*, London, 1958.

NIMROD, *Memoirs of the Life of John Mytton*, London, 1903.

R. ONSLOW, *The Heath and the Turf*, London, 1971.

V. ORCHARD, *Tattersalls*, London, 1953.

H. PERKIN, *The Age of The Railway*, Newton Abbot, 1971.

H. PERKIN, *The Origins of Modern English Society 1780–1880*, London, 1972.

J. PORTER, *Kingsclere*, London, 1896.

J. PORTER and E. MOORHOUSE, *John Porter of Kingsclere*, London, 1919.

P. B. POWER, *Some Observations upon the Question 'Will Horse Racing Benefit Worthing'*, London, 1859.

A. R. PREST, *Consumers' Expenditure in the United Kingdom 1900–1919*, Cambridge, 1954.

C. RAMSDEN, *Farewell Manchester*, London, 1966.

C. RAMSDEN, *Ladies in Racing*, London, 1973.

H. REEVE (ed.), *The Greville Memoirs*, London, 1874, 1885 and 1887.

J. RICE, *The History of the British Turf*, London, 1879.

G. RICHARDS, *My Story*, London, 1955.

C. RICHARDSON, *The English Turf*, London, 1901.

C. RICHARDSON (ed.), *Racing at Home and Abroad. Vol. 1. British Flat Racing and Breeding*, London, 1923.

E. RICKMAN, *On and Off the Racecourse*, London, 1937.

E. RICKMAN, *Come Racing with Me*, London, 1951.

J. RICKMAN, *Homes of Sport: Horse Racing*, London, 1952.

R. RODRIGO, *The Racing Game*, London, 1960.

LORD ROSSMORE, *Things I Can Tell*, London, 1912.

B. S. ROWNTREE and G. R. LAVERS, *English Life and Leisure*, London, 1951.

H. ROUS, *On the Laws and Practice of Horse Racing*, London, 1850 and 1866.

W. RUSSELL, *The Reminiscences of Jock Thirlestane, Yokel and Detective at Musselburgh Races in Days Gone Bye*, Edinburgh, n.d.

J. M. SCOTT, *Extel 100: The Centenary History of the Exchange Telegraph Company*, London, 1973.

S. W. SEARLE, *The Origin and Development of Sunninghill and Ascot*, Chertsey, 1937.

P. W. SERGEANT, *Gamblers All*, London, 1931.

M. SETH-SMITH, *Bred for the Purple*, London, 1969.

S. SIDNEY, *The Book of the Horse*, 1875(?).

T. SLOAN, *Tod Sloan*, London, 1915.

A. SOUTAR, *My Sporting Life*, London, 1934.

E. Spencer, *The Great Game*, London, 1900.

The Sportsman, *British Sports and Sportsmen – Past Sportsmen* (2 vols), London, 1920(?).

The Sportsman, *British Sports and Sportsmen – Racing*, London, 1920.

The Sportsman, *British Sports and Sportsmen – Breeding and Agriculture*, London, 1926.

R. Stone and D. Rowe, *The Measurement of Consumer Expenditure and Behaviour in the U.K. 1920–1938*, vol. 2. Cambridge, 1966.

Earl of Suffolk (eds.). *Racing and Steeplechasing*, London, 1886 and 1907.

Earl of Suffolk, H. Peck and F. G. Aflalo (eds.), *The Encyclopaedia of Sport*, London, 1900.

D. Sutherland, *The Yellow Earl*, London, 1965.

Sylvanus, *The Bye-Lanes and Downs of England*, London, 1850.

W. Tait, *Magdalenism*, Edinburgh, 1840 and 1842.

F. M. L. Thompson, *Victorian England: The Horse Drawn Society*, London, 1970.

F. M. L. Thompson, *English Landed Society in the Nineteenth Century*, London, 1971.

Thormanby, *Famous Racing Men*, London, 1882.

C. C. Trench, *A History of Horsemanship*, London, 1970.

Victoria County Histories of England.

A. E. T. Watson, *The Turf*, London, 1898.

A. E. T. Watson, *The Racing World and Its Inhabitants*, London, 1904.

A. E. T. Watson, *King Edward VII as a Sportsman*, London, 1911.

R. Weir, *Riding*, London, 1895.

J. Welcome, *Fred Archer: His Life and Times*, London, 1967.

J. Welcome, *Neck or Nothing: The Extraordinary Life and Times of Bob Sievier*, London, 1970.

T. Weston, *My Racing Life*, London, 1952.

J. C. Whyte, *History of the British Turf* (2 vols), London, 1840.

E. L. Woodward, *The Age of Reform 1815–1870*, Oxford, 1954.

A. Wykes, *Gambling*, London, 1964.

THESES

K. Allan, 'The Recreations and Amusements of the Industrial Working Class in the Second Quarter of the Nineteenth Century with special reference to Lancashire', M.A. thesis, University of Manchester, 1947.

D. C. ITZKOWITZ, 'Peculiar Privilege: A Social History of English Foxhunting 1753–1885', Ph.D. thesis, University of Columbia, 1973.

R. MILLER, 'Gambling and the British Working Class 1870–1914', M.A. dissertation, University of Edinburgh, 1974.

M. B. SMITH, 'The Growth and Development of Popular Entertainment and Pastimes in the Lancashire Cotton Towns 1830–70', M.Litt thesis, University of Lancaster, 1970.

Index of Horses ⌐

Research Epilogue: A Guide To Further Reading ⌉

It is always a sign that a subject has achieved academic respectability when doctorates are awarded in the area. Two emerged under my supervision: Iris M. Middleton, *The Developing Pattern of Horse-Racing in Yorkshire 1700–1749: An Analysis of the People and the Places*, PhD thesis, De Montfort University (2000); John Tolson, *The Railway Myth: Flat Racing in Mainland Britain 1830–1914*, PhD thesis, De Montfort University (2000). Others include Paul Khan, *The Sport of Kings: A Study of Traditional Social Structure Under Pressure*, PhD Thesis, University of Wales (1980), Michael P. Filby, *A Sociology of Horse-racing in Britain: A Study of the Social Significance and Organisation* of Horseracing, PhD Thesis, University of Warwick (1983), Susan C. Macken, *Economic Aspects of Bloodstock Investment in Britain*, PhD Thesis, University of Cambridge (1986), Mark Clapson, *Popular Gambling and English Culture, c. 1845 to 1961*, PhD Thesis University of Warwick (1989), Deborah Ann Butler, *Indentured and Modern Apprenticeship in the Horseracing Industry: A Gendered Analysis*, PhD Thesis University of Warwick (2011).

General histories of the flat have been written by Mike Huggins, *Flat Racing and British Society 1790–1914* (London: Frank Cass, 2000) and *Horseracing and the British, 1919–1939* (Manchester: Manchester University Press, 2003) and of National Hunt racing by Roger Munting, *Hedges and Hurdles* (London: J. A. Allen, 1987). Wray Vamplew & Joyce Kay's *Encyclopedia of British Horseracing* (Abingdon: Routledge, 2005) avoided recycling old material and examined some previously neglected areas such as the link between racing and the arts, the church and alcohol. It looked at the social, economic and political forces that shaped the development of the sport and emphasised the historical duality of continuity and change. A collection of original work on racing features in Rebecca Cassidy (ed.), *The Cambridge Companion to Horseracing* (Cambridge: Cambridge University Press, 2013).

Regional histories of racing have been written for Scotland

(John Burnett, 'The Sites and Landscapes of Horse Racing in Scotland before 1860', *Sport Historian* 18.1 (1998), 55–75; Joyce Kay and Wray Vamplew, 'Horse–Racing ' in Grant Jarvie and John Burnett (eds.), *Sport, Scotland and the Scots*, (East Linton: Tuckwell, 2000), 159–173), Wales (R.J. Moore-Colyer, 'Gentlemen, Horses and the Turf in Nineteenth-century Wales', *Welsh History Review* 16 (1992/93), 47–62), the North-East of England Mike Huggins, 'Horse-Racing on Teesside in the Nineteenth Century: Change and Continuity', *Northern History*, 23 (1987), 98–118 and '"Mingled Pleasure and Speculation': The Survival of the Enclosed Racecourses on Teesside, 1855–1902', 3.2 *British Journal of Sports History* (1986),158–172. A general geography can be found in R.W. Tomlinson, 'A Geography of Flat-racing in Great Britain' *Geography 71–3 (1986), 228–239*

The timing of race meetings in one locality in the eighteenth century has been examined by Iris Middleton and Wray Vamplew ('Horse-Racing and the Yorkshire Leisure Calendar in the Early Eighteenth Century', *Northern History* 40 (2003), 259–276) and the effect of railway development on meetings and other aspects of the sport a century and a half later by John Tolson and Wray Vamplew ('Derailed: Railways and Horse-Racing Revisited', *Sports Historian* 18.2 (1998), 39–49 and 'Facilitation not Revolution: Railways and British Flat Racing 1830–1914', *Sport in History* 23 (2003), 89–106).

Social anthropologist, Rebecca Cassidy, takes us into the class and kinship relationships of Newmarket, a major centre of all things horseracing, in two books [(*Sport of Kings: Kinship, Class and Thoroughbred Breeding in Newmarket* (Cambridge: Cambridge University Press, 2002) and *Horse People: Thoroughbred Culture in Lexington and Newmarket* (Baltimore: Johns Hopkins University Press, 2007)]. Racegoers and their behaviour are one aspect covered by another social anthropologist Kate Fox, [*The Racing Tribe: Watching the Horsewatchers* (London: Metro, 1999)]. Mike Huggins takes a look at one particular crowd in 'Art, Horse Racing and the 'Sporting' Gaze in Mid-Nineteenth Century England: William Powell Frith's *The Derby Day*', *Sport in History* 33.2 (2013), 121–145 and historical misbehaviour in the form of the racetrack gangs in the interwar years are the subject of Heather Shore, ('Criminality and Englishness in the Aftermath: The Racecourse Wars of the 1920s', *Twentieth Century British History* 22.4 (2011), 474–497 and 'Rogues of the Racecourse: Racing Men and the Press in Interwar Britain' *Media History, 20.4 (2014)* 352–367). Joyce Kay considers how racecourse executives treat the next generation of racegoers ('A Blinkered Approach? Attitudes towards Children and Young People in British Horseracing and Equestrian Sport' in *Idrottsforum* (2008)).

Class has inevitably featured in racing history research. Mike Huggins provided a revisionist view that gave the middle classes a greater role in racing than had been envisaged in *The Turf* ('Culture, Class and Respectability: Racing and the English Middle Classes in the Nineteenth Century', *International Journal of the History of Sport*, 11 (1994), 19–41; 'A Tranquil Transformation: Middle-Class Racing "Revolutionaries" in Nineteenth-Century England', *European Sports History Review* 4 (2002), 35–57). John Pinfold went higher up the social scale with his 'Horse Racing and the Upper Classes in the Nineteenth Century', *Sport in History* 28.3 (2008), 414–430).

Most jockeys emanated from the working class, though in the nineteenth century gentlemen riders occasionally competed against the professionals (Wray Vamplew and Joyce Kay, 'Captains Courageous: The Gentleman Rider in British Horseracing 1866–1914', *Sport in History* 26 (2006), 370–385). Wray Vamplew ('Still Crazy after All Those Years: Continuity in a Changing Labour Market for Professional Jockeys', *Contemporary British History* 14.2 (2000), 115–145) has surveyed the life and times of jockeys, but we still know so little about these diminutive men who risked life and limb every time they went to work, who faced the stress of public and private appraisal, constant weight-watching with its associated health risks, and the demeaning struggle to gain employment in an over-supplied labour market. How, for example, did the barely literate Fred Archer manage to arrange 667 rides in 1885?

In contrast to the paucity of historical research on jockeys there has been a significant expansion in the literature on the modern jockey and their weight-loss practices, the medical problems, both physical and mental, they face in trying to reduce their weight, and the impact that weight watching has on their racetrack performance (Michael J. Caulfield and Costas I. Karageorghis, 'Psychological Effects of Rapid Weight Loss and Attitudes Towards Eating Among Professional Jockeys', *Journal of Sports Sciences* 26.9 (2008), 877–883; Eimear Dolan, et al., 'Nutritional. Lifestyle, and Weight Control Practices of Professional Jockeys', *Journal of Sports Sciences* 29.8 (2011), 791–799; Martin Tolich and Martha Bell, 'The Commodification of Jockeys' Working Bodies: Anorexia or Work Discipline?' in Chris McConville (ed.), *A Global Racecourse* (Melbourne: ASSH, 2008), 101–114.); George Wilson, et al. 'Rapid Weight-Loss Impairs Simulated Riding Performance and Strength in Jockeys: Implications for Making Weight', *Journal of Sports Sciences* 32.4 (2014), 383–391). Injuries, employment conditions and industrial relations have also featured in recent research by *Michael Turner, P. McCrory and W. Halley*, 'Injuries in Professional Horse Racing in Great Britain and the Republic of Ireland during 1992–2000', *British Journal of Sports Medicine 36* (2002), 403–409 and Janet Winter, 'Industrial Relations-Lite? The Management of Industrial Relations in the UK Thoroughbred Training Industry' in Chris McConville (ed.), *A Global Racecourse* (Melbourne: ASSH, 2008), 87–100. Although the bulk of the information relates to jockeys in the past decade or so, there is no reason to believe that this could not be applied to more historical periods

Other groups have undergone even less historical scrutiny than jockeys. For trainers, Mike Huggins made use of the regional and local press to look at eighteenth and nineteenth-century Yorkshire practitioners and examine their background, methods and finances *Kings of the Moor: Yorkshire Racehorse Trainers 1760–1900* Teesside University Papers in North Eastern History, 1991. Some of these men were major local employers but we know nothing of their workers as we have only two academic studies of stablehands and those are for the late twentieth century (Michael .P.Filby, 'The Newmarket Racing Lad: Tradition and Change in a Marginal Occupation', *Work, Employment & Society*, 1 (1987), 205–224; Janet Winter, 'Industrial Relations-Lite? The Management of Industrial Relations in the UK Thoroughbred Training Industry' in Chris McConville (ed.), *A Global Racecourse* (Melbourne: ASSH, 2008), 87–100).

The history of women in horseracing has been one of struggle against male domination of the sport (Wray Vamplew and Joyce

Kay, 'Horse Racing' in Karen Christensen, Allen Guttmann and Gertrud Pfister (eds.), *International Encyclopedia of Women and Sports* (New York: Macmillan Reference, 2001), 537–544). Deborah Butler shows that women began to work in the British horseracing industry in the late 1960s, early 1970s when, in order to be accepted, they had to be as strong, tough and able as the 'lads' ('Not a Job For 'Girly-Girls': Horseracing, Gender and Work Identities', *Sport in Society* 16.10 (2013), 1309–1325). Laura-Jayne Roberts, and Malcolm MacLean show that discrimination against female riders still exists (*'Women in the Weighing Room: Gender Discrimination on the Thoroughbred Racetrack'*, *Sport in Society*, 15.3 (2012), 1–15).

Racehorses themselves feature prominently in Wray Vamplew & Joyce Kay's *Encyclopedia of British Horseracing* (Abingdon: Routledge, 2005) and the dangers of the sport to the animals in R.B. Williams et al. 'Racehorse Injuries, Clinical Problems and Fatalities Recorded on British Racecourses From Flat Racing and National Hunt Racing During 1996, 1997 and 1998', *Equine Veterinary Journal* 33.5 (2001), 478–486.

Racing and gambling have been long-time bedfellows, the former providing the vehicle for wagers and the latter, eventually, helping finance the racing industry. Academic studies such as David Dixon, *From Prohibition to Regulation* (Oxford: Oxford University Press, 1991) and Mike Huggins, 'The Manchester Betting World', *Manchester Regional History Review*, 20 (2009), 24–45 have focussed on the asymmetric legal position of higher-class and working-class gambling. Revisionist works [David C. Itzkowitz, 'Victorian Bookmakers and Their Customers', *Victorian Studies* 32 (1988), 7–30; Carl Chinn, *Better Betting with a Decent Feller* (Hemel Hempstead: Aurum, 1991); Mark Clapson, *A Bit of a Flutter* (Manchester: Manchester University Press, 1992] have tried to rehabilitate late nineteenth-century bookmakers as respectable small businessmen but many did exhibit criminal characteristics [Mike Huggins, 'The First Generation of Street Bookmakers in Victorian England: Demonic Fiends or 'Decent Fellers' *Northern History*, 36 (2000), 129–145]. For an overview of the changing location of betting see Peter Jones, David Hillier and David Turner, 'Back Street to Side Street to High Street: The Changing Geography of Betting Shops', *Geography* 79.2 (1994), 122–128 *and for a discussion of how gambling on the horses can be regarded as a leisure practice* D.M. Saunders and D.E. Turner 'Gambling and Leisure: The Case Of Racing', *Leisure Studies* 6.3 (1987), 281–299. Unhappily, although betting adds to the drama and excitement of a race, it can also lead to corruption. Mike Huggins ('Lord Bentinck, the Jockey Club and Racing Morality in Mid Nineteenth-century England: the "Running Rein" Derby Revisited', *International Journal of the History of Sport*, 13 (1996), 432–444) has demonstrated the level of deceit attached to the nation's premier classic race in early Victorian times and John Gleaves, the reaction to doping in racing at the turn of the twentieth century ('Enhancing the Odds: Horse Racing, Gambling and the First Anti-Doping Movement in Sport, 1889–1911', *Sport in History* 32.1 (2012), 26–52).

It fell to the Jockey Club to try and restore the integrity of racing. There has been an assumption the Jockey Club was in control of British racing from its foundation in the mid eighteenth century, but Wray Vamplew ('Reduced Horsepower: the Jockey Club and the Regulation of British Horseracing, *Journal of Entertainment Law* 3 (2003), 94–111) has shown that up to the 1860s, apart from Newmarket and a few other elite courses, the Club had some influence but little power. Similarly Joyce Kay 'From Coarse to Course: The First Fifty Years of the Royal Caledonian Hunt, 1777–1826', *Review of Scottish Culture* 13 (2000/01), 30–39) has made it clear that the Royal Caledonian Hunt Club was not as influential north of the border as previously thought. For a detailed study of power relations in the sport see Christopher R. Hill, *Horse Power: The Politics of the Turf* (Manchester University Press, 1988.

One thing missing from *The Turf* was any theoretical underpinning of the overall arguments. This was partially rectified in a later work, *Pay Up and Play the Game* (Cambridge: Cambridge University Press, 1988) which applied the economic concepts of rent, utility maximisation and others to several sports including horseracing. Then, with Joyce Kay, a challenge was mounted to Guttmann's theory of modernisation when applied to horseracing. We suggested that too little attention had been given to the roles of gambling, professionalization and commercialisation ('A Modern Sport? From "Ritual to Record" in British Horseracing',

Ludica 9 (2003), 125–139). Although many in horseracing have little interest in the history of their sport, save for recent form as a guide to betting, the British turf possesses, in the *Racing Calendar*, the longest continuous sporting periodical in the world. Its usefulness as an historical source has been discussed by Joyce Kay ('Still Going After All These Years: Text, Truth and the *Racing Calendar*', *Sport in History*, 29 (2009), 353–366). Along with the stud books this allows us to know more about the genealogy of eighteenth and early nineteenth-century thoroughbreds than of many of their owners and certainly most of their riders. Breeders, however, do look to the past though perhaps they have been too accepting of early data as geneticists have revealed errors in the official records (E.W. Hill et al., 'History and Integrity of Thoroughbred Dam Lines Revealed in Equine mt Variation', *Animal Genetics* 33 (2002), 287–294). Joyce Kay has pointed out idiocy rather than errors, in that races, specifically designed to improve the breed, actually allowed geldings to be entered which obviously undermined the rationale ('Closing the Stable Door and The Public Purse: The Rise and Fall of the Royal Plates', *Sports Historian* 20 (2000), 18–32). Although R.J. Moore-Colyer ('Gentlemen, Horses and the Turf', 53); has argued that many Welsh gentlemen who engaged in the breeding business did so with profit as an important motive, Mike Huggins has shown that only a minority of nineteenth-century Yorkshire breeders made a profit though their deficient accounting procedure often presented them with a different picture ('Thoroughbred Breeding in the North and East Ridings of Yorkshire in the Nineteenth Century', *Agricultural History Review*, 42 (1994), 115–125). Conservatism seems to have been a watchword in the British breeding industry. Rebecca Cassidy ('The Social Practice of Racehorse Breeding', *Society and Animals*, 10.2 (2002), 155–171) considers the resistance to new reproductive technologies, including artificial insemination and R.J. Moore-Colyer & J.P. Simpson ('High-Caste Corinthians: Amateurism and the Bloodstock Industry 1945–75' *International Journal of the History of Sport* 21.2 (2004), 277–296) note a dogged indifference to the realities of social and economic change within the industry.

Amongst modern works looking at the economics of the bloodstock industry are Margaret A. Ray, 'Advertising and

Pricing Policies in the Equine Breeding Industry or Sex and the Single Stallion', *Applied Economics* 23.4, (1991), 755–762 and Conor Parsons and Ian Smith, 'The Price of Thoroughbred Yearlings in Britain', *Journal of Sports Economics* 9.1 (2008), 43–46. More generally the specific economics of the horseracing industry have been discussed by Wray Vamplew ('The Economics of British Horseracing' in Wladimir W. Andreff and Stefan Szymanski (eds.), *Handbook of the Economics of Sport*, Edward Elgar, London, 2006, 374–378).

Britain exported the sport, including bloodstock, race names, racing models and the style of governance, to its formal and informal empires. Some of this can be traced in Mike Huggins ('The Proto-globalisation of Horseracing, 1730–1900: Anglo-American Interconnections', *Sport in History*, 29 (2009), 367–391) and in Andrew Lemon (Horse Racing: An English or an International Sport?' in Chris McConville (ed.), *A Global Racecourse* (Melbourne: ASSH, 2008), 1–11). In contrast Donna Landry and Rebecca Cassisdy look at an international flow the other way (*Noble Brutes: How Eastern Horses Transformed English Culture* (Baltimore: Johns Hopkins University Press, 2008 and Rebecca Cassidy 'Turf Wars: Arab Dimensions to British Racehorse Breeding', *Anthropology Today* 19.3 (2003), 13–18).

General Index]